D1382843

Economic Efficiency and Social Justice

Economic Efficiency and Social Justice

The Development of Utilitarian Ideas in Economics from Bentham to Edgeworth

John Bonner

Edward Elgar
Aldershot, UK · Brookfield, US

Published by
Edward Elgar Publishing Limited
Gower House
Croft Road
Aldershot
Hants GU11 3HR
UK

Edward Elgar Publishing Company
Old Post Road
Brookfield
Vermont 05036
US

British Library Cataloguing in Publication Data

Bonner, John
   Economic Efficiency and Social Justice:
   Development of Utilitarian Ideas in
   Economics from Bentham to Edgeworth
   I. Title
   330.01

Library of Congress Cataloguing in Publication Data

Bonner, John
   Economic efficiency and social justice : the development of
utilitarian ideas in economics from Bentham to Edgeworth / John
Bonner.
   224 p. 22 cm.
   Includes bibliographical references and index.
   1. Economics—Great Britain—History. 2. Utilitarianism—Great
Britain—History. I. Title.
   HB161.B72 1995   95–19606
   330.15—dc20   CIP

ISBN 1 85278 295 1

Printed and bound in Great Britain by Ipswich Book Co. Ltd., Ipswich, Suffolk

Contents

Preface

This book has been a long time in preparation. The idea for an introduction to the classical utilitarians was suggested nearly seven years ago, but the necessary reading and preparation went ahead in a haphazard fashion, with many more stops than starts. Not until the academic session of 1993-4, when the author was fortunate to be granted leave of absence, was concentrated work possible. His slow and old fashioned mind is unable to cope with interruptions and diversions. Much credit for the manuscript's eventual appearance, therefore, is due to the University of Leicester for being so generous and to Edward Elgar for being so patient.

Originally intended to fill a gap in the secondary literature (there being almost too much on each classical utilitarian in the round and practically nothing on their common interest in the special field of economic policy), the project gradually developed self indulgent tendencies. The history of economic ideas is not a popular subject. Students prefer to study vocational courses and absorb yet more quantitative techniques. Their teachers have to concentrate on journal articles at the sharp end of economics in order to make a mark in the research selectivity exercises. Those who determine to write books of this kind, therefore, can afford to adopt different priorities. They can relax and start to enjoy the experience. They can wander off course and include things that are not strictly relevant but which they find fascinating. The story of the classical utilitarians is certainly full of temptations of this kind. Hopefully, enough of them have been resisted to enable readers to understand why utilitarianism is still relevant to the current debate about social welfare and justice among economists, philosophers and political scientists.

1. Introduction

A recent text on welfare economics declares that 'few to-day pay much attention to classical utilitarianism'.[1] It seems a strange judgement to make. Economists such as John Harsanyi, Peter Hammond, Jonathan Riley and Y-K Ng, and philosophers such as Richard Hare, Paul Kelly, David Lyons, and Donald Regan continue to revisit and revise the work of just the people who are supposed to have been forgotten. Indeed, there is scarcely any modern contribution to the debate about ethics and public policy which fails to mention the utilitarian argument, whether in praise or rebuttal. For economists, as Kenneth Arrow has pointed out, the connection is all too close.

> Recommending a policy is making a choice, and the inevitable question arises, by what criteria should a choice be made? While the subject abuts closely on the philosophers' theories of justice, in fact the only philosophical influence has been that of the classical utilitarians, which is, to a large extent, the work of economists.[2]

Welfare economics is still conducted with concepts and a language largely derived from these sources. This book attempts to explain the policy recommendations of those economists who were classical utilitarians. What precisely was the nature of their beliefs? How did their philosophy influence their economics? Why was their theory of justice so persuasive? Although they agreed on the central tenet of their faith (to use the pursuit of happiness as the guide to policy), there were important differences in the way in which they interpreted its meaning, and in the policies they advocated.

Lionel Robbins put the close association between British economics and utilitarianism in the nineteenth century down to an historical accident. At the other extreme, Elie Halévy suggested that utilitarianism, or philosophical radicalism (sometimes referred to as philosophic radicalism), was another name for classical economics, and Leslie Stephen thought the Political Economy Club was an organ of utilitarian propaganda.[3] The truth seems to lie somewhere in between.. Adam Smith was no utilitarian. The rise of Benthamism eclipsed the influence of his theory of morals. Ricardian economics was not wholly acceptable to Jeremy Bentham, and Benthamite economics not wholly acceptable to David Ricardo.[4] While Ricardo was a friend and admirer of Bentham, his acceptance of the general objective of 'the greatest happiness of the greatest number' was little more than a gesture to what he found uncontroversial and vaguely comprehensive. He never bothered with the details nor made any contribution to the development of the utilitarian creed. Thomas Malthus was hardly a Radical, taking a more extreme view of the wages fund and the poor law than Ricardo, and having even less contact with the immediate utilitarian circle. Nassau Senior may have mixed with Bentham's disciples, and even sympathised with some of their objectives, but he remained a Whig. Although these same Benthamites are said to have been instigators of many of the social reforms in the nineteenth century, it is important to distinguish between the policies they advocated, along with most economists, and the philosophical foundations underlying those policies, which they shared with only a few. Perhaps the historical accident was that utilitarianism remained a peculiarly British phenomenon for so long.[5]

The Troops

The choice of those economists who can be properly regarded as part of the classical utilitarian tradition, what Joseph Schumpeter would have called the 'troops', is comparatively easy. Jeremy Bentham, James Mill, John Stuart Mill, Stanley Jevons, Henry Sidgwick, and Francis Edgeworth are the leading figures.[6] It has to be admitted that they were not all equally involved with economics and philosophy. Bentham, for example, spent only part of his enormous energies on economics, but his contribution to the theory of normative economics was profound. In any case, no study of utilitarianism is complete without the founder. James Mill is included because his economics had more influence on his son than is usually recognised and because his commitment to Benthamism, in nearly all its forms, was unquestionable.

John Stuart Mill, who is often described as the last of the truly classical economists, became famous for challenging the views of his father James Mill and godfather Bentham and the content of the education they had designed for him. Only after careful examination of alternative philosophies did he turn to formulate a revisionist version of utilitarianism. These differences with the mainstream of utilitarian thought, on matters of principle as well as policy, make him the least typical member. Stanley Jevons, one of the first of the neo-classical economists, took quite another route. He was converted to 'happiness' doctrines without the help of Bentham. Only later did he come to appreciate the virtues of 'old Mr Jeremy', particularly when he wanted to attack John Mill. Jevons regarded the influence of Ricardo and Mill on economics as almost wholly pernicious. He strongly defended what he regarded as true 'utilitarian economics' and had a more serious interest in utilitarian philosophy than is usually acknowledged. But it was Sidgwick who was the most famous philosopher of classical utilitarianism. He was also the last English philosopher to write a major text in political economy. Edgeworth, like Jevons, and to a lesser extent John Mill, is worthy of high esteem as an economist independently of any utilitarian connections or beliefs. Nevertheless, when he did write as a utilitarian, his interpretation was the most extreme, and his vision of the greatest happiness principle as applied to economics the most pure and mathematical. The impact these ideas have had on subsequent developments in welfare economics is only equalled by those of Sidgwick and Bentham himself. Thus, if John Mill was the reformer, Sidgwick, and Jevons and Edgeworth (who both fell under the influence of Herbert Spencer[7]) were the restorers of orthodoxy. With Arthur Pigou, the first neo- or 'provisional' utilitarian,[8] the classical period comes to end.

The Problems

Samuel Hollander has drawn attention to the distinction between the History of Economic Analysis and the History of Systems of Political Economy.[9] In Schumpeter's terms, a system of political economy is

> an exposition of a comprehensive set of economic policies that its author advocates on the strength of certain unifying (normative) principles such as the principles of economic liberalism, socialism, and so on.[10]

There are difficulties, however, in treating utilitarianism as one example of a system of political economy, with general or the greatest happiness representing its unifying principle. An historian of systems of political economy will want to explain how this set of policies was arrived at, test it for internal consistency, and study how it has responded both to changes in economic circumstances and to the challenge of competing ideologies. An historian of economic analysis will be more concerned with how the utilitarian economists argued as economists, and with the techniques of analysis they employed, than with the policies they advocated. Unfortunately, classical utilitarianism was not just a system of political economy. A mix of sensationalist psychology, ethical hedonism, classical (and later neo-classical) economics, and democratic politics, it was supposed to apply to all of what were called the moral and now are called the social sciences. That is to say, its subject matter could just as well be the reform of the law, the structures of colonial government, education, social policy, or the suffrage, as that of banking, trade, the labour market or the tax system. Moreover, its distinguishing feature for economics was less the policies themselves than the philosophical justification it gave them. In Frank Hahn's words, utilitarianism 'made discussion of policy possible', it 'gave reasons why one is better than another'.[11] It provided a unifying normative theory that economics either lacked or believed it did not need.

The first problem then is selection. Some way has to be found of sorting out those parts of the enormous literature produced by the classical utilitarians which are directly relevant to this normative exercise. Issues of economic policy may be easily distinguished from the rest, but the philosophic justification is common to the whole programme and has to be understood, at least in its essentials. The task is not made easier by the fact that the discussion of these issues was not confined to books and essays on economics, but appeared under the heads of all the other moral or social sciences, in particular under law, politics and philosophy. The second problem concerns the elusive nature of the unifying objective. To say that the greatest happiness should be the end of economic policy is to beg several other questions. Is happiness a state of mind or a state of the world? Can happiness be subjective feelings of well-being as well as the objective circumstances that satisfy desires for well-being? Feelings may not always correlate with circumstances. Sometimes the classical utilitarians emphasised the importance of what was going on in the individual's mind and at other times the importance of the evidence of the individual's requirements. The problem with the former is that there may not be one state of mind common to all sensations and there may be some things desired that are not really states of mind. The problem with the latter is that people may not always know what is in their true interests and their desires have to be censored, idealised or educated.

Another problem concerns the differences between the quantity and quality of happiness. Can some kinds of happiness be more sophisticated or on a 'higher' plain than others, and therefore not comparable on the same scale of quantity? It may be that some individuals are incapable of appreciating the full strength of these higher pleasures. Similarly, how broadly is happiness to be defined? Basic information about income and wealth, and the private happiness they bring, should perhaps be expanded to include circumstances like freedom, liberty, and relative inequality, and feelings like sympathy and benevolence. Has this broad happiness ceased to be utilitarian? Is it any longer operationally significant? Monks might be said to be maximizing their own happiness in the next world. But is that a very helpful description of their behaviour? Above all else, what methods are available to add these different 'happinesses' together? The measurement of happiness could become the ultimate test of the viability of utilitarianism.

There is one further problem. Greatest happiness was meant to be the foundation of a theory of moral behaviour and public decision-making. Classical utilitarians welcomed the opportunity to deduce their ethics from individual psychology, and to carry over the same associations into their economics. Its critics in economics and philosophy have found this link between psychological and ethical hedonism its weakest point. Alfred Marshall, for example, tried to distance economics from what he understood to be hedonism. Although words like utility and pleasure were a common inheritance, and many of the leading British economists of the nineteenth century were avowed followers of Bentham, Marshall rejected any necessary connection between utility maximising behaviour and a moral creed. The fact that most people in the ordinary business of life seemed to follow their self-interest, could not be used as a foundation for a theory of how they ought to behave.[12] At the same time, he was not shy of pointing out his own version of the way to a better life. Individuals should think of their duties to others, be righteous and honest, work hard, develop their higher faculties, and learn to relax. Statesmen should wrestle with the problems of inequality, poverty and unemployment. Economists should help define the general ends of economic policy as well as assess the means to achieve them, and while defending the advantages of economic freedom, recognise the value of altruism and the opportunities for collective action. The difference between him and his predecessors was that he did not believe these conclusions could be simply deduced from the pursuit of pleasure and the avoidance of pain.

Ethics and Economics

There are at least two questions to be asked about the link between
psychological hedonism and ethical hedonism. The first concerns
whether 'ought' statements can be derived from 'is'statements. Even if
it can be shown that individuals universally pursue happiness, does it
follow that happiness is the only good? The second concerns the
reconciliation of private interests with the public good. How can it be
shown that the pursuit of self-interest, of individual happiness, leads to
the welfare of all, general happiness? Marshall seemed to be trying to
answer the second in his rejection of hedonism. But instead of offering
the Categorical Imperative of Kantian philosophy ('I ought never to
act except in such a way that I can also will that my maxim should
become a universal law'[13]) as the alternative ethical premise, he turned
to a watered-down version of utilitarianism, in which true happiness
supposedly came only with self-respect, and self-respect only with the
promotion of social progress. Because economics was, for Marshall, a
science, pure and applied, rather than a science and an art, ethics
could not be one of its major concerns. A generous if rather vague
commitment to the improvement of the human race, including the
development of character and morals, had to be sufficient. (Not so
very different from the way in which Ricardo accepted the greatest
happiness principle.) For many of those who followed Marshall, and
who wanted to explore economics as an art, to make judgements about
economic policy, the basis might be broader, and more detailed, but it
had to exclude any traces of the psychology of happiness.

None of the argument about deriving the 'ought' from the 'is'
undermines the legitimacy of either of them, taken separately.
Psychological hedonism may continue to be a persuasive theory of
how individual's behave. Economists may continue to make normative
judgements, to be prescriptive as well as as descriptive. The same
economist may make both kind of statements, as long as they are
presented independently of each other, as long as it is not assumed
that one follows from the other. In any case, modern utilitarianism has
shown that ethical hedonism can be pursued, in economics and
philosophy, quite successfully without any commitment to
psychological hedonism. So there is no need to take sides in the
dispute.[14] It is important, nevertheless, to recognise that economists
have always fallen back on utilitarian terminology and assumptions to
help justify their policy conclusions. Concepts like diminishing
marginal utility and aggregate utility seem indispensable. Cost-benefit
analysis, and similar examples of applied welfare economics return to

earlier exercises in the measurement of utility and the construction of inter-personal comparisons. Most revealing of all, any attempt to discuss the equity or fairness of taxation starts, and usually finishes within the limitations of a utilitarian ethic.

Pigou, the founder of welfare economics, managed to retain most of the results of utilitarian economics by changing many of the words used to describe its objectives, like 'welfare' instead of 'utility' and 'satisfaction' instead of 'the surplus of pleasures over pains', and by fudging the issue between ordinal and cardinal measurement.[15] Nor did the triumph of the New Welfare Economics over 'provisional' utilitarianism, as might have been expected, completely destroy the connection. Paretian judgements for improvement (some people being made better-off without others being made worse-off), presume some notion of overall economic welfare as the desirable end, even if it is not put in the form of a maximand. The information permitted to be to used in making these judgements was much more restrictive: no interpersonal comparisons or cardinal measurements of utility, just ordinal preferences. But individuals were still assumed to be rational maximisers and the pursuit of self-interest continued to be justified because such behaviour led, in ideal conditions, to the best overall outcome. The New Welfare Economics, like the utilitarians, 'ground the social good on the good of individuals'.[16]

Since then there has been a considerable revival of interest in utilitarian welfare economics. Use of consumer surplus measurements in cost-benefit analysis, for example, has encouraged another look at the provisional or quasi-utilitarian concepts of Marshall and Pigou, and the debate about compensation tests that followed them. Positivist methodology had persuaded economists, for a time, to lose confidence in their ability to make value judgements about changes in economic welfare, indeed to abstain from making ethical statements of any kind. The development of social choice theory, and somewhat paradoxically the refinement of the two fundamental theorems of general equilibrium welfare economics, have forced them to think again about the ethical nature of their assumptions. Facts and values, means and ends, are not so easily separated. Economists want to argue that some 'states of affairs', are better than others. They also imply that some behaviour is more appropriate or acceptable to this better state of affairs.

The concept of utility, of course, is more likely to be associated with the history of the theory of subjective value than with ethics. Consumer behaviour used to be based on the maximization of personal happiness, utility, or welfare, as a function of the goods and services available, and subject to a budget constraint. In modern versions of the theory, emphasis is placed on the rationality of choice, with consumers choosing a most preferred bundle of commodities from the set of feasible alternatives. Yet to make assumptions about rational decision-making may be to imply a minimal utilitarian definition of individual well-being.[17] Furthermore, the classical utilitarians had a pre-occupation (most classical economists shared the same pre-occupation) with the beneficial social effects of the rational pursuit of private interests. Their positive statements had normative consequences. Being rational was also part of being good. A simple version of utilitarianism might regard individual utility maximisation as a means to an end. It is good because it leads to a good outcome for the economy as a whole (maximum aggregate utility), not because it is good in itself. Perhaps the vision is too narrow to carry full conviction. As one critic has put the matter,

> the paradigm about self-interest leading to a workable and perhaps even optimal social order without any admixture of 'benevolence' has now been around so long that it has become intellectually challenging to rediscover the need for morality.[18]

The modern theory of choice seems to be more inclusive. It can be descriptive, normative and prescriptive. From being about how individuals actually behave, it can be transformed into how they ought to behave if they were looking after themselves properly, or how they need to behave if the economy is to perform efficiently.[19] It may even be able to accommodate some notion of choosing for others, how to help them look after themselves better, and how helping them may even benefit us. There is nothing inherently irrational about benevolence.

Value judgements in economics, in other words, are not just about institutions. Keeping promises, honouring contracts, and telling the truth are other examples of the kind of behaviour crucial to the success of competitive markets. Treated as self-evident truths, often enshrined in the law, their ethical content is often forgotten. It is certainly more usual to start with policy conclusions based on judgements about 'states of affairs' as the matter of welfare economics and ethics. But 'states of affairs' can be complete descriptions of society's arrangements, from the way individuals are treated by others, whether they are allowed to own property and on what terms, their rights in employment, their liberties as citizens and so on, to the organisation of industry, and the role of government. Or they can be limited to one particular dimension, like the distribution of personal incomes or the system of company taxation. The great attraction of utilitarianism is that it can provide a single principle to guide all the value judgements economists are likely to make about behaviour and social states. Its great drawback is that all possible ends have to be reduced to one, happiness.[20] Modern economics has plumped for a neutral and even thinner alternative. The objective becomes not happiness and pleasure but the satisfaction of revealed preferences, or the widening of choice. Unfortunately, similar criticisms apply. What precisely do these preferences reveal? Is any kind of uninformed preferenc acceptable? Is the widening of choice still good when the things chosen have unpleasant consequences? At the same time, modern economics remains true enough to its utilitarian origins in avoiding pluralistic ends.

Method of Proceeding

Some kind of organising principle is required to tell the story of the classical utilitarians and their economics. Otherwise there would be too many loose ends and diversions. One solution would be to reformulate what they had to say so that it could be compared directly with modern analysis. By fully specifying the assumptions they appeared to have made, turning their vague generalisations into explicit statements, and allowing their arguments to be fully developed under what are now understood to be the laws of logic, an unambiguous and consistent version of classical utilitarianism would emerge. In other words, an axiomatic classical utilitarianism could be tested against current axiomatic models of both neo or quasi-utilitarianism and non-utilitarian social choice theories. 'Benthamite' social welfare functions are now commonly in use, and an attempt has already been made to put John Mill's utilitarianism into axiomatic form.[21] The exercise could be repeated for all the others.

There are three reasons why this solution has not been adopted. First, the classical utilitarians had sharp disagreements about fundamentals and each would require a very different model. Although a precise description of these disagreements is valuable, the same result can be reached following a simpler route. Second, fitting the work of the classical utilitarians into the straight jacket of mathematical language, subject to strict rules of reasoning, could be counter-productive. The vagueness of their generalisations was sometimes deliberate. Matters of importance might be left out and the result would not be history. Third, the axiomatic approach is technically demanding. Diverting the time and energy necessary to learn and then manipulate the power of such rigorous mathematics is not required for this limited exercise. It would be wrong, nevertheless, to ignore the advances that have been made by philosophers and economists in recent years, including those using axiomatic methods. In particular, there is now a much clearer picture of the implications of utilitarianism for welfare economics and social choice. This information will be helpful in the study of the political economy of classical utilitarianism.

Part of each chapter, therefore, will be concerned to discover how close the classical utilitarians, who were economists, came to what is currently described as 'classical utilitarianism'. In all, seven characteristics have been selected to form the ideal template. The list must not be taken as offering a complete description of utilitarianism, new or old. There is no law or education, for example, and most of the pure philosophy has been evaded. The perspective is set by the concerns of welfare economics and social choice theory.

1. A Single Overriding Objective

Utilitarianism is one of those theories of individual and collective action in which a magnitude of some kind is allowed to establish a preponderance between alternatives. It defines what is a private interest, what is in the public interest, where public interest overrules private interest, and where the private interests of some people can outweigh the private interests of others. It reduces all other objectives to the same ultimate standard, to be assessed on the same level. It is the opposite of pluralism. The ultimate magnitude could be votes in elections, or strength of opinion, or credits in heaven. Here the only desirable end is happiness or general utility.[22] It would be foolish to deny the validity of the argument that the pursuit of happiness and the avoidance of pain are vital ingredients in most people's lives, and forms part of their view of what is right or wrong. But there are other feelings to be taken into account, like justice and fairness, honour and desert, which might lead to different actions. Not everyone agrees that they can all be reduced to the end called utility.

2. Consequentalism

The choice between alternatives is determined by their consequences. Behaviour is purposive, has a goal or final cause, is teleological. The value of actions is to be found in the state of affairs they produce, and not in intention or desert. Extensions of consequentalism in the direction of the theory of choice mean that individual behaviour can be predicted once the set of consequences of alternative actions have been specified. Individuals always choose the best outcome available. Extensions of consquentalism in the direction of the theory of morals mean that judgements of outcomes are impersonal. Only the good state of affairs matters, not who brought about or caused that state. The theory is agent-neutral. Utilitarianism, of course, is not the only form of consequentalism. Indeed, it is very difficult to find a moral theory which ignores consequences altogether. Consequences, on the other hand, do not have to be measured by the same standard. Desirable states of affairs could be multi-dimensional, and judged according to pluralistic objectives.[23]

3. Welfarism

The assessment of consequences is restricted to information contained in individual utility functions (but more than is included in ordinal individual preference functions). Non-utility information is irrelevant. So too is the identity of the people enjoying the utility. Like consequentalism, welfarism is strongly neutral between persons. Economists might find welfarism attractive because it seems to absolve them from the need to worry about strictly non-economic variables like democracy, individual rights, or social justice. Important though these are, the argument goes, their evaluation is best left to others. Economists would be wrong if thought this was implied by utilitarian consequentalism, because its distinction between utility and non-utility information leaves too much much open. Utility information can be quite rich. State terrorism, for example, will make some citizens very unhappy. Their individual (dis)utility functions will surely reveal the pains they suffer. A non-economic factor can have utility consequences. The subtle difference is that the existence of torture and false imprisonment, as part of the state of affairs, can be judged bad (or good) only when their effects show up in individual utility functions. No other kind of judgement is allowed. On this basis, if torturers enjoy their work, that too has to be counted. Income distribution provides another example of how utilitarian welfarism works. The deprivations of the poor and the enjoyments of the rich will show up in their respective utility functions, that is all. Re-distribution will only be recommended if it can be shown that total utility, the sum of all individual utilities, thereby increases. There is no basis for a condemnation of the existence of extreme inequality (or state terrorism), as a matter of principle. Feelings of sympathy, charity and love, associated with these different circumstances, present an even deeper difficulty. They could be treated as utility information, and included as the affect of interdependencies in individual utility functions. Perhaps they can even be measured. Some people may be happier in the knowledge that other people are not being tortured. The rich may be happier when they have made sacrifices so that the poor are suffering less. Of course, there is also the darker side of human nature: feelings of envy and hatred. On what grounds can one be included and the other excluded?[24] Not strictly utilitarian ones?

4. Individualism

Utilitarianism is atomistic in two senses. One is an adherence to methodological individualism, to the notion that the utility of the community is simply the sum of the utilities of the individuals who are its members. The whole is not greater than the sum of the parts. The other is the belief, closely related to the economist's notion of rationality and the pursuit of self-interest, that individuals are the best judges of their own welfare or happiness. Interference with their choices, therefore, has to be exceptionally justified. In either case, the individual unit is the source of all utility. But whilst utilitarians hold consistently to the first kind of individualism, they are ambivalent about the second. Utility is counted at both the community and the individual level. Utilitarianism is a theory of both government and individual behaviour. As well providing a clear vision of what the public good means, it calls for a legislative programme to achieve the maximisation of aggregate utility. Individuals may not always be the best judges of their collective welfare. The unfettered pursuit of private interests may produce conflict rather than harmony. Citizens have to be educated in the public virtues, and their selfishness harnessed to the common advantage. Utilitarianism possesses a potential for social engineering. To reduce the possibility of a serious divergence between the pursuit of private and social utility, utilitarians tend to stress the underlying similarities in the psychology and beliefs of apparently different people.[25]

5. Equality

Each person is to count for one. Everyone is equal before the law and to be treated equally by the government. No person's utility is to be worth more than any one else's utility. This is sometimes put in the form of an anonymity requirement. As under welfarism and individualism, the personal identity of the recipients of utility should not matter. Having large inequalities in the distribution of personal income may be good or bad by utilitarian standards, but if (some of) the rich change places with the poor, and relative income levels remain the same, that is no reason for the judgement to change. Utilitarianism has always had a bias towards equality because it assumes that the enjoyment of income or wealth increases at a diminishing rate as income and wealth increase. The poor will make better use, in utility terms, of the superfluities of the rich than the rich themselves. Such a conclusion should be linked to the utilitarian theory of human psychology mentioned above. People are supposed, in this context, to have similar capacities to process pleasure, to be equal 'pleasure machines'. If not, then the pursuit of maximum aggregate utility will lead away from rather than towards equality in income distribution.[26] In any case, the utilitarian bias towards equality has always been severely tempered by its concern for practical effects on security and incentive.

6. Aggregation

The decision on whether one state of affairs is better than another depends on the sum of personal utilities. Only the total matters; not how it is divided up, nor the identity of the individual units. Inequalities in distribution are bad for just one reason; they lower the sum of utilities. Keeping more people alive is good, if total enjoyment is thereby increased. For most utilitarians, lower pleasures count as much as higher pleasures, the pleasures of the un-deserving as much as the deserving, and the economic as much as the non-economic. Sum-ranking alternative social states is one way of describing the process. The ultimate objective, however, is to maximise aggregate utility or welfare.[27]

7. Measurement

For these purposes, utility has to be something that can be quantified. Utilitarianism has always claimed to have a scientific approach to the social sciences: facts, precision and calculation rather than prejudice, obscurity and conjecture. So the cardinal measurement of utility with full inter-personal comparability would be extremely useful. In the perfect world of the hedonistic calculus, it should be possible to tell not just how many units of utility an individual enjoys, or how many more the same individual enjoys in one situation compared to another, but how many more the individual enjoys compared to another individual in the same situation, what their combined utility units amount to in different situations, and so on. These requirements are very demanding. There is the problem of measuring individual utilities; the choice of units, their scale and origin, and whether utility is to be measured like temperature or height. Then there is the problem of making inter-personal comparisons, and whether attempts to put oneself in the position of others can yield meaningful judgements about levels of and changes in their utility. Finally there is the problem of aggregation, of how this inter-personal utility information can be transformed into quantities of social utility. Unfortunately, the range of practicable measurements is wide and imperfect. There may be cardinal numbers for individual utility which cannot be used for inter-personal comparisons; inter-personal comparisons that can only be based on ordinal measurements; and no sum-totals of utility at all. Sum-totals of proxies for utility may have to suffice.[28]

The Utilitarians and Classical Utilitarianism

Bentham's writings contain references to all seven; some in considerable detail, others merely in outline. His followers concentrate on a narrower range, rarely the same and usually with a different emphasis. They all agree that greatest or general happiness should be the object of public policy. Either explicitly or implicitly, they also take consequences (in happiness) as the basis of judgements about actions. There are serious disagreements about the nature of this happiness, what it can include, how broadly it should be defined, and how accurately it may be measured. There are utilitarians who tend to be paternalistic, and others who stress the importance of individual rights; some who see value in the link between psychological and ethical hedonism, others who wish to make a clean break. Most of them draw egalitarian conclusions from the application of utilitarianism to distribution in principle but draw back from them in practice; one takes the opposite line. Utilitarianism is elusive because it is always changing. At each stage in the development, some of its assumptions have been shared with non-utilitarian economists. Whether the latter have always been conscious of the association is another matter. Nineteenth century versions of utilitarianism, therefore, are no more completely or purely 'classical' than those of the twentieth. The purpose of the list of 'classical' characteristics is pedagogic: to illuminate rather than replicate reality.

Without some leavening, any analysis confined to the closeness of the match between the classical utilitarians and this template would make for a dull, stodgy and un-historical book. What they did, how they were educated, who they met and read, what challenges they and the society in which they lived had to face, are equally important parts of the story. Each chapter will, therefore, offer a biographical sketch and attempt to put the work of the authors in a wider context. Empire, particularly India and Ireland, the rise of the industrial working class, the growth of towns, the beginnings of mass democracy, and the threat of poverty, inequality and unemployment, provided the inspiration for utilitarian policy. Most of this material is secondary. When dealing with matters of principle and theory, however, the classical utilitarians are usually allowed to speak for themselves. The choice and arrangement of the passages quoted is intended to distinguish their respective interpretations of the greatest happiness doctrine and, in particular, its bearing on the problems of political economy and welfare economics. Finally, it has to be remembered that the critics the classical utilitarians thought they were answering came from the ranks of philosophers, not economists. Even those economists who disliked or were embarrassed by utilitarianism, found its combination of welfarist consequentalism and a single (quantifiable) maximand all too convenient. They saw little profit in arguing out their doubts about the rest. On the other side, those philosophers who mounted challenges to the utilitarian hegemony, most notably F.D. Maurice, William Whewell, F.H. Bradley and T. H. Green, offered no basis for an alternative political economy. They had other concerns and owed different allegiances.

Notes

1. Hahnel and Albert (1990) p.14. It is only fair to add that the authors put classical utilitarianism in the proper historical context.
2. Arrow (1984) in Preface to *Collected Works* Vol I.
3. Robbins (1952) p.141, Halévy (1928), Stephen (1950).
4. Viner (1949) gives a much more balanced view of the association.
5. But see note 5 in Chapter 2.
6. Dasgupta and Heal (1979) p.260 make Sidgwick the last of the classical utilitarians.
7. Spencer is excluded on two grounds: his version of utilitarianism was rejected by most of the utilitarians; and he was no economist.
8. The description 'provisional' is taken from Robbins (1938).
9. Hollander (1985) p.602.
10. Schumpeter (1954) p.38.
11. Hahn (1982).

Notes continued

12. Marshall (1959) note on p.14, and Marshall (1975). Marshall has often been criticised for moralising. But he offered a course on Bentham while lecturing in the moral sciences and at least appreciated there was a problem to be faced.
13. Kant (1948) p.67.
14. For further discussion of the topics covered in this section the reader can consult Klappholz (1964), Roy (1989), Redman (1991), and Sen (1987 and 1993).
15. Pigou (1960) and (1962). It is remarkable how careful he was in avoiding utilitarian language as well as all references to utilitarian economists. Only in the later work on public finance was aggregate utility mentioned, or Sidgwick and Edgeworth allowed to make an appearance.
16. Arrow (1963) p.22.
17. As suggested by Strasnick (1979) p.64.
18. Hirschman (1981) p.299.
19. See Bell, Raiffa and Tversky (1988).
20. There is a powerful passage in Robbins (1952) which describes the need for prescription to have a goal, a test for good and bad consequences, in addition to positive facts.
21. Strictly speaking, they are Benthamite social welfare functionals, because social welfare is derived from individual utility functions rather than individual utility orderings. The Mill exercise is to be found in Riley (1988).
22. This characteristic might be thought to summarise aspects of the other six, but it is important to stress the power of the single objective to break ties and provide answers where other approaches are indecisive. For many utilitarians, taking general happiness to be the ultimate objective is the only assumption they can agree wholeheartedly about. The notion of preponderance is taken from Held (1970). See also Lyons (1965) p.vii.
23. Consequentialism has been defined by Scheffler (1988) to mean producing the best overall outcome from an impersonal point of view, giving equal weight to the interests of everyone. A narrower concept is employed here to bring out the similarities as well as differences between utilitarianism and other philosophies. Williams (1973), Sen (1979b), Sen and Williams (1982), Williams (1985) and Hammond (1986) are useful sources.
24. Welfarism has been examined extensively by Sen (1979b) and (1979c).
25. The Mills and Edgeworth were very interested in psychology and the similarities between individuals. Harsanyi (1976, 1982, 1986) is a modern neo-utilitarian who stresses the importance of a common human nature. See also under Equality and Measurement below. Sen introduces the conflict between individual rights and welfare in (1970) and develops it further in (1976). Although the target is the Paretian welfare criterion, there are many echoes of the debate within and around utilitarianism.
26. Bentham mentioned the possibility. Sidgwick saw that the implications could be difficult. Edgeworth enjoyed spelling them out. Sen (1973) completed the story.
27. As will be seen, John Mill was uneasy about maximisation and this way of looking at aggregation. If it were the only characteristic that mattered, then he could not be described as a utilitarian.
28. The obvious references for the problems of measurement start with Robbins (1962) and Majumdar (1958), and continue into Sen (1973, 1979a, and 1982). Interesting observations on inter-personal comparisons and extended sympathy are to be found in MacKay (1986) and Hurley (1989).

2. Jeremy Bentham

Bentham's Life and Character

On his death, it has been said, there were 126 boxes full of Bentham's work and 1 box full of Bentham.[1] Apart from visits to Paris in 1770 and to Russia between 1785 and 1786, nearly all of his 84 years (from 15th of February 1748 to 6th June 1832) seem to have been spent writing at home in London. As a gentleman of some means he was invited to stay at other people's country houses, and for a time had one of his own. But he was essentially a metropolitan. Educated at Westminster School and The Queen's College, Oxford, the intention was for Bentham to follow his father into the law; and although he was admitted to the Bar in 1769, he never practised. Instead, he assumed the role of a legal theorist and social reformer, devoting his considerable energies in a largely unsuccessful attempt to persuade governments and statesmen, leaders of opinion and his fellow intellectuals, anyone who might influence public policy, of the virtues of his many radical schemes.

William Hazlitt, who met and talked with him, made much fun of the situation.

> His name is little known in England, better in Europe, best of all in the plains of Chile and the mines of Mexico. He has offered constitutions to the New World, and legislated for future times. He has lived for the last forty years in a house in Westminster ... like an anchorite in a cell, reducing law to a system, and the mind of man to a machine.

On the serious side, the same essayist could also be very astute about Bentham's achievements and habits as a scholar.

> Mr Bentham is not the first writer (by a great many) who has assumed the principle of UTILITY as the foundation of just laws, and of all moral and political reasoning: his merit is, that he has applied this principle more closely and literally; that he has brought all the objections and arguments more distinctly labelled and ticketed, under this one head, and made a more constant and explicit reference to it at every step of his progress, than any other writer.[2]

17

As the founder of a school of applied philosophy called the 'philosophic radicals' or 'utilitarians', he was to have a more powerful and longer lasting influence than any of his critics imagined.

Bentham felt his own failures very keenly. Between 1792 and 1794, for example, he launched an expensive campaign for the construction of a model prison, which he, Bentham, would manage, called the Panopticon. A Bill to enact the proposal passed through the House of Lords; but subsequent negotiations with the government collapsed.[3] Unhappily, he never received proper recognition for the power and originality of his ideas at home. He was neither a prosperous businessman, nor a Member of Parliament, nor even a Professor at a University. Abroad, the situation was rather better. Some of his work was published in France and he became an honorary citizen of the French Republic in 1792. There were translations in other languages and several foreign governments expressed a wish to adopt his proposals. Of his productivity, there can be no doubt. In the 45 years, from the printing of his first book, a *Fragment on Government* in 1776, there came a steady stream of pamphlets, articles and manuscripts, most of which were to appear posthumously, and some of which still remain unpublished. It has been estimated that he must have written, on average, fifteen folio pages every day of his life.

If Bentham's personal history seems uneventful, the times through which he lived were marked by dramatic changes to the economy and social fabric of Britain and to its power, prestige and influence in Europe, North America and India. The strains imposed by the agricultural and industrial revolutions at home, the growth of population, the costs of the long drawn out struggle for dominance with France (for 36 of the years between 1756 and 1815 Britain was at war), the burdens of the national debt, the debates about the effectiveness of British trade and monetary policy, the consequences of the loss of the American colonies, the scandals that surrounded the role of the East India Company, and the example of the French Revolution, challenged both received opinions and established institutions. Bentham was not alone in recommending radical solutions. He welcomed the French and American Revolutions, but found them flawed by an adherence to what he regarded as the dangerous nonsense of natural rights. Nor, in spite of the honour bestowed on him, could he condone the violence of the new regime in France. Bentham always put the security of the person as his first priority. In fact, he was something of an authoritarian figure in his early years, an indifferent Tory until 1790, believing in his ability to persuade those in power to introduce the radical changes necessary for the future progress of the nation. Only when he became disillusioned by their short-sightedness and lack of response, was he converted to the cause of representative democracy. After 1815, he even became a reluctant participator in parliamentary elections.

Marx ridiculed Bentham as a 'purely English phenomenon' and as 'a genius by way of bourgeois stupidity'.[4] Whilst he was not the last to mistake the genius for a fool, he was right to point to the peculiarly insular nature both of 'Mr Jeremy's' intellectual legacy and of his eccentricities. Until the twentieth century, the development of utilitarianism as a philosophy of the social sciences was confined to Britain (the only possible exception being Gossen[5]); and the habit of calling his walking stick 'Dapple' and his sacred tea-pot 'Dick', his love of cats and a hypochondria that led at times to psychosomatic blindness, do suggest a certain kind of Englishman. Some of the doubts about the quality of his work also stem from the fact that he was, and is difficult to read. Again, Hazlitt has a valid point to make:

> Every possible suggestion finds a place, so that the mind is distracted as much as enlightened by his perplexing accuracy ... His words have been translated into French, they ought to be translated into English.

Over fond of inventing new words, or of using old names for new purposes (some of which like 'international' and 'maximise' have been adopted as common usage, others like 'Brithibernia' for the Union of England, Scotland and Ireland, or 'dyslogistic' as the opposite of eulogistic, have failed to stick), of expressing his thoughts in note form, or in long lists and tables, rather than in continuous narrative, and of leaving manuscripts unfinished, he may well have confounded those he wished to convert.

Mathew Arnold's remark that he freed himself from the obligation to consider Bentham's ideas because Bentham had not considered anyone else's, was unfair. Bentham did recognise his indebtedness to others, often in fulsome terms. Nevertheless, there was some evidence of a lack of intellectual sympathy, and a curious selectivity. For example, whilst Locke, Helvetius, Becharia, Hume and Priestly received due praise; and Adam Smith of *The Wealth of Nations* was idolised; Adam Smith of *The Theory of Moral Sentiments* was ignored, Rousseau, read and derided,[6] and Blackstone heard and read, and then used as a convenient scapegoat for all the real and imagined evils of contemporary jurisprudence. Bentham was self confident, assertive and abrasive. Yet it would be wrong to conclude that he was an isolated or lonely figure. He enjoyed a long association with a Whig magnate, the Earl of Shelburne, played chess with William Pitt, and went for long walks with David Ricardo. Other friendships had important consequences for the direction and dissemination of his work. Etienne Dumont, whom he met in 1788 at Bowood, the country house of Shelburne, was a political writer from Switzerland who accepted responsibility for publishing versions of Bentham's writings (in French as Hazlitt indicates) and thus making his ideas more widely known for the first time. James Mill, whom he met in 1808, introduced Bentham to the world of radical politics and, perhaps more importantly, to his son John Stuart Mill. The father was an uncritical admirer and populariser of the Benthamite philosophy; the son became its most accomplished interpreter and revisionist.

It is unfortunate that the presentation of so many of Bentham's ideas was left to others. His reputation has relied too much on the translated selections of Dumont, on the 11 volumes of his papers edited by John Bowring, published between 1838 and 1843, and, not least, on the personal judgements of critical admirers like John Stuart Mill. Only now, thanks to the efforts of the Bentham Committee at University College, London, are accurate editions of all his work being produced. At the start, the editors planned volumes under nine subject heads: Principles of Legislation, Penology and Criminal Law, Civil Law, Constitutional Law, Political Writing, Judicial Procedures, Economics and Society, Philosophy and Education, and Religion and the Church. Much remains to be done, but the 17 volumes published so far (9 of correspondence and 8 of text) reveal how careful the interpreter of Bentham's views has to be, given his habit of revising and occasionally contradicting earlier positions he had taken up. A more informed and better balanced view of Bentham emerges. He cannot be lightly dismissed as pedantic bore or a prophet without honour. In spite of the absurdity of some of his enquiries and the turgidity of much of his prose, even those who finally reject the doctrines of Benthamite utilitarianism cannot fail to be impressed by the depth of his scholarship and the breadth of his vision. Not the least important lesson to be learnt from a more careful reading of what Bentham wrote, is that he often foreshadows the supposed amendments and corrections of his followers and, on occasion, can be found to overtake them in their supposed radicalism.

The long if still partial list of his writings gives an astonishing picture of sustained effort and expanding interests. (Several titles have been abbreviated.

1774/76   A Comment on the Commentaries (NP) (Legislation)
1776   A Fragment of Government (P) (Legislation)

1780	Introduction to the Principles of Morals and Legislation (P) (Full version in 1789)
1782	On Laws in General (NP)
1787	In Defence of Usury (P)
	Panopticon (Letters) (P) (Penology)
1793/95	Manual of Political Economy (P)
1794	Proposals for a Mode of Taxation (P)
1795/96	Proposals for the Circulation of a Paper Currency
1800	Circulating Annuities (P)
1801	The True Alarm (P)
	In Defence of a Maximum (P)
1801/4	Institute of Political Economy (P)
1814/19	Deontology (NP) (Moral Philosophy)
1815/17	A Table of the Springs of Action
1816/17	Chrestomathia (P) (Education)
1818	Church of Englandism by 'An Oxford Graduate' (P)
1823	Influence of Natural Religion on the Temporal Happinessof Mankind by 'Philip Beauchamp' (P)
1825	Not Paul but Jesus by 'Gamaliel Smith' (P)
1825/26	The Constitutional Code (Vol. 1) (unfinished) (NP)
1829	Article(s) on Utilitarianism (P) (Philosophy)
1830	Official Aptitude Maximized: Expense Minimized. (P) (Constitutional Law)

Wherever possible, the dates given are for writing rather than for publication. Only those manuscripts marked with a (P) were published complete, as written, and in the year given. Those marked with (NP) remained unpublished. In other words, much of his most important work appeared in parts and posthumously. 'On Laws in General', for example, was not discovered until the 1930's. His religious volumes were printed under pseudonyms, probably from fear of being charged with blasphemy. Even Bentham seemed indifferent to their fate.

The Father of Utilitarianism

Like the *philosophes* of the eighteenth century, Bentham was anxious to apply the methods of the physical sciences to the study of human society. Advances in the understanding of the way in which the natural environment worked had already been achieved. Now it was time to discover the natural order, or the underlying mechanism of the social structure. The search for the laws of individual and collective behaviour led to an examination of the role of self-interest. If such a powerful motive was to be unleashed, how could social cohesion be preserved? Did a natural harmony exist, or did it have to be engineered? Acceptance of selfishness and the rejection of conventional restraints also raised the issue of morality. Where were virtue, duty, and honour to be found? How could sympathy and benevolence be explained? Again, Bentham shared the view of many of his contemporaries that a new code to guide private and public conduct had to be constructed, out of reason rather than established Church ethics. They wanted to preach a new religion. He strove to realise a more practical but equally remarkable ambition. Bentham belived that the principle of utility could serve as the unifying theme for the answers to these questions. It could be applied scientifically to the study of human behaviour; it showed how self-interest could be reconciled with the common good; and it offered the basis for a theory of personal and collective ethics. If citizens and governments always acted to maximise the greatest possible surplus of pleasure over pain, then all obstacles to social progress would be swept away. Above all else, he was intent on devising a programme of radical reform for the law, for government, for education, and for the economy. No wonder he hinted at becoming the Newton of the moral sciences.

There were several versions of the philosophy of happiness on offer in eighteenth century. William Paley, for example, published in 1785 a popular Christian version of the notion of virtue as doing good to mankind in obedience to the will of God, and for the sake of everlasting happiness.[7] Neither the law of honour, nor the law of the land, nor custom, nor even the Scriptures provided sufficient or reliable guides to right conduct. Instincts of pains and pleasures, including the pains and pleasures of the next world, revealed the will of God. Bentham, as a determinedly secular thinker, would have found this kind of argument anathema. A very different illustration of the same principle can be found in William Godwin's anarchist plea of 1793. He also believed that the true object of moral and political life was pleasure and happiness, and that Justice required the greatest sum of pleasure and happiness. He was even prepared to claim that a scale of happiness could be calculated for different individuals.[8] Bentham would have found the foundation for these views equally unacceptable. He was a radical not a revolutionary, who attacked anarchy as the new constitutional disease.

To be fair, Bentham did not claim to have invented the principle of utility. (In spite of what J.S. Mill thought, he could claim to have used the word 'utilitarian'). Whilst acknowledging intellectual debts to

David Hume, Hartley, Helvetius and Beccaria,[9] he held that it was a phrase about the greatest happiness of the greatest number in a 1768 pamphlet of Joseph Priestley which made him cry out like Archimedes on the discovery of the fundamental principle of Hydrostatics, 'Eureka'.[10] By 1780, he was boldly stating that,

> Nature has placed mankind under the governance of two sovereign masters, pain and pleasure. It is for them alone to point out what we ought to do, as well as to determine what we shall do. On the one hand the standard of right and wrong, on the other the chain of causes and effects, are fastened to their throne.[11]

Bentham had more trouble in showing how these sovereign masters were linked to the sum of interests. Several years later he was to take care in defining the way in which the individual contributed to the overall objective.

> Utilitarianism states as the only proper end in view of the moralist and the legislator the greatest happiness of the greatest number. And as the only means by which any individual can be engaged to operate toward it, the happiness of the same individual: viz; either by indicating or creating an interest operating upon him as a motive and engaging him to operate towards that end.[12]

He is now suggesting that individuals will not always be motivated to take into account the interests of the greater number. Their self-interest must be somehow harnessed, may even have to be manipulated, to the greater end. They must come to see their own happiness as including the happiness of others. Bentham returned to this theme over and over again.

Such was the basis of Benthamite philosophy. They remain, with the amendments and refinements of successive generations, its hallmarks. What emerges from Bentham is clearly both a theory of psychological hedonism and a theory of ethics. All actions, including those done for moral reasons, are motivated by the pursuit of pleasure and the avoidance of pain. Bentham believed that seeking pleasure and avoiding pain followed naturally from the psychology of human beings and, in turn, would lead to the best state of the world for the communities to which they belonged: universal happiness. He saw no conflict between is and ought statements, between use of the principle of utility as a standard of right and wrong and an explanation of cause and effect. He did recognise, however, that it is one thing to approve or disapprove of every act of an individual, or of a government, in terms of their contribution to the greatest happiness of the greatest number, and quite another thing to expect every act to automatically have that effect.

Natural Harmony

Of course it should not be forgotten that another idea given much prominence in the 18th century, and among the founders of the new science of political economy, was that of a natural harmony of interests between competing individuals. If all individuals followed their own interests (in Bentham's terms maximised their utilities), the 'hidden hand' of competitive markets would ensure that the maximum possible number of interests was satisfied. Selfish behaviour would have unintended and beneficent social consequences. Bentham accepted the idea of a natural order as long as it meant an empirically observable phenomena of social interaction. He could not abide its description as a divinely constructed part of a controlled universe. Natural rights, for example, were

> simple nonsense: natural and imprescriptible rights, rhetorical nonsense, nonsense on stilts.[13]

A right had to be shown to be advantageous to society before it could be established. He feared that they would otherwise become the enemies of law and the tools of the despot.[14]

The self-regarding motive, on the other hand, could be shown to have a vital role in society. All human minds possessed feelings of self-regard and sympathy for others, though in different proportions:

> But in self-regard even sympathy has its root; and if, in the general tenor of human conduct, self-regard were not prevalent over sympathy, even over sympathy for all others put to-gether, no such species as the human could have existence.[15]

Where Bentham appeared to disagree with the idea of 'natural' harmony was in his denial that this essential motive, this driving force of material progress, could do the job on its own. In places, he implies that there had to be controls, otherwise society would disintegrate. Even when concentrating on political economy, he refers to the danger of war with all.[16] Individuals had to be educated, guided, moulded and persuaded, to ensure that their pursuit of self-interest could be reconciled with universal happiness. Those who would attempt this exercise need to be realistic and very well informed.

> To deny the selfish principle would not diminish its force: but to diminish its force, the knowledge of it is essential. To diminish the principle is impossible. To direct it so it may agree with the general interest is practicable...[17]

The creation of the conditions in which the harmony of interests can be realised becomes the responsibility of government. For Bentham, this implies a certain amount of social engineering.

Bentham's position on the natural order in society might seem little different from that of Adam Smith. Neither could be described as doctrinaire advocates of laissez faire. Both agreed that, on occasion, self-interest and competition could be opposed to public interest. They may have differed on the number and nature of these exceptions, not on the general rule. Similarly, Bentham's comments on the relative strengths of self-regard and extra-regard, on concern for close kin and friends compared to distant neighbours and strangers, echo those of Smith. It is rather surprising, therefore, to find evidence of a deeper tension between them. Bentham often starts with a minor difference on a detail of economic reform, which then is turned into a violent disagreement with Smith on fundamentals. While making out the case for an upper limit to the rate of interest, which he knew contradicted Smith's view that the government should keep its hands off, Bentham could not resist firing off a broadside.

> I have not, I never have had, nor ever shall have, any horror, sentimental or anarchical, of the hand of government. I leave it to Adam Smith, and the champions of the rights of man (for confusion of ideas will jumble together the best subject and the worst citizens on the same ground) to talk of invasions of natural liberty, and to give as a special argument against this and that law, an argument the effect of which would put a negative upon all laws.[18]

The estrangement also surfaced when Bentham felt that his utilitarianism was being threatened. In his marginals to the *Springs of Action*, Smith's teaching on the propensity to truck, barter and exchange is attacked for substituting 'smoke for light' (why not simply say, individuals maximise utility?) and for suggesting that aversion to wealth has a place in the human breast alongside the desire for wealth.[19]

It is not that Bentham lost respect for Smith. On the contrary, further on in the same piece, Smith, David Hume and Thomas Reid are credited with cultivating moral sense in Scotland after it had been all but abandoned in England. It is rather that he may have felt overshadowed by Smith the moral philosopher. After all, Smith had a prior claim to be the author of a study that was explicitly non-utilitarian in the Hume sense of that word. *The Theory of Moral Sentiments* had been first published in 1759, and gone through six editions; the last, with major amendments, appearing just before his death in 1790. In an advertisement to this final version, Smith had claimed that it fulfilled

an earlier promise to give an account of the 'general principles of law
and government'. Yet nowhere did Bentham actually mention this
contemporary alternative to much of his own efforts. He must have
been aware of its existence. It had been well-received and widely
discussed in London.[20] Was Bentham exhibiting his lack of intellectual
sympathy, his incurious selectivity, in deliberately ignoring the great
man's favourite book? Or was he fearful of admitting the strength of
the opposing view? The latter interpretation would explain his distress
over Smith's concept of the propensity to truck, barter and exchange.
Nowhere in the *Wealth of Nations* is reliance placed on the pursuit of
simple, all-inclusive utility. The division of labour is not attributed
directly to human wisdom 'which foresees and intends the general
opulence to which it gives occasion'. On the contrary, the existence of
a 'system of natural liberty and justice' is treated as a necessary
condition for the success of economic society, as something to be
created. Thus Bentham would have found much more to upset him in
the language of the *Theory of Moral Sentiments*. Propensities of
wonder, surprise, and admiration; designs of the Almighty;
considerations of merit and duty; and above all else, the notion that the
'toil and bustle of this world' serves 'vanity' not 'ease or pleasure'.

The Nature of Utility

The nature of utility bothers philosophers more than economists. Utility
can be interpreted as a state of mind, of being happy; or it can be
interpreted as a state of the world, of circumstances which might be
expected to lead to happiness, and thus be desired or preferred. The
problems of taking either interpretation have already been discussed in
the Introduction. Economists favour desire or preference accounts
because they seem to be more objective. Behaviour can be observed
and the inference drawn that people are better off when they move to a
more preferred state of the world. Economists need not become
involved in making deeper judgements: whether being better off in this
sense really means an increase in 'goodness'. They need not pretend to
be getting inside people's minds. They can, of course, be mistaken
about the evidence and about the ability of people to choose what is
good for them. Bentham, who was both a pychological hedonist
(believing that people seek happiness) and an ethical hedonist
(believing that seeking happiness was morally good), used states of
mind and states of the world accounts of utility.

> By utility is meant that property of any object, whereby it tends to produce benefit, advantage, pleasure, good, or happiness (all this in the present case comes to the same thing) or (what comes again to the same thing) to prevent the happening of mischief, pain, evil, or unhappiness to the party whose interest is concerned.[21]

and again, utility is

> a vain word, a word devoid of meaning ... only to those who do not understand that it refers ... to human feelings: feelings painful and pleasurable, pains and pleasures.

In the deveopment of his ideas about morality, however, he gave priority to feelings. Painful and pleasurable feelings are essential to produce the best states of the world. They are the basis of what he called all the other 'fictions'. Take them away, he said, and concepts of justice, duty, obligation and virtue, and even happiness, which people are supposed to desire, lose any meaning.[22]

Practical Benthamism

However difficult and controversial these concepts were to prove to be for Bentham's successors, they seemed to have had no influence on the growing acceptance of what might be called practical Benthamism. Although he had only a small band of dedicated disciples at his death, and not one piece of legislation to his name, that was soon to change. Already in the 1820's, F.D.Maurice was reporting that Benthamism was the prevalent faith among the young intellectuals at Cambridge.[23] Meanwhile, the second generation of philosophic or philosophical radicals, as the utilitarians were originally called, made up in energy and influence for any shortcoming in numbers. It is possible to exaggerate their contribution to the great reforms of the British legal and political system in the nineteenth century. One subsequent celebrator of Bentham's prophetic powers, claimed no fewer than twenty major enactments, from the extension of the suffrage and the overhauling of the jury system to clean water and cheap postage, in his name. Certainly there were direct links between Bentham and some of the great reformers of the 19th century. Edwin Chadwick who tirelessly promoted sanitation, for example, helped nurse Bentham during his last illness. But other pioneers of social improvement, like the Earl of Shaftesbury, would have found their inspiration in a more traditional form of evangelism. A more balanced view would stress the importance of the contribution of the utilitarians to the general climate of reform rather than the number of men and woman who were directly moved to implement Benthamite proposals.[24]

By contrast, the utilitarians suffered the same condemnation as the classical economists for being unsympathetic to the condition of the working classes, and in particular for being the main supporters of the dreaded workhouse system. Whether fair or not, that has to balanced against Bentham's hidden programme. Considerable doubt must be expressed about whether all of Bentham's followers in the nineteenth century fully appreciated, or were prepared to admit, the advanced nature of his radicalism, from the support of female suffrage, and artificial means of birth control, to anti-clericalism and the legalisation of homosexuality. Nevertheless, he was far from being a popularist. His attitude to contemporary leaders of working class and lower middle class movements was one of disdain. They failed to attain what he regarded as proper standards of intellectual debate, and often advocated extreme and violent solutions. Andrew Bain, the biographer of James Mill, quotes Bentham on his attitude to Hunt and Cobbett, 'as vapid animals devouring one another in a drop of water'. Violence was an ever present threat to security of society.

> ...the danger now is from the great multitude; in respect of the disposition to unruliness which has been, and continues to be, propagated, with but too much success, among the lower orders, among those (let it never be out of mind) of whom is composed the vast majority of people.[25]

He even found an excuse to accuse the Irish of being particularly susceptible to idleness and drunkenness. Utilitarians could have sympathy for the plight of the lower orders; they could not stand with them on the barricades. Their task was to build a rational and realistic basis for government and legislative reform, not to promise an immediate utopia.

Bentham's Economics

Bentham's reputation as an economist has never stood very high. Ricardo was cool. The Mills read and professed Ricardian rather than Benthamite economics. Jevons may have tried to break from the Ricardian traditione, but there is no evidence that he found any inspiration in Bentham's economics. Sidgwick read John Mill and Jevons, while Edgeworth read almost everyone. Neither seemed to have read Bentham on economics. It is hardly surprising, therefore, to find Marshall balancing his view of Bentham as one of the most influential of Adam Smith's immediate successors with the remark that he wrote very little about economics. Keynes was even more dismissive:

Bentham was not an economist at all. Indeed, he held him partly responsible for the worst excesses of Marxism. Marxism became the reductio ad absurdum of Benthamism by overvaluing the economic and materialist criterion.[26] Thanks to the efforts of Jacob Viner, Lionel Robbins, Werner Stark, Terence Hutchinson and others, we now have a much better informed picture of Bentham the economist.

The critics did have an excuse. Only a small proportion of the manuscripts which he specifically devoted to the subject, mainly written in the years between the 1770's and 1804, have ever been published. Of those, perhaps ten percent fill the three volumes edited by Stark. Yet Bentham first achieved fame as a writer on economics with the publication of his pamphlet *In Defence of Usury* in 1787. Taking issue with Adam Smith on the desirability of legal limits to the rate of interest, Bentham was careful to express his indebtedness in fulsome terms,

> as far as your track coincides with mine, I should come much nearer to the truth were I to say that I owe everything to you.[27]

Adam Smith, in turn, is credited with recognising the force of Bentham's attack on his position. The point of the episode, however, is Bentham's use of the phrase, 'as far as your track coincides with mine'. As has already been explained, their tracks did not coincide very much, even in economics. Bentham's vision was very different. He was preoccupied with the use of political economy as an art. Many of his pamphlets and articles were about ways of improving the effectiveness of monetary and fiscal policy. Ingenious schemes for easing the burden of the national debt, for the taxation of inherited wealth, and for a new paper currency were pressed hard. He made pioneering attempts to exploit the crude statistical evidence then available about the performance of the economy, and gave original twists to contemporary themes like the strategic role of the country banks in the determination of the supply of money, and the Physiocratic separation of agricultural and manufacturing output.

Though fertile and powerful enough in their own right,[28] they failed to impress wider audience. Bentham had no more success with economic reform than he had with penal reform. The failure of his scheme for circulating annuities was an especially bitter blow. Ricardo, in contrast, swept all before him. Although Bentham shared the beliefs of the other classical economists in free trade and the virtues of private enterprise, his own agenda for permitted government interference was much longer.[29] Part of the explanation for this lack of influence must be found, once again, in his style. His pamphlets do go on. They do not read like the work of a analytical economist. They lack clarity and precision, virtues that Ricardo showed to perfection when writing about similar subjects. Any reader of *In Defence of Usury*, for example, will soon grow tired of wondering where Bentham's argument is leading. Is he for or against? Is Adam Smith right or wrong? The point eventually emerges. Smith was mistaken in clinging to the idea that there were some benefits in the regulation of interest rates. (Bentham seemed to contradict himself later, see his *In Defence of a Maximum*.) Bentham once claimed that Ricardo was his spiritual grandson, with James Mill as the intermediary. It would be more accurate to say that Ricardo was James Mill's instructor in economics even if Bentham was the dominant intellectual influence in nearly everything else. There is no evidence that Bentham shared Ricardo's fascination with economic theory, or understood the importance of the debates that took place between Ricardo and Malthus on the subject of value, distribution and growth. It is equally apparent that most of Bentham's contemporaries among the classical economists failed to appreciate what the utilitarians were about.[30]

It is not surprising, therefore, to find that Bentham compared his little treatise, the *Manual of Political Economy*, written in the years 1793/95, to Adam Smiths *Wealth of Nations*, as what a book on the art of medicine is to a book of anatomy or physiology. He never attempted a treatise on the pure science of economics, and the *Manual* was followed by another exercise in normative economics, the *Institute of Political Economy*. Yet, although none of his particular cures for policy problems proved to have a lasting impact, his general application of the principle of utility became the source of two essentially different strands in the subsequent development of economics. One is the subjective utility theory of value and the other welfare economics. The latter is the principle subject of this book.

Bentham himself failed to exploit the potential of a utility theory of value. Like Smith and Ricardo, when he wrote that utility meant the property of a thing to produce benefit or happiness, he was referring to value-in-use, not value-in-exchange. Whether he followed the line of Ricardo's argument in defending the labour theory of value and holding that utility was a necessary but not a sufficient condition for the phenomenon of exchange value, is not known. What is certain is that Ricardo could explicitly reject utility as the measure of relative value and still remain committed to the greatest happiness principle as a guide to policy.[31] Perhaps he had second thoughts about using it as the basis for a scientific project, but in this sense at least he was a

Benthamite. Some classical economists, like Nassau Senior and J.R. McCulloch, were content to be Ricardians in value theory and non-Benthamite in policy. Others, like the Mills, were strongly Ricardian in value theory and strongly Benthamite in policy. When the so-called marginal revolution came along, most of those who helped to develop the subjective utility theory were indifferent to the rest of Benthamite philosophy. Only Jevons among them saw a necessary connection between the two themes. Sidgwick went back to Ricardo on value thory and back to Bentham on policy. Edgeworth was to be ambiguous about both. The true Benthamite interest in the measurement of marginal utility, for example, derives from a practical concern to maximize aggregate utility, and not with exchange value. The Austrian school has an epistemiology of its own to support subjective value.

Welfare Economics

Bentham distinguished between economics as a science and economics as an art. In much the same way as Pigou was to argue some 130 years later,[32] the science was the pure theory that shed light and served as the guide, while the art applied the science and produced the fruit of economic policy. It is impossible to have one without the other; but it is the fruit that makes the effort of understanding the science worthwhile. Unlike most of his contemporaries, however, Bentham wanted to see fruit ripening on many trees. His ambition encompassed all the social sciences. This breadth of interest has two important implications. The first is that only a small proportion of Bentham's views on economic policy can be found in his purely economic writings. The second is that his approach to economic policy was bound to be influenced by his general philosophy. Normative statements are to be found in both the science and the art of each related subject. He was a theoretician of the normative

In order to promote policies that would increase the well-being of individuals and the communities to which they belong, the failings of existing institutions have first to be revealed and then appropriate reforms designed. It was not simply a matter of deciding whether, for example, the repeal of the Corn Laws, or the reform of the Poor Law, or the introduction of a tax on inherited wealth would increase general happiness. There were larger and more general issues at stake. Bentham was interested in the distribution of personal incomes and the strength of the case for equality, in the defence of the institution of private property, in the merits of private choice in a market economy, and in the proper limits to the role of the government. Fairness and efficiency were to be judged in terms of the same principle, that of the greatest happiness. If redistribution of income or wealth from the rich to the poor could be shown to increase the net total of happiness, having taken careful account of all the possible pains, then the redistribution was to be recommended. If parts of the existing system of taxation could be shown to impose more damage on the people who paid them than they confered benefit on the community at large, then they should be swept away. If the state could provide badly needed services that individuals were unable to provide for themselves (or might not be willing to provide for themselves), then the general presumption against government interference should be relaxed (and the government actually make the provision itself or force individuals to make the provision for themselves).

The underlying assumptions that Bentham made in order to arrive at these policy conclusions (the way in which he applied the principle of utility to economics and the other social sciences) form the basis of utilitarian welfare economics. As has already been suggested, evidence of all seven 'ideal' characteristics of 'classical' utilitarianism can be found in his writings. Unfortunately, these vary in quality and scope very widely. Some of the documents quoted in the Stark editions, for example, are really compilations of extracts from the Bowring editions, where no attempt was made to distinguish one sub-discipline from another.[33] In any case, Bentham rarely keeps to the point when he is writing on any subject, often introducing economic subjects into philosophical or legal manuscripts. But thanks to the efforts of the dedicated editors of the Bentham Project, much more of it is now available.[34]

1. Utility as the Single Objective. In his strictly economic manuscripts, Bentham is cautious about the possibilities of applying the principle of utility. He takes Adam Smith to task for not putting as the sole or principal part of his enquiry into the *Wealth of Nations*, how the law ought to be, what ought and ought not to be done. There is too much science and not enough art. Yet Bentham himself is content to use wealth as a proxy for utility. The wealth of the community, he says, is clearly the sum of the wealth of the people in the community. Utility is occasionally mentioned, but in a neutral sense and, at first, without explicit reference to pleasure, happiness, or the avoidance of pain.[35] The connection between the art of government in matters of political economy and the maximisation of aggregate utility comes later. The object or general aim of the sovereign is then defined in terms of the happiness of the several members of the community taken together, and with reference to the whole of time. Even on such matters as taxation and redistribution, he is content to let money income or wealth stand for happiness or utility.

There can be no doubt, however, that happiness or utility is always the ultimate end. When emphasising the practical importance of the subordinate aims of subsistence, security, abundance and equality, all measured in wealth or income, Bentham will only recommend them provided they lead to utility or happiness. Political economy, he insists, will be a study without meaning if there is no reference to the effects of legislation on human feelings. Subsistence is defined as the minimum level of material wealth necessary for mere existence, so that without it there can be no enjoyment. The first duty of government, in political economy, is to provide subsistence for all its citizens. The second duty is the provision of security, which means for Bentham, as it did for Smith, defence from threats and violence of fellow citizens and of the home government, as much as from foreign citizens and governments. It also means laws that protect private property and contracts, and give the right of redress against the corruption and extortions of government officials. Security and subsistence are the foundations of an efficient market economy: the necessary conditions for the achievement abundance and equality. Thus while Bentham is generally against government interference in the sphere of political economy, always regarding legislation as a necessary evil, he makes an exception for security. The legislator is always properly engaged in the pursuit of law and order. Subsistence and abundance should follow once security had been establishment.

Abundance means the total wealth of the country, opulence or the per capita wealth of the citizens of the country. When attempting to measure total happiness, therefore, the size of the population, populousness, is taken into account as well as opulence. (The combination of Malthusian worries about the growth of population and philosophical speculation about the optimum population of a country has fascinated utilitarians since Bentham.) In the *Institute of Political Economy*[36] populousness is desirable not just because it increases the number of people hopefully enjoying some abundance, but also because it increases the number of men available to defend this abundance from external threat. Although equality is mentioned at this point in the development of Bentham's thought, there is no elaboration of what it means and how it contributes to happiness.

In his non-economic manuscripts, Bentham is painstaking in the way in which pleasures and pains are analysed. The groundwork is laid in his *Introduction to the Principles of Morals and Legislation*. The value of pains and pleasures depends on their intensity, duration, certainty or uncertainty, propinquity (nearness) and remoteness. For an act which might give rise to pleasures and pains rather than the pleasures and pains themselves, there are two other circumstances to be taken into account: fecundity and purity. These relate to the power of the acts to generate the desired, or undesired effects. Bentham is not finished. Having detailed six or eight circumstances (depending on how they are counted) that affect the value of pains and pleasures, he goes on to distinguish fourteen different kinds of pleasure and twelve different kinds of pain.

Although he insists that there is no such thing as a bad motive, and no justification for distinguishing between the same amount of utility derived from different kinds of enjoyment, the pursuit of pleasure and the avoidance of pain do not have to be purely self-regarding. In Bentham's *Deontology*, benevolence can be admitted as a proper motive, provided it contributes, directly or indirectly, to the utility of the individual affected by the condition of others.

> To deny the existence of ... this social affection would be to talk in the teeth of all experience ... But the pleasure I feel at the prospect of bestowing pleasure on my friend, whose pleasure is it but mine? The pain which I feel at the sight or under the apprehension of seeing my friend oppressed with pain, whose pain is it but mine?[37]

For Bentham, prudence, probity and beneficence are the three qualities of character contributing to human happiness. Regard for the individual's own, ultimate interests is thus expanded to encompass obedience to social conventions and laws, positive acts of charity, and the negative acts of refraining from harming others. The individual may even learn to adopt habits which conform to public opinion and attract the approval of others, build up a fund of goodwill, but only because they increase that individual's own feelings of happiness.[38] Utility remains the final test of what is prudent, proper and beneficent.

When it comes to the happiness of the community and the rule to be followed by the legislator, Bentham is forced by the misrepresentations of his greatest happiness principle, to introduce amendments. It is 'the greatest number' part that causes all the trouble. So the single objective finally becomes

> the greatest happiness of the greatest number of members of the community: of all without exception, in so far as possible: of the greatest number, on every occasion on which the nature of the case renders it a matter of necessity, to make sacrifice of a portion of the happiness of a few, to the greatest happiness of the rest.[39]

Those occasions when maximising aggregate happiness requires balancing gains to the majority against losses to a minority, Bentham still hopes will be small. But he now recognises that when they happens the balancing will be very difficult. In fact, he goes so far as to accept that the calculation of the net effects of every piece of legislation may be impossible.[40] To compound the problem, he elaborates on a new dimension of happiness built around the concepts of security expectation and disappointment prevention. Pain or disutility can arise if members of a community suffer disappointment at not being allowed to enjoy the protection of the law which they had believed was properly theirs. They should have confidence that they will be able to develop their own projects for a better life without interference from other people and the abuse of state power. Failure to realise their own future utility plans is very damaging, and providing this kind of protection is a prime responsibility of the utilitarian legislator.[41]

Allowing the sacrifice of the interests of some people to be compensated or outweighed by the advantage to others, puts Bentham's principle of the greatest happiness of the greatest number clearly into the category of preponderance theories. One situation, one set of circumstances, or state of the world for individuals in a community, is said to be better, because it yields more utility. The greater is the stength of this magnitude, the greater is the public good. Different states of the world can be ranked in order of merit. There is a way of comparing and adding up the utility of different people, and arriving at an overall judgement. The total of utility may be greater, at least in exceptional circumstances, when the utility of some members of the community actually goes down (has to be sacrificed). Most importantly in Bentham's theory, the utility of each person is a function of a wide range of economic, political and social factors. The simplifications of the narrow economic sphere are left behind. The nature of the magnitude that predominates, is multidimensional.

2. Consequentalism. Utilitarianism and consequentalism seem inseparable. Happiness, or the surplus of pleasure over pain, is the only thing that matters. All acts must be judged by their happiness or utility outcomes. Bentham is always clear on this point. In the *Introduction* he argues that the general tendency of an act is dependent on its total consequences.[42] In the subsequent discussion, he dismisses two alternatives to the principle of utility; one he calls aestheticism and the other sympathy/antipathy. Aestheticism is taken to mean another kind of consequentalism, in which acts are judged according to whether their effect is to reduce happiness. Sympathy/antipathy is taken to mean an approach which tries to ignore consequences and approves or disapproves of acts merely because someone feels moved to approve or disapprove. In other words, it is based on no good reason at all.[43] An almost identical argument is to be found many years later in his *Article on Utilitarianism*. The only refinement is that the rejection of principles like sympathy/antipathy or benevolence/malevolence has become an attack on 'ipsedixitism'. Ipsedixitism is the view of right and wrong in human conduct which is based implicitly or explicitly on the declared opinion of the writer or speaker making the judgement, simply because they say so, and again with no apparent reason.[44]

Bentham holds that ipsedixitism is fatally flawed because it will not recognise the need for an external standard of what is right and wrong, and mistakenly relies on moral judgements of the form: it is good because it conforms to our moral intuition or obeys the moral code which we all accept. He will not accept any appeals to the laws of nature and reason, or to natural justice, equity, or good order. Utility is the only sensible external standard. He is equally firm on moral judgements about intentions. Consequences can be described as good or bad, but motives, interests or desires taken by themselves are neither good nor bad..

> Now pleasure is in itself a good ... the only good ... and pain is the only evil ... it follows, therefore, immediately and incontestably, that there is no such thing as any sort of motive that is in itself a bad one.[45]

Motives, interests and desires, can have good outcomes depending on the circumstances of the acts they produce. For example, acts done out of self-interest might have good effects, while those done out of sympathy might have bad effects.

3. Welfarism. Utilitarianism is a special case of consequentalism. Outcomes are important, not possibilities, and are to be judged strictly in terms of pleasures and pains. Bentham has a very broad view of the factors that caused happiness. He argues that ignoble pleasure count as much as noble pleasure. Push-pin can be as good as poetry to some people. Any attempt to distinguish between them on the grounds of an all embracing and non-utilitarian concept of the good, is dismissed as nonsense. Those who follow such a path end up with a summum bonum, a sovereign good, which

> consists in virtue, it consists of this and t'other: it consists in anything rather than pleasure. It is the Irishman's apple which was to be made of nothing but quinces.[46]

Bentham seems to saying that everything can be included, in the sense of being counted, as long as it is under the heading of utility: all virtues and vices, wealth, degrees of equality, good works. Some people may think they are acting out of pure benevolence, but in reality they are pursuing utility because they want others to see them performing good works. They take pleasure in being admired by others.

The love of justice, for example, can be analysed into simple elements of pleasure: into the pleasure of self-preservation against the harmful acts of others and the government, the pleasure (pain?) of sympathy for others suffering injustice, the pleasure of sympathy for the community with its collective interest in the maintenance of justice, and even the pleasure (pain?) of antipathy towards those committing acts of injustice. A similar list of 'simple' pleasures are derived from the love of liberty.[47] Why else, Bentham asks, should these things be desirable? In the language of the modern interpretations of classical utilitarianism, his approach is still welfarist because it reduces all apparently non-utility information to individually experienced pleasures (and the avoidance of pains). Bentham never doubts that (enough) people desire justice and liberty, so that justice and liberty will always be counted as good. But there is still no absolute standard, no final judgement of right and wrong, apart from the general principle of utility. He also seems to admit that it can be applied indirectly through the interests of the community, in addition to the direct interests of individuals. There is a hint that individuals can conceive of a collective good.

4. Individualism. Like the Physiocrats and Adam Smith, Bentham insists that individuals are the best judges of their own welfare. They have no need of a higher authority to tell them how to gain their happiness and avoid their pains. In his earlier economic writings, Bentham states the general presumption in favour private choice.

> With few exceptions, and they are not considerable ones, the attainment of the maximum enjoyment will be most effectively secured by leaving each individual to pursue his own particular maximum of enjoyment as he is in the possession of the means.[48]

> Generally speaking, ... no one knows what it is for your interests to do, as you yourself: no one who is disposed with so much ardour and constancy to pursue it.[49]

From the start, he is highly suspicious of any notion of society as an organic whole, in which the whole was somehow greater than the sum of the parts.

> The community is a fictitious body, composed of the individual persons who are
> considered as constituting as it were its members. The interests of the community
> then, is what? ... the sum of the interests of the several members who compose
> it.[50]

Nevertheless, Bentham takes human beings to be social animals who
live in regulated communities, because they recognise the benefits of
co-operation and the protection given by the system of laws. There are
collective needs to be met, and he wants governments to serve the
interests of all members of the community, not just a small privileged
minority, and certainly not just themselves.

In his later economic writings, exceptions to the general rule of
minimising government interference grow more important. Individuals
sometimes lack the inclination, the power, or the knowledge to do for
themselves what would increase their welfare, or when the spontaneous
exertions of individuals could not be expected to provide projects that
would increase national wealth.[51] Furthermore, individuals may have
the inclination, the knowledge, and the power, in terms of wealth, to
provide certain services for themselves, and still not be able to proceed
in the absence of the necessary market structures. They may not have
the necessary knowledge. They may not be able to persuade others to
join in a co-operative venture. Self-interest can be destructive.

> That the uncoerced and unenlightened propensities and powers of individuals are
> not adequate to the end without the control and guidance of the legislature is a
> matter of fact of which the evidence of history, the nature of man, and the very
> existence of political society are so many proofs.[52]

But the phrase 'political society' can cover a wide spectrum of public
and private provision. Purely personal interests compete with interests
as members of a family, as members of voluntary and public bodies
within general society, as citizens of the state, even as citizens of the
world.[53]

For Bentham of the *Institute of Political Economy*, the most
important work of the legislator concerns the provision of security in
all its branches. Security is 'the seed of abundance', the protection of
the individual against the 'mischief', and the 'apprehension of
mischief' wrought by other individuals and governments. Individuals
must still have a protected sphere, free from the danger and fear of
interference, in which to develop their own projects.[54] For Bentham of
the *Constitutional Code*, this legislature will be the product of
representative democracy, with frequent elections and the power of

recall. The actions of its administrators are to be subject to as many checks and balances he could devise, to minimise possible corruption and bureaucratic waste. Even so, the list of possible government ministries and public responsibilities is long, much longer than those of his contemporaries among the classical economists. Apart from stressing the importance of the public production and dissemination of knowledge useful for the proper working of the private enterprise economy, he recommends hospitals and work houses for the poor, insurance against unemployment and ill-health, education for the children of the poor, and a public health system. It reads like an early manifesto for the social market economy.

5. Equality. The first sense in which Bentham uses the word equality is in equal treatment for all individuals before the law. Every person's interests, well-being, utility, liberties and rights should count the same. No one's happiness can be shown to have any stronger claim than any other's.[55] There should be no discrimination in favour of the rich and powerful. The second sense in which he uses the term is in the personal distribution of income and wealth. In certain circumstances, a more equal distribution will increase aggregate utility. Absolute equality is distinguished from practicable equality. A distribution in which everyone has exactly the same income or wealth only has a place in a subject like physics. In human societies, too much equality will undermine the incentive to production. On the other hand, a reduction in the degree of inequality which falls short of this extreme, can increase total utility by strengthening the security and abundance of the poorer members of the community. Bentham further complicates the notion of practicable equality by mentioning that individuals may have different sensibilities of enjoyment, or different capacities to convert units of income or wealth into utility. The implications of this crucial admission are not examined.

Without subsistence there can be no enjoyment and, therefore, no utility. Above subsistence (i.e. some abundance), utility would be positive and rising, but it will not rise in proportion. Property and wealth are used interchangeably to mean the 'articles' of subsistence and abundance. The relation between their increase and the increase in happiness, 'the increase of pleasure by extent', and the argument for equality, is most clearly set out in Bentham's unfinished *Civil Code*.

1. Each portion of wealth is connected with a corresponding portion of happiness.
2. Of two individuals, possessed of unequal fortunes, he who possesses the greatest wealth will possess the greatest happiness.

3. The excess of happiness on the part of the most wealthy will not be so great as the excess of his wealth.

4. For the same reason, the greater the disproportion between the two masses of wealth, the less the probability that there exists an equally greater disproportion between the masses of happiness.

5. The more nearly the actual proportion approaches to equality, the greater will be the total mass of happiness.[56]

In other *Pannomial Fragments*, the same conclusion is reached by a slightly different but revealing route. After stating that the quantity of happiness will not increase in the same proportion to wealth, Bentham expands his description of individual experience.

in other words, the quantity of happiness produced by a particle of wealth (each particle being of the same magnitude) will be less and less at every particle; the second will produce less than the first, the third than the second, and so on.[57]

(In case it is thought that this relation exists for Bentham only between happiness and stocks of wealth, passages in Stark's selection called *The Psychology of Economic Man* contain references along exactly the same lines to money income and pleasure.)[58]

Taken together with his discussion of taxation, this analysis offers both an embryonic notion of the diminishing marginal utility of income, and prepares the way for the later nineteenth century case for re-distribution from the rich to the poor, on utilitarian, greatest happiness, grounds. Taxes for Bentham are a necessary evil. The best tax is on the consumption of luxuries, followed by those on property and property transfer. In general, taxes should be designed to be paid by those most able to pay. Ability to pay is related to the individual's wealth and income. Comparing a day-labourer, just above subsistence level, with a monarch, who has abundance to the full, it is clear that the monarch will be better off. But it is not clear by how much. He might be enjoying twice the level of utility, or one and a half times the utility of the labourer. It will be safer to conclude, Bentham writes, simply that the monarch would not enjoy much additional utility if he has more income, whereas the labourer's capacity to convert additional income into additional utility is at the maximum.[59] Now the implication is that aggregate utility will increase if some of the monarch's abundance is given to the labourer.

Yet security is always put first. Security is the seed of subsistence and abundance. Re-distribution is a dangerous exercise because it can threaten abundance, destroy incentives (expectations of the enjoyment of the fruits of labour), and create uncertainty. Moreover,

What an apparatus of penal laws would be required to replace the gentle liberty of choice, and the natural reward of the cares which each one takes for himself.[60]

These costs (the second order effects of equality) have to be set against any gain in aggregate happiness as a direct result of the re-distribution (the first order effects). A balance should be maintained. The fabric of society is undermined by the extremes of inequality and equality. Continued progress towards greater equality is desirable, but it should be gradual. It is safer to wait, for example, until the rich die. Then any re-distribution can be achieved with the minimum of pain and smallest disincentive effects. A stronger case can be made out for equality of opportunity. The security-providing and disappointment-preventing principles combine to show that the distribution of property (and other means like education) should never be so unequal as to deny any sections of the community reasonable expectation of securing their own well-being.[61]

6.Aggregation. When Bentham first tries the words 'the greatest happiness of the greatest number' they are more likely to have been describing the good and happiness of the majority of the members of any state.[62] Later, he recognises that happiness of all without exception, is a comforting if unrealistic motto. Similarly, when describing the responsibilities of government, the overriding principle becomes:

Greatest happiness of the greatest number maximised,; national subsistence, abundance, security, and equality maximised; official aptitude maximized; expenses, in all shapes, minimized.[63]

Given that security, equality and subsistence can conflict, the second part of the statement needs refinement. He has already faced up to the possibility that, in exceptional cases, the sacrifice of a few for the many may be justified. Thus the happiness, and unhappiness, of different people has, in principle, to be compared.

The number of people is one crude measure of total happiness. More people means more receptacles for enjoyment. Of course, Bentham accepts that population growth is limited by the means of subsistence, and so opulence is relative to population. Maximising happiness is a function of both the number of people and wealth per person.[64] In spite of realising the difference, he avoids making wealth per person the deciding factor, because he still worries about the need for men to defend the country. Similarly, although the sum of happiness is seen as dependent on the distribution of wealth and income among the population, he worries about the way in which redistribution creates winners and losers. Thus, when comparing the sacrifice of losers with the advantage of the gainers, he argues against simplistic interpretations of his formula for the relation between wealth or income and utility. The example of a community consisting of 4001 people is used to illustrate the dangers. Start, he says, with a situation in which all 4001 receive equal happiness. Now take away from 2000 of them all their happiness and give it to the remaining 2001; distributing the happiness transferred among this majority in any way thought best. Total happiness, he maintains, will have declined because the unhappiness of the losers will exceed the happiness of the gainers.[65]

Bentham's reasons for this asymmetry are interesting. First, he stresses the importance of the size of the minority. The larger the minority, the more likely will the outcome be a reduction in total happiness. Second, he believe that losses are more keenly felt than gains:

> Sum for sum, and man for man, the suffering of him who incurs a loss is always greater than the enjoyment of him who makes a gain.[66]

There is no further explanation. Nor does he attempt to follow up the possible links between this asymmetry and the balancing of gains and losses in a wider policy context. Third, he refers again to the disappointment-preventing principle. The minority suffer a destruction of their expectations of future abundance. The majority enjoy no similar and additional benefit. Finally, maximizing total utility should not be contemplated if it requires a minority to live in a state of misery. That is pushing things too far.

In the adding-up of total utility, each individual's utility is supposed to count the same. Paradoxically, Bentham again provides a set of reasons why individuals should not be treated as identical pleasure machines. Detailed examination of the nature of individual utility leads him to conclude that variations in personal circumstances can result in very different capacities to convert income or wealth into utility.

> the quantity of felicity habitually experienced by a gloomy, or ill-tempered or gouty, or otherwise habitually diseased monarch, is not as great as that habitually experienced by an habitually cheerful, and good tempered and healthy, labourer.[67]

Again, the argument is not taken to its logical conclusion. If it is true, what about the good-tempered labourer compared to the gloomy labourer, or the diseased landlord compared to the healthy landlord? Bentham fails to explain how these different experiences and intensities of utility can be put together. He seems to want to confine himself to quantity rather than quality variation. He will admit that the diseased monarch cannot enjoy the same number of units of pleasure from push-pin or poetry as the healthy labourer; he is reluctant to claim that poetry offers a higher quality of pleasure; and for that reason alone, be worth more units to the educated writer than push-pin to the ignorant labourer. He gets close to making inter-personal comparisons of utility; he stops short of awarding them any operational significance

7. Measurement. Not only does Bentham use terms such as pleasure, happiness, utility and felicity interchangeably in his legal, political and philosophical works, he also uses terms like property, wealth and income in his economic works as if they mean the same. They are taken to represent claims on material well-being, and the more of them anyone has, the happier they will feel. But he knows that to make judgements about the utility of individuals and communities something more precise is required. How can it be shown that the gloomy landlord enjoys twice as much happiness as the cheerful labourer? How can it be proved that the surplus of pleasure over pain in the country with free trade is higher than in the country without? In some passages Bentham appears to suggest that there are no answers to these questions; in others he falls back on using money as a proxy value.

Political arithmetic is a phrase Bentham himself uses to describe the kind of normative economics he preaches. By that he means the application, in a particular and complete fashion, of arithmetic calculation to happiness and all its elements.

Without Calculation, the principle of utility might float useless in sea of words with other phantoms of the imagination.

However, the calculus falls far short of an all-comprehensive reckoning because pleasure is not directly ponderable or measurable, and therefore money had to be used as its general source and representation.[68] In the sphere of economics, at least, a little progress can be made. Unfortunately, the examination Bentham has already conducted of the relationship between income or wealth and utility suggests a representation that is vague.

Take thereupon an individual: give him a certain quantity of money, you will produce in his mind a certain quantity of pleasure. Give him again the same quantity, you will make an addition to the quantity of his pleasure. But the magnitude of pleasure produced by the second sum will not be twice of the pleasure produced by the first.[69]

It may well be less than twice, he says, as the reader would will expect from the earlier analysis. By how much less, only the individual concerned can tell. Most people may be observed to behave as if they receive less than proportionate increases in utility from increases in money income, but there is still no way in which the degree or intensity of this increase can be accurately measured. There are no units of happiness or utility.

It is difficult to avoid the conclusion that the issue has been evaded. In Viner's opinion, this moral arithmetic makes no attempt to actually measure pains and pleasures, and is just a preliminary exercise to clear the ground. Money income provides information only on the general direction of the change in utility. By Bentham's own argument, an extra £50 to a healthy labourer need not indicate the same extra utility to a gloomy landlord. If two people's incomes increase, then both enjoy more happiness and the sum of their happiness increases. In the absence of envy, it might also be argued that an increase for one, and a steady state for the other, will have the same effect, as far as direction is concerned, on the sum. Nothing can be said, however, about the size of the increases; and nothing can be said for sure about the effects of any direct redistribution between them. Even taking from a rich and healthy landlord and giving to a poor and unhealthy labourer might not increase their total happiness.

Notes

1. Burns (1962).
2. Hazlitt (1969) pp.19 and 23.
3. Never was a man worse used than Bentham, according to William Wilberforce. The experience may well have driven him to form harsh opinions about the system of British government. Quoted in Firneaux (1974) p.49.
4. Marx, *Capital* Vol. 1., (Marx 1938 ed.) ftn p.622.
5. Gossen, Herman Heinrich (1810 to 1858), the 'unknown' economist who was a strict hedonist in politics and ethics and introduced a very original formulation of the the principle of marginal utility. Perhaps he was more interested in the mathematics of subjective utility than the greatest sum of pleasure. Jevons found him very sympathetic. In spite of the fact that some of Bentham's writings were available in German in the 1830's, there is no evidence of any direct influence on Gossen. Although they acknowledged the the same predecessors (including Helvétius, Beccaria, Priestley and Paley), Gossen's hedonism was different from Bentham's utilitarianism. See the introduction by Nicholas Georgescu-Roegen to Gossen (1983).
6. In a letter to Etienne Dumont, in 1802, Bentham admits to being fascinated by Rousseau but 'could never bring himself to to fancy so much as for a moment ... the smallest ray of intelligence'. Bentham (1988) p.26.
7. Paley, (1825). According to Keynes, this William Paley was the great grandfather of Margaret Paley Marshall. Keynes (1972e).

Notes continued

8. Godwin (1985), where happiness even gets into the subtitle.
9. Helvetius (1758) particularly chapt. XXIV, and Beccaria (1767), p.2. The former used the phrase 'the greatest happiness of the greatest number', and the latter had 'pleasure-pain calculating machines' and 'social utility'. Hume's versions of the role of utility in the theory of morals came under attack from Adam Smith. See Smith (1976), particularly pp.305-6. See also Haakonssen (1981).
10. *An Article on Utilitarianism - the Long Version*, in Bentham (1983b) p.292.
11. Bentham (1970a) p.11.
12. From *A Table of the Springs of Action*, in Bentham (1983b).
13. *Anarchical Fallacies*, in Bentham (1962) Vol.II p.500.
14. See *Supply without Burthen* in Bentham (1952) Vol. 1., pp.334-35.
15. Bentham (1983a), vi.31.A8.
16. *Manual of Political Economy*, in Bentham (1952) Vol. 1.
17. Bentham (1983b) p.57.
18. *In Defence of a Maximum*, in Bentham (1952) Vol. 3.
19. Bentham (1983b) p.291.
20. See Introduction by Raphael and Macfie to Smith (1976).
21. Bentham (1970a) p.12.
22. From *A Table of the Springs of Action*, in Bentham (1983b) p.89.
23. Quoted in Allen (1978).
24. Ogden (1932) p.19 is the source of the first claim. David Roberts (1974) and Stephen Conway (1990) provide a more balanced view. Samuel Finer (1972) argues that Bentham's thoughts and attitudes did play a predominant role, if not the Benthamites themselves, in many nineteenth century reforms.
25. Quoted in Bain (1882)
26. Marshall (1959) Appendix B. Keynes (1972a) p.279, and (1972b).
27. Bentham (1952) Vol. 1.
28. Hutchinson (1956).
29. Robbins (1952) and (1970).
30. See Viner (1949).
31. In a letter to Maria Edgeworth on the potato and the problems of Ireland, Bentham's 'the greatest happiness of the greatest number' is expressly mentioned, see Ricardo (1952), Vol. IX, 13 Dec.1822. In letters to Malthus and Mill, however, he doubts whether happiness, our own or other people's, can be known with any certainty. See Ricardo (1952), Vol. VII, 4 Sept.1817 and 30 Aug.1815.
32. Pigou (1960) Preface and Chapt. 1.
33. They are given the titles of *The Philosophy of Economic Science* (Vol. 1) and *The Psychology of Economic Man* (Vol. 2).
34. Bentham (1968 *et. al.*)
35. See his *Manual of Political Economy* in Bentham (1952) Vol. 1, p.224.
36. Bentham (1952), Vol. 3 pp.307-09.
37. Bentham (1983b) p.148.
38. op. cit., pp.182-84.
39. Bentham (1983a) p. 136.
40. See below under Aggregation and Measurement.
41. See Bentham (1977) p. 231, and in *Article on Utilitarianism*, Bentham (1983b) pp. 295-296. A theory of distributive justice has recently been built on the Disappointment-Preventing and Security-Providing principles found in Bentham's work. See Kelly (1990) See also under Individualism and Equality below.
42. Bentham (1970a) p.74.
43. op. cit. p 179.

Notes continued

44. Bentham (1983b) pp. 304-305.
45. Bentham (1970a) p.100. See also *A Table of the Springs of Action* in Bentham (1983b).
46. Bentham *(*1983b) p.134.
47. op.cit., p 97.
48. The Manual, in Bentham (1952) Vol. 1 p 337.
49. The *Institute of Political Economy* in Bentham (1952) Vol. 3, p 333.
50. Bentham (1970a) p.12.
51. The *Manual* in Bentham (1952) Vol. 1, pp 337-338.
52. op. cit. p.310.
53. From *Dedacologia*, Appendix A to Bentham (1983b) pp.333-334.
54. Bentham (1993) pp.309-310.
55. Bentham (1962) Vol. II p.271 and Vol. IV p.540.
56. op. cit Vol. I., pp.304-305.
57. In Bentham (1952), Vol. 1, *The Philosophy of Economic Science*, p.113. in Bentham (1962), Vol. III, pp.224-230.
58. Bentham (1952), Vol. 3, pp.440-441. Also in Bentham (1962), Vol IV, *Codification Proposals*.
59. Bentham (1952) Vol. 3, pp.443-444.
60. *The Civil Code*, Bentham (1962) Vol. I, p.311.
61. Kelly (1990).
62. *Article on Utilitarianism* in Bentham (1983b) p 291.
63. Bentham (1983a), VII. 2. p.137.
64. Bentham (1952), Vol. 3, p. 361.
65. *Article on Utilitarianism* in Bentham (1983b) pp.309-310.
66. Bentham (1952) *The Manual*, Vol. 1, p 239.
67. Bentham (1962), Vol. II p.271.
68. op. cit., Vol. IV p.540.
69. op. cit., Vol. IV p.541.

3. James Mill

The Mills

Bertrand Russell records in his autobiography how, by the time of his birth in 1872, his parents had drifted away from traditional religion and become disciples and friends of John Stuart Mill, 'from whom both learned to believe in birth control and votes for women'. In fact, his mother had written to invite this 'Saint of Rationalism' to become one of the new infant's godparents. Much to her surprise, she received a favourable reply: John Stuart Mill did not think it would conflict with his beliefs.[1] In the event, he had little time to discover what duties of supervision and instruction he thought he had assumed, dying only a year later. The same could not be said of John Mill's own sponsors. He had been only two when his father first met Bentham. Their close, if occasionally troubled, friendship meant that the founder of utilitarianism, who still had twenty four years to live in 1808, could help direct the education of James Mill's eldest son. Of course, there was much more to the intellectual legacy of John Mill than birth control and votes for women; and although Bertrand Russell was never convinced by philosophical utilitarianism, thinking it to be false if noble in intent, he did carry on the radical, libertarian, and rationalist tradition of Bentham and the Mills well into the twentieth century.

How the first link in the chain of utilitarian thought was forged is an extraordinary story. Bentham and James Mill enthusiastically adopted the late eighteenth century belief that education had the power to mould the mind of a child. John Mill was chosen by them to be the subject of an experiment in isolation and control. From the age of three to sixteen he worked at home, under the direction of his father, on a programme of study, more classical than utilitarian, that for ambition and pace would strike horror into the hearts of the most committed of modern scholars. In turn, he was expected to act as monitor to his younger brothers and sisters, passing on to them such instruction as his father thought fit. Bentham and James Mill seemed to have found the ideal pupil: John Mill was precocious, assiduous and remarkably obedient.

It has been suggested that whereas Bentham's picture of an ideal society was like his model prison (the Panopticon), James Mill's picture was like his model schoolroom. James Mill certainly approved of the Panopticon, emphasising the need for it to be 'a circular building, of the width of a cell', 'the cells all open inwards, having an iron grating instead of a wall', so that the prisoners can be kept under continuous supervision by the keepers, who are placed in a narrow 'inspection tower', built specially for this purpose in the central space. Moreover, by means of windows and blinds, the keepers can see without being seen. There is much in this design to conjure up the image of a spider and its web. He also supported Bentham's scheme for a Chrestomathic (useful knowledge) schooling for the children of the masses, 'which left the elements of hardly any branch of knowledge unprovided for'. Apparently that was not enough for his eldest son, who would be raised to the level of those 'with the wealth and time to acquire the highest measure of intelligence', without going to school or university. If James Mill had faith in the progress of the human mind, and in its rapid progress as the fulfilment of human destiny, he had little faith in the established insitutions of his day to deliver such perpetual improvement. Like the legal and political structures of the state, they had become obstacles to social improvement. Thus utilitarians concerned to do good in society should parallel those in the classroom who, 'best qualified in morality and intellect', try to transmit 'their teaching through subordinate monitors to numerous but eager pupils, until the whole room was a murmur with earnest diligence'.[2]

As a summary of Bentham's and the elder Mill's vision of the world, in Schumpeter's sense of a vision, this is probably unfair and incomplete. Nevertheless, it gives a flavour of what a Benthamite education must have meant, in attitudes and prejudices as well as in content. There was a similar partiality in popular descriptions of James Mill as a cold, hard, calculating, and unimaginative rationalist. Certainly he was very earnest and painstaking, and became a fervent exponent of (almost) everything Benthamite; but his own education and background was very different. Intended for the Church, he had been reared in Scotland, become first a Whig, and, allegedly for personal reasons, taken against everything aristocratic. Bentham, by contrast, had no time for religious doctrine, flirted with the upper classes and English Toryism, and even hoped, through his brother, to influence Catherine the Great. Whilst both became radical democrats with a strong faith in the general progress of the human race, Mill adopted a more reserved position, never, as his eldest son suggested, building 'unreasonable hopes on any one event or contingency'. His final rejection of religious belief came about because he found it impossible to accept that 'a world so full of evil was the work of an Author combining infinite power with goodness and righteousness'.[3] More significantly for utilitarianism, he brought with him to England the influence of the philosophers of the Edinburgh school, and the last remnants of the eighteenth century Scottish enlightenment. This view of society and history was very different from that of Bentham.

There is one other common feature in the lives of James Mill and his son that has some importance. For thirty years, one or both of them were servants of that unique institution in the history of British conquest and trade, the East India Company. Of course, they had to make a living. Bentham was the son of a rich and successful father (and brother). In spite of the financial costs of his failed attempts to promote reform, he always managed comfortably on private means. Ricardo made a large fortune on the money markets, when cut off from the support of his family and its business. James Mill had no money of his own and for most of his life had to struggle to make ends meet. Necessity and the prospect of secure employment, therefore, pushed them in the Company's direction. What is of interest is that neither of them came to regret the association or feel the need to justify their role as radicals in helping to govern India. They must have been aware of Adam Smith's lengthy strictures on the Company in Part III of Book V of the *Wealth of Nations*, and Bentham's doubts about the benefits of colonialism to the colonial power. It is true that James Mill joined after the Company's loss of the monopoly on trade with India, so they had no links with the worst scandals of its commercial activities. Even so, he will be found in 1832 still defending the economic effectiveness of the tax on opium; and his son claiming that India was fortunate to be governed by those who lived there, and who made it their professional interest, rather than directly by the Westminster government. These early utilitarians believed that Britain had a special mission in India, and that their doctrines were an essential guide to the correct relationship between imperial and subject peoples.

James Mill

James Mill was born at Northwater Bridge on the North Esk river near Montrose in 1773, the son of a cobbler and small-holder. His mother, who seemed to have been a determined and dominating character, had changed the family name from Milne to Mill, so to sound less Scottish. It was she who first encouraged him to study. After attending the parish school and Montrose Academy with evident success, he came to the attention of Lady Jane the wife of Sir John Stuart of Fettercairn (Sir John's mother, who must have been equally dominant, forced a change in the family name from Belsches in 1797). Their support enabled him to attend Edinburgh rather than the nearer Aberdeen University. He stayed there for seven years, apparently living with the Stuart family and acting as tutor to their daughter Whilhelmina. The original intention was for him to enter the ministry of the Church of Scotland. Before submitting to instruction in divinity, he followed the normal M.A. courses in Latin, Greek, Mathematics, Moral and Natural Philosophy and some Political Economy, graduating in 1794. It was then that he came under the influence of Dugald Stewart, Professor of Moral Philosophy. James Mill left the University in 1797 with a licence to preach, but proved unable to support himself from such itinerant earnings and had to return to private tuition. By 1802, at the age of twenty-nine and with no real prospects, he accepted an offer from his patron to travel with him to London.[4]

On arrival, Mill set out on a career as a journalist, trying wherever possible to use contacts with other Scots already in publishing to help him find work. Whether such behaviour makes him an example of that 'superb specimen of the unspeakable Scot, the Scotsman on the make in London',[5] there is some evidence that he tried to remove all traces of the Scottish idiom from his writing. Indeed, so reluctant was he to speak of his life before London that his eldest son had to write to friends of his father in Scotland in order to discover the basic facts of the family background. Perhaps he was shy of humble origins and, in the light of his growing radical opinions, reluctant to reveal previous dependence on aristocratic subsidy and clerical ambitions. On the other hand, he called his eldest son John Stuart (John Belsches Milne would not have had the same ring), his first daughter Wilhelmina, another Jane, and was pleased to receive Sir John and Lady Jane at his house whenever they were in town.

By 1805 he felt confident enough of his success to marry a Harriet Burrow, whose mother kept an establishment for lunatics in Hoxton.

The new *Literary Journal* had given him more permanent employment in 1803, and he was probably earning up to £500 per annum from editorials, articles and essays by the time of his marriage. It was doubly unfortunate that this journal folded in 1806, because he had already decided to give up other regular sources of income and concentrate on writing a history of British India. Eleven years were to pass before the mammoth task was completed, and his name made. In the meantime, he had to support a growing family. Life at home could not have been very relaxed or happy. Eventually, the East India Company provided a stable source of income, £800 a year to start with (in 1819), rising to £1,200 by 1832, and his financial problems gradually disappeared. More surprisingly, employment by the Company did not stop him writing. His son was to be similarly uninhibited. Mill died while still in office, in 1836, only four years after Bentham.

1808 had been an important year for Mill because he began friendships with two people who were to influence his future work and, in turn, be influenced by him. He met Ricardo as a result of the publication of 'Commerce Defended', an essay in which Mill defended free trade against the criticisms of Spence and Cobbett. They became close during the Bullionist controversy, taking daily walks together. Later, the Mill family would visit the Ricardo country house, Gatcomb Park, and Mill himself played an important role in the completion of Ricardo's *Principles of Political Economy and Taxation*. The meeting with Bentham marked the start of a longer if more troubled relationship. Mill became converted to Bentham's utilitarianism and served as one of its most successful propagandists. Bentham helped the Mills solve their housing problems and took a keen interest, as has been explained, in the education of John Stuart. They did, however, have their differences. Mill sometimes resented his financial dependence on Bentham; Bentham sometimes found Mill's manner domineering and oppressive. Whereas Mill was a dogmatic adherent of Ricardian economics, Bentham could be more independently minded, even unorthodox, on matters relating to monetary policy and trade. Whereas Bentham found writing in plain English very difficult, Mill's relentlessly didactic mind was able to produce clear and persuasive prose, on tap.

There are contemporary reports of Mill which suggest a dour Scot, still Presbyterian in moral earnestness if no longer in faith, who took a dim view of unalloyed pleasure, who believed in the idea of progress as the philosophy of history, and in education as its chief engine, but doubted whether much could be done to relieve the suffering of the great mass of the world's population.

> The state of defective food and excessive labour, is the state in which we find the great bulk of mankind; the state in which they are either constantly existing, or into which they are every moment threatening to fall.[6]

George Grote, a friend and admirer, had to admit their were faults to his character. He was prone to cynicism and asperity, overly critical of others, even of the great and good.[7] Others found him approachable and modest. Maria Edgeworth, who knew Ricardo as well as Mill, may have been expecting something rather different, given his public reputation. Yet after a meeting in March of 1819, she reported quite favourably on the impression he made.

> Mr Mill British India chief figurante. But he is not the least of a figurante nor a showman but a person of excellent sense and benevolence, speaking fluent sense and giving information for pleasure of all his hearers, not for his own glory.[8]

He must have possessed enough charm and agreeableness to persuade large numbers of influential people to his point of view. His letters to Bentham during their period of estrangement were remarkably tolerant and diplomatic, and he maintained long friendships with such disparate characters as Ricardo and Henry Brougham. This man of facts and calculation was, like Thomas Gradgrind, 'basically decent and humane'.[9]

It must be admitted that Mill had few doubts about his intellectual superiority or of the leading role that he saw for his class (he tended to called it the middle rank rather then class). An advocate of representative democracy and of the extension of the franchise to all adult men, and an opponent of all aristocratic interests, he nevertheless wanted the educated and professional members of society to determine its general welfare by their advice and example.

> It is to be observed, that the class which is universally described as both the most wise and the most virtuous part of the community, the middle rank, are wholly included in that part of the community which is not the Aristocratical ... Another proposition must be stated ... It is, that the opinions of that class of the people, who are below the middle rank, are formed, and their minds are directed by that intelligent and virtuous rank, who come the most immediately in contact with them ... to whom they fly for advice and assistance.upon whom they feel an immediate and daily dependence ... to whom their children look up as models for their imitation, whose opinions they hear daily repeated, and account it their honour to adopt.[10]

(Mill could keep up this kind of superior rant for a long time). The point is quite clear in the context of a popular franchise. Majority opinion could be relied upon to be sensible, not extreme or partisan. There is also a wider lesson to be learnt. Mill's benevolent paternalism becomes one of the common themes of utilitarian thought in the nineteenth century.

The development of Mill's ideas, his movement away from the Whigs and any residual attachment to Christianity, was a gradual process that had begun before he met Bentham; just as Bentham had become a democrat before he met Mill. Nor was utilitarianism the only influence that shaped his interests after 1808. The record and content of his major publications shows the importance of Ricardian economics, Malthusian population theory, Scottish historicism, and radical politics, as well as Benthamite policies on the reform of education, prisons, law and administration.

1804	Essay on the Impolicy of a Bounty on the Exportation of Grain
1807	Commerce Defended (both pamphlets)
1808	Thomas Smith on Money and Exchange.
1817	History of British India (6 volumes)
1819/1823	Essays on Government, Jurisprudence, Liberty of the Press, Education, and Prisons and Prison Discipline.
1821	Elements of Political Economy
1829	An Analysis of the Phenomenon of the Human Mind. (2 Volumes)
1830	Essay on the Ballot and Fragment on Mackintosh
1836	Whether Political Economy is Useful (essay)

In fact, direct references to Bentham's greatest happiness principle are infrequent. Mill was more of his own man than is often supposed. His utilitarianism was an underlying theme or general presumption rather than a detailed theory to be applied in everything he wrote.

The Scottish Enlightenment

When Adam Smith had finished the *Wealth of Nations*, David Hume teased him for allowing it to be sold to the English:

> How can you so much as entertain a thought of publishing a Book, full of Reason, Sense, and Learning, to those wicked, abandoned Madmen?[11]

The Scots could then afford to look down on the English. There was nothing in England to compare with the scope and originality of the intellectual contribution that those north of the border had made in the years between 1740 and 1790. Bentham lamented the way in which the English had neglected moral philosophy and let the Scots take the lead; but there was much more than moral philosophy in the Scottish Enlightenment. As a particularly productive, if relatively objective and moderate branch of a movement of renewal that swept through eighteenth century Europe, its main theme was the progress of society. The study of law, history, politics and political economy, and philosophy, was combined to produce an explanation of the mechanisms of social development. 'Meta-sociology', 'historical sociology', and 'philosophical anthropology' have all been terms used to describe their approach.[12]

Most of the contributors to the new science of society were to be found in Scotland's great universities: Adam Smith and his teacher Frances Hutchinson, Thomas Reid (Adam Smith's successor in the Chair of Moral Philosophy), and John Millar (another admirer of Adam Smith), Professor of Law, all at Glasgow; Dugald Stewart, who inspired James Mill and whose lectures in political economy James Mill might have attended, Adam Ferguson (Dugald Stewart's predecessor in the Chair of Moral Philosophy), and William Robertson (the Principal of the University), all at Edinburgh. David Hume (and Lord Kames, his kinsman and mentor) was one of the exceptions to this domination by professional academics. Hume was a devoted friend of Adam Smith, a philosopher of world class, perhaps the greatest Britain has ever produced, and a writer of innovative and provocative history, but which could not really be described as 'meta-sociology'. Apart from a re-examination and rediscovery of classical wisdom, the Scottish Enlightenment drew inspiration from work on the continent by the philosophers of natural law, Grotius and Pufendorf, and of Montesquieu, the Physiocrats, and later Condorcet. France was certainly more important to them than England, as a country to visit and as well as a source of published ideas. Of course, they drew upon the writings of Hobbes and Locke, but Mandeville was probably the only eighteenth century writer in that 'abandoned' country who they felt worthy of attention.

Conjectural history (the construction of a model of what was supposed to be the natural progress of society) was one of projects popular in the group. Adam Smith, for example, saw four stages of development from barbarism to civilisation, each with its own level of economic activity and technology, political and social structures. The most primitive stage was hunting, gathering, and fishing: poor, small in size, with no private property and no government. The second stage was just above subsistence level, predominantly pastoral and nomadic, with property emerging in the accumulation and transfer (from one generation to another) of herds, leading to inequalities in wealth and power, and some form of despotic government. Next came agriculture (or feudalism), marked by cultivation in residential communities, with property in land, greater wealth but also greater inequalities, landless peasants who were dependent upon and subject to landlords, arbitrary justice, and conflicts between local and national authorities. Finally, there arrived the fourth stage of commerce (and manufacturing), the richest and most civilised, where the division of labour and the use of machines was advanced, the power of landlord balanced by that of the new proprietors, the growth in the importance of towns, good government encouraged, individual liberties defended, and inequalities in wealth reduced.

Examples were taken from across the world to illustrate societies at different stages of development. Scotland was presumed to be entering the commercial stage, just behind her larger and richer neighbour England. The Act of Union, liberalisation among the Presbyterian clergy, the relative strength of the 'middle rank' of persons, and the absence of an expensive Royal court, have all been adduced to explain the comparative intellectual advantage of Scotland. Be that as it may, as an educated member of a civilized nation (the new Union), James Mill would have had few inhibitions about passing judgement on backward societies. This sense of natural superiority, this belief that an understanding of the processes of economic and social development was now available, strengthened by the tools of legal and economic analysis he had more recently learnt from Bentham and Ricardo, gave him the confidence to embark upon a history of India.

He also took from both the Scottish and English sources the notion that the free interaction of self-interested individuals need not result in chaos. In the economic sphere, at least in the most progressive societies, there were beneficial social consequences to be obtained from competition among agents who sought only private gain. Unlike the other classical economists, who seemed to think that motivation needed no further elaboration, Mill absorbed some of the Scottish tradition's uneasiness about the destructive potential of pure self-interest. Adam Smith was not the only member to worry that civilization might bring a weakening of relations between individuals, and to look for an ideal balance between the selfish and benevolent affections. Mill, the utilitarian, was perhaps more optimistic about the possibilities of harnessing egotistical individuals to serve the common good. Carefully designed legislation and the right kind of education were the practical solutions.

Bentham and Mill had an interest in psychology and ethics. It is difficult to imagine Ricardo asking, as Smith asked, 'Wherein does virtue consist? ... by what power or faculty of the mind is it recommended to us'. Bentham's answers, however, were very different from those of the Scottish philosophers. Most of them denied, for example, that sympathy could be deduced solely from selfishness; and the sense in which Mill used words like 'virtue', 'propriety', 'prudence', 'benevolence' and even 'utility', reveals something of his intellectual life before Bentham. His intention, undoubtedly, was to show how these moral rules could ultimately be reduced to the standard of the greatest happiness.[13] But in the process, they are often given independent, non utilitarian justifications. Moreover, in his own examination of the nature of pleasures and pains, Thomas Reid, the so-called common sense philosopher, is as important an influence as Bentham.

James Mill on Pleasures and Pains

In making the case for parliamentary democracy, Mill expresses a view of human nature that emphasises selfishness and envy. If there were no government, there would be a Hobbesian world in which each person would be subject to the exploitation of others. Under an aristocratic form of government, the threat would come from just a few; under a Monarchy just from one. There is no relief to be expected from an appeal to the benevolence of the rulers, nor from exhaustion in their search for gratification.

> That one human being will desire to render the person and property of another subservient to his pleasures, notwithstanding the pain and loss of pleasure which it may occasion to that other individual, is the foundation of government.[14]

Thomas Macaulay made a famous attack on such an apparently cynical and one-sided approach, and Mill replies, quoting Plato and Hume among others, in defence of awarding universal prominence to self-love among the motives of human conduct.[15] Mill's declared objective is good government and that means creating an identity of interests between those who enact the laws and the rest of the community. The only way to achieve this identity is to have a legislative assembly of elected representatives. The representatives will be dissuaded from pursuing sectional interests by the threat of defeat at the next election.

All this has apparently nothing to do with the Rights of Man or liberty. Representative democracy is desired for good government, and good government for the greatest happiness. Nevertheless, it needs to be supported by certain rights and liberties. Mill is true to Bentham in rejecting ipse dixitism and the notion of natural rights, but not rights as such. In his *Jurisprudence*, the establishment of individual rights is depicted as an essential object of the social union, the system of government and the law.

> in other words that the weak may not be deprived of their share of good things, it is necessary to fix, by some determination, what shall belong to each, and to make choice of certain marks by which the share of each may be distinguished. This is the origin of right. It is created by this sort of determination, which determination is either of the whole society, or of some part of the society which possesses the power of determining for the whole. Right, therefore, is factitious and the creature of will.[16]

Furthermore, the people need to form correct judgements about the conduct of their representatives and the acts of the government. They need freedom of expression, of criticism and enquiry.

> Without knowledge then, of what is done by their representatives, in the use of the powers entrusted to them, the people cannot profit by the power of choosing them, and the advantages of good government are unattainable.[17]

The liberty of the press, as he calls it, a press free from government influence and undue legal constraints, becomes an important means to this end. So too is the intellectual elite who will have the time and energy to understand and voice the constructive criticism. The value of their commitment to the exercise of reason and the pursuit of the truth cannot be overestimated. Although Bentham shared Mill's belief in a free press and the protection of the weak by factitious rights, he may not have gone so in emphasising the role of the elite. For Mill, the exercise of reason and the search for truth seem almost to be desirable in themselves.[18]

A rather similar departure from strict utilitarianism is evident in his writings on education. He begins with a utilitarian recommendation for the mind to be trained to understand the causes of happiness and its achievement.

> To attain happiness is the object: and, to attain it in the greatest possible degree, all the means to that end, which the compass of nature affords, must be employed in the most perfect manner.[19]

But the happiness to be achieved is not purely selfish. How individuals affect the happiness of others must also be taken into account. Learning about the perfect way to promote personal pleasures and avoid personal pains, is the easiest part of the exercise. Self-love provides all the incentive that is needed. The qualities which produce the maximum happiness in others require more careful instruction.

> A man can affect the happiness of others, either be abstaining from doing them harm, or by doing them positive good. To abstain from doing them harm, receives the name of Justice; to do positive good receives that of Generosity.[20]

Benevolence is the name given by Mill to the combination of Justice and Generosity, and when it is developed to the highest degree possible, the individual will gain command over other people's wills by 'exciting their love and admiration'. He admits that the opposite is possible: command over other people's wills could be achieved by developing those qualities that 'excite their terror'. The power of pain and cruelty can also be learnt. The wrong kind of education will then produce a 'bad man'.

   Much the same strange mix of the philosophies of the Ancients, as Mill called them, to-gether with the Scottish Enlightenment, and Bentham, is carried over into his studies of psychology. Traces are to be found in the essay on *Education*. After examining the theories of Locke, Hume, Hartley, Reid and Condillac, he provisionally concludes that the 'character of the human mind consists in the sequences of its ideas', and that these sequences of ideas or trains of thought are associated with, follow the same order of cause and effect as the impressions and sensations of experience. Thus the role of education is to encourage, by using the twin powers of Custom and Pain/Pleasure, those 'trains' that lead to good (utilitarian) outcomes. Apart from Benevolence, Intelligence and Temperance are the other virtues or qualities of the character most to be desired. Benevolence is seen to work in harmony with the them.

> In reality, as the happiness of the individual is bound up with that of his species, that which affects the happiness of one, must also, in general, affect that of the other.[21]

Although the references to universal happiness, and training through associations with pain and pleasure, are consistent with Benthamism, there is also much use of notions like 'virtue' and 'temperance', which might serve 'ipsedixist' ends.

Mill provides further evidence of his independence with the publication in 1829 of the *Analysis of the Human Mind*. John Stuart believed that his father was much superior to Bentham in understanding human nature, and saw this work as giving him the honour of serving as 'the reviver and second founder of Associationist Psychology', (the first being Hartley).[22] After the six volumes on Indian history, these two volumes on the relationship between human understanding and experience, must represent James Mill's most ambitious project. Whether they reached the standards of originality and excellence claimed by his son, has to be decided elsewhere. What is interesting is that the son uses them in retrospective support for his own departures from Benthamite orthodoxy. The utilitarian nature of the interactions between individuals is given further examination.

> It is obvious ... that the grand cause of all our pleasures are the services of our fellow creatures; since Wealth, Power and Dignity, which appear to most people to sum up the means of human happiness, are nothing more than the means of procuring these services. This is a fact of the highest possible importance, both in morals, and in Philosophy.[23]

In terms of morals, the pleasures of others attract an individual's benevolent feelings. Acts which lead to the pleasure of others, or reduce their pains, in turn affect the pleasure of the actor, albeit in an indirect manner.

> In the first place, we have associations of pleasure with all the pleasurable feelings of our Fellow-creatures. We have associations of pleasure, therefore, with those acts of ours which yield him pleasure. In the second place, those are the acts which procure to us one of the most highly valued of all the sources of our pleasures, the favourable disposition of our Fellow-men.[24]

Unlike Bentham, Mill seems to admire the *Theory of Moral Sentiments*. He even makes a direct reference to its author's views on the love of praise and fear of blame which .

> that remarkable phenomenon of our nature, eloquently described, but not explained, by Adam Smith, that, in minds happily trained, the love of Praiseworthiness, the dread of Blameworthiness, is a stronger feeling, than the Love of actual Praise, the Dread of actual Blame.[25]

Bentham and Mill, of course, are supposed to have provided the missing explanation. But Mill fails to grasp the vital factor in Smith's distinction between praise or blame, on the one hand, and the thing that ought to be the natural and proper object of praise or blame, even when not actually praised or blamed, on the other. There is, in Mill, no room for the impartial spectator.

Perhaps Mill strays furthest from narrow utilitarianism when he tries to tackle the problem of immoral acts and how they can be reconciled with motives of pleasure and pain. He uses the example of adultery to illustrate his solution.

A man is tempted to commit adultery with the wife of a friend; the composition of the motive obvious. He does not obey the motive. Why? He obeys the motives which are stronger. Though pleasures are associated with the immoral act, pains are associated with it also; the pains of the injured husband; the pains of the injured wife; the moral indignation of mankind; the future reproaches of his own mind.[26]

Moral indignation and future reproaches of the mind seem remote from simple pleasures and pains. Moreover, he recognises that the 'other' motives could be weak. Bad education might devalue the moral senses, and the development of conscience might never encouraged. Pleasure would triumph over morality. So what remains is the beginnings of an argument for general rules of conduct that preserve public morality, and maximize aggregate happiness, rather than the determination of individual acts by the private calculus of immediate pleasures and pains.

James Mill and India

As a large financial and territorial corporation, the East India Company depended upon its Charter from the British government to survive and, in turn, continued to exert a powerful influence on politics at Westminster. It even had a role in the development of the study of economics, establishing the first Chair in the subject (strictly a Chair in History and Political Economy), at Haileybury, its college in Hertfordshire, in 1805. The holder was Malthus. By 1819, it had been convinced of the need to improve the quality of its central administration. Mill was recruited along with two other outsiders, Edward Strachey and Thomas Love Peacock, as a man of 'great intellectual and literary ability' to prepare the Court of Director's dispatches. Although the generally favourable reception of Mill's *History* must have weighed heavily in the Court's judgement as to his suitability for the post, he had powerful backers like Ricardo. He began in the revenue department, as a Chief Assistant Examiner, was

put over the other two newcomers in 1823, and became Chief
(Political) Examiner in 1831. Put simply, Mill helped to supervise the
government of India by correspondence (what today, no doubt, would
be called distance government); serving as a member of a kind of
economic planning staff in London. By 1834, all the Company's
trading activities ceased and it concentrated exclusively on being the
political agent for the British government in the sub-continent. Both
the Mills regarded that as an ideal arrangement.

Office hours were from 10 to 4. Unlike many of their colleagues,
the Mills kept regular time. Peacock satirised the day in verse:

> From ten to eleven, ate a breakfast for seven;
> From eleven to noon, to begin was too soon;
> From twelve to one, asked 'What's to be done?'
> From one to two found nothing to do;
> From two to three, began to foresee
> That from three to four would be a damn bore.[27]

The Mills found plenty to do. James Mill produced some of his most
radical and substantive pieces during the years of employment. None
of them, however, come close to the *History of British India* in length.
Its six volumes must have involved prodigious effort, particularly in
the collection and arrangement, for the first time, of evidence from
many diverse sources. Volumes one and two contain a detailed
examination of Hindu society and of its Mohammedan conquerors; the
rest is a history of the British in India, and, therefore, a history of the
British East India Company. Mill paints the perspective in his
introduction with glowing, imperial tones.

The study of India is part of the knowledge of 'my country, its
peoples, its government, its policy, and its laws; it is a study of the
transactions of the British nation, to which the affairs of India have
given birth'. He also foresees the objection that he was a writer who
had never been to India, and who had only a slight acquaintance with
any of its languages. His defence is that no one with "qualifications
which alone can be acquired in India' is better fitted to write such a
history than him. Mill's own background and education, what he had
learnt from the Scottish Historical School, from Ricardo and Bentham,
will serve him well in the task. To understand India requires

> the most prefect comprehension of the principles of human society; or the course,
> into which the laws of human nature impel the human being ... and ... a clear
> comprehension of the practical play of the machinery of government,[28]

in all its aspects. This he possessed, or so he must have supposed, by 1819. One of his main objectives is to dispel any illusions about the level of civilization in India. The Mohammedan Conquerors may have had 'a degree of intellectual faculties rather higher, be rather less deeply involved in the absurdities and weaknesses of a rude state of society, and attained a stage of civilization, in some little degree, higher' than the Hindus, but the whole sub-continent languishes under a corrupt and debased, political and religious despotism.

It is when he examines the astronomical and mathematical science of the Hindus, that Mill waxes most eloquently about their deficiencies.

> Exactly in proportion as Utility is the object of every pursuit, may we regard a nation as civilized. Exactly in proportion as its ingenuity is wasted on contemptible or mischievous objects, though it may be, in itself, an ingenuity of no ordinary kind, the nation may be safely be denominated barbarous.[29]

The contrast between civilization and barbarism is fully in keeping with the Scottish historical tradition. Equally consistent with the Scottish philosophers, if not with Bentham, is the use of the word 'utility'. Here Mill gives it the meaning of appropriate, fitting, well-suited, or designed for a given end, rather than directly giving pleasure or happiness. Pleasure may even be derived, as Adam Smith suggested, from contemplating a well-suited or designed artifice, including something as complicated as a political or legal system.

His solution to the problem of India, his way of raising the masses out of misery and deprivation, is threefold: the reform of government, the reform of laws, and the reform of taxation. In contrast to the evangelical tradition in India, the utilitarians want to abolish God and substitute human for Divine justice. Education is important but pointless as long as poverty rules the land. Economic growth has to be stimulated from within the economy by removing the restraints of an archaic system of government, and by directing native ingenuity into the pursuit of useful objectives. Taxation is the one area of reform where the teaching of Bentham and Ricardo come together. The theories of greatest happiness and differential rent point in the same direction. Land is the only proper source of government revenue because its taxation minimises the loss of total happiness. Only the landlord suffers.

A typically Benthamite statement about the role of government is set out by Mill in his *Essay on Government*:

the lot of every human being is determined by his pains and pleasures ... Human pains and pleasures are derived from two sources; they are produced, either by our fellow-men, or by causes independent of other men ... the concern of Government is with the former of these two sources ... its business is to increase to the utmost the pleasures, and diminish to the utmost the pains, which men derive from one another.[30]

Whether Mill deliberately restricts the role of government in this way, by denying that it should intervene to relieve at least the consequence of natural disasters and disease, must be questioned. He is undoubtedly keen to stress the importance of the quality and efficiency of an administration. In the *History of India* he argues that

The form of government is one, and the nature of the laws for the administration of justice is the other, of the two circumstances by which the constitution of the people in all countries is chiefly determined. Of these primary causes no result to a greater degree ensures the happiness or misery of the people, than the mode of providing for the pecuniary wants of the government.

Thus the system of taxation must have two desirable qualities.

The first is, to take from the people the smallest quantity possible of their annual produce. The second is, to take from them that which is taken with the smallest possible hurt or uneasiness.[31]

Mill goes on to list the other attributes of good taxes, which will be familiar to anyone with a knowledge of Adam Smith's canons, like keeping down the cost of collection, and the dangers of uncertainty, of inequality in the treatment of tax-payers, and of creating new impediments to production.

There is no further examination of the meaning of minimising unhappiness, and no extension of the argument to other forms of taxation. Mill has practical rather than theoretical concerns. He recommends, in effect, land nationalisation for India. In keeping with British experience, classical economics might suggest adoption of capitalist agriculture, the institution of private property in land, and the restriction of government interference to the minimum necessary for the maintenance and protection of a competitive economy. Mill's habitual dislike of any aristocracy, allied with the Ricardian argument about the landlords class opposing the interests of every other class in society and thus being an obstacle to economic progress, leads him to devise an alternative policy. for the special conditions of the Indian political economy.

Nine-tenths probably of the revenue of the government in India is derived from the rent of land ... and to me that appears to be one of the most fortunate circumstances that can occur in any country; because in consequence of this the wants of the state are supplied really and truly without taxation ... without any drain either upon the produce of any man's labour, or the produce of any man's capital.[32]

As the sole landlord, the State could offer 20 to 30 year leases directly to the peasant cultivators, thereby eliminating the intermediate class of tax collectors with property rights in the land.

Given the backwardness of Indian agriculture, the peasant cultivators will be barely above subsistence level and, therefore, enjoying very little utility in strict Benthamite terms. Any policy that relieves them of unnecessary burdens and encourages improvements in agricultural efficiency ought to add to total happiness. When rents are confined to the net product of land, the 'tax' will be related to the differential fertility of the land leased by the peasants, and not calculated as some proportion of what they lease or the gross return on farming. Mill suffers no illusions about the administrative difficulties involved in assessing and collecting such a 'tax', nor about the temptation for the government to increase its revenue by pushing rents above their pure economic level. His tax proposals are, after all, part of a strategy for revenue and expenditure. Government should provide sound administration, law and order, and little else. These are the indispensable conditions for economic progress. Any extension of public expenditure, such as investment in the infrastructure of the economy, is usually unnecessary. A large army might be an unpleasant requirement for the secure government of India, but even its cost has also to be controlled.

There are several lessons to be learnt from the story of Mill and the subcontinent. First, his policy was never implemented in full. Although his view of rent as a source of government revenue continued to be influential, there were alternative strategies, and some of them had already become entrenched in the bureaucracy of British rule. Second, the dominant influence on him was Ricardian rather then Benthamite. The greatest happiness principle could have been used to support one or more of these alternative strategies; only the Ricardian theory of rent and Mill's own reading of the problems of the agricultural system justified his. Third, he failed to apply the same rent and tax argument to Britain. His policy was for export only. No doubt political and economic realities at home made an important difference. He assumed that his readers would understand the subtleties. Fourth, the government always meant the East India Company. Mill may have criticised the Company on matters like the training of its staff, but he never lost faith in the superiority of an agency over direct rule from Westminster. Under the latter, Ministers of the Crown would have an incentive to hide the true nature their involvement in the government of India, to prevent inspection, lull suspicion and avoid responsibility. Fifth, Mill never thought that Indians resented being ruled by foreigners. Such feelings might exist among Englishmen, not among the peoples of Asia. Thus, whilst he saw no reason why well-qualified Indians should be excluded from senior administrative positions, he believed that it was unhealthy for them to look for advancement in government employment. They should be encouraged instead to develop their own resources and abilities, as cultivators, merchants, and manufacturers.[33]

James Mill and Economics

James Mill was a loyal follower of Adam Smith and Ricardo, taking issue with their critics and elaborating their doctrines. There is, accordingly, very little specifically utilitarian to be found in his economic writings; nothing about subjective utility, measurement of utility, equality of incomes, or the greatest happiness of the greatest number. Before meeting Ricardo he had published two essays on contemporary issues of economic policy. The first, 'An Essay on the Impolicy of a Bounty on the Exportation of Grain', in 1804, reviews the history of the Corn Laws and their effects, and then advocates the abolition of all bounties on the export and all restrictions on the import of grain, on the grounds that the community will greatly benefit from a slightly lower price, and farmers from a steady, regular price. In passing, Mill both attacks Malthus for holding protectionist opinions, and defends landlords and corn dealers against the charge that they are responsible for every increase in prices. They are only doing what every other class does in similar circumstances, 'and it is unjust to require more sacrifice of them than of others'.

The second essay, 'Commerce Defended', appeared in 1808,[34] and ridicules Cobbett and Spence for daring to suggest, among other things, that land rather than manufacturing is the only real source of wealth, that trade with other countries might actually result in a loss, that the National Debt is not a burden, that taxes can be productive, and that supply does not always create its own demand. Mill clearly embraces every tenet in the Ricardian orthodoxy. Whilst there can be over-production of particular commodities, there cannot be over-production of commodities in general, for the production of commodities 'creates, and is the one and universal cause which creates a market for the commodities produced'. This tendency to absolute certainty and 'the excessive use of deductive reasoning', as Edgeworth was to note,[35] has tended to diminish the appeal of Mill's work in political economy. He could also be very heavy handed. As one of the founders of the Political Economy Club in 1821, he invented a 'catechism' which each member would be asked at the commencement of its meetings:

> Do you know anything in the legislation or practice of this country, not recently under consideration of this Society, peculiarly at variance with the principles of Political Economy and has anything occurred to you with respect to the measures of remedying such evils?[36]

There is no record of his suggestion being followed.

After 1808, Mill and Ricardo grew close. They wrote to each other on a regular basis, and for a time went for daily walks.[37] Mill and his family often stayed with the Ricardos at their country house, Gatcomb Park. Ricardo admired Mill's intellectual abilities and seemed to enjoy his friendship. But it was less intimate, shorter and calmer than the friendship between Mill had Bentham. The influence that Mill exerted over Ricardo's *Principles of Political Economy and Taxation* has been the subject of dispute. Evidence points to the conclusion that although Ricardo had the idea of publishing a book before he met Mill, he would not have finished it without Mill's help. Mill read drafts, advised on presentation, constantly cajoled the author into completing promised chapters, and generally boosted his confidence. Ricardo was generous in recognising his indebtedness.

> If I am successful in my understanding it will be to you mainly that my success will be owing, for without your encouragement I do not think that I should have proceeded, and it is to you that I look for assistance of the utmost importance to me, the arranging of the different parts, and curtailing what may be superfluous.[38]

What Mill did not contribute were economic ideas. He accepted the Ricardo's theoretical system without question, welcomed its correction of the errors of Adam Smith, and wished only to make it available to a wider audience.

How Mill's own *Essentials of Political Economy* came to be published in 1823 is quite another story. John Stuart Mill records in his *Autobiography* that his father took him through a complete course of political economy in 1819. The father gave 'lectures' to the son on their walks (everyone seemed to go for long walks), and the son would submit a written account the next day. This draft was then discussed and re-written until a 'clear, precise, and complete' version emerged. John also read the appropriate chapters of Ricardo and reported daily to his father on 'the collateral points which offered themselves in our progress'. The written outline of the whole course thus constructed, served as the basis for James Mill's little book, designed as 'a didactic treatise ... fit for learners'. In scope, the *Essentials* was limited to four inquiries: to explain the laws of production, distribution, exchange, and consumption. Whereas every effort is made to ram home the lessons of Ricardian economics, and Malthus again taken to task for arguing that there can be a general glut or an 'excess of production in the aggregate', there are few visible traces of anything specifically Benthamite.

One exception is to be found in the section[39] (appearing only in the second edition) where Mill deals with the effects of direct taxes. He asks a question which might have been expected to stimulate a utilitarian answer: 'whether it is equitable to levy the same rate of tax upon all incomes?' Instead, he first argues that this is an issue of general policy rather than of political economy, and then, after admitting that most other books on political economy attempt an answer, offers a rather confused solution of his own. He recognises the difficulty of finding an acceptable definition of ability to pay and wants to take into account, in addition to the absolute size of annual income received, its permanence or certainty, the tax-payer's length of life, and the extent of inheritance. Happiness is mentioned, but only in connection with the difference it makes to the tax-payer to know that 'their incomes are to pass to their children at their deaths'. No suggestions are made as to how this happiness might be measured. After worrying about the effect of proportional income and inheritance taxation on the incentive to accumulate large fortunes, he proposes one guiding principle:

A tax operating fairly, ought to leave the relative condition of the different classes of contributors the same after tax as before. In regard to the sums required for the service of the state, this is the true principle of distribution.[40]

Redistribution seems to be ruled out. Fairness is about maintaining the status quo.

Mill chooses the concept of an annuity to facilitate the comparison of differences in the individual circumstances of those receiving income, either of rent, profit or wages. Suppose, he says, one man receives £100 per annum from the rent of land. The source of his income is secure. He owns the land in perpetuity. It might be worth 30 year's purchase. (The numbers only make sense if it is assumed that 30 years purchase means it is worth thirty times the annual income, i.e. £3,000) Another man receives £500 per annum in salary from an office. The source of his income is insecure. He can lose his post. Accordingly, it was worth only 6 years of purchase (also £3,000). These incomes should be treated equally for tax purposes. What does being treated equally mean in practice? A clue is given a little later when, having examined the effects of different kinds of income on the children of recipients, he attempts to summarise the results of the section:

> If one income is worth half as many year's purchase as another, it ought to be half as much taxed; if it is worth one-third of as many year's purchase, it ought to be taxed one-third, and so on.[41]

The principle seems to have vertical as well as horizontal equity implications. But how is it to be interpreted? The only practical method is to impose the same rate of tax on the actual incomes of all taxpayers, for example 10%. In other words, a proportional income tax. In this way taxpayers would be left with same annuity values, or the same relative annuity values as before. Whether Mill intended this conclusion is not clear. He certainly steers away from any Benthamite argument about the diminishing utility of sacrifice. There is no suggestion here that a recipient with twice the income will suffer a smaller proportional utility sacrifice from an equal proportional tax.

Another instance of where Mill comes close to Benthamite issues in economics occurs in his discussion of the motives to save. The question of higher and lower pleasures is immediately introduced.

> When a man possesses ... food, clothing, lodging, and all other things sufficient only for comfortable, but pleasurable existence, he possesses the means to all the substantial enjoyments of human life. The rest is in a great measure fancy.[42]

Not everyone, he goes on to suggest, will be able to appreciate the difference, just as some people will never see the point of sacrificing present for future satisfactions. Unfortunately those who do, will also see that future satisfactions are often of an inferior kind.

> There are two sets of men; one, in whom the reasoning power is strong, and who are able to resist a present pleasure for a greater one hereafter; another, in whom it is weak, and who can seldom resist the charm of immediate enjoyment ... The class, on the other hand, in whom reason is sufficiently strong to form a due estimate of pleasures, cannot fail to perceive that those which they can obtain by adding penny to penny, after all the rational desires are satisfied, are not equal to

the pleasures which, in the circumstances we have described, they must relinquish to obtain them.[43]

The net result is a disinclination to save. Towards the end of the same discussion, Mill suddenly switches to the connection between optimal population and the happpiness of society. The problem, as he sees it, is to restrict the number of births and stabilise the size of the population, before the return on capital invested in land falls too far. A surplus must remain after the needs of the labouring classes have ben met, so that economic growth can continue. Maximum happiness, however, is also a function of the type of person who is being made happy. It means supporting as many people as possible who are neither very rich nor very poor.

> It is also, in a peculiar manner, the business of those whose object it is to ascertain the means of raising human happiness to its greatest height, to consider, what is that class of men by whom the greatest happiness is enjoyed. It will not probably be disputed, that ... the men of middling fortunes, in short, the men to whom society is generally indebted for its great improvements, are the men who, having their time at their disposal, freed from the necessity of manual labour, subject to no man's authority, and engaged in the most delightful occupations, obtain, as a class the greatest sum of human happiness.[44]

Mill never misses an opportunity to extol the virtues of the people in the 'middle rank', and their role in society seems to be at the heart of his notion of utilitarianism. He seems to condemn the remaining members of the community either to a life of unproductive and unthinking idleness, in the case of the rich, or to hard labour for (at best) liberal wages and no leisure, in the case of the poor. Neither state brings much happiness.

Just before his death, Mill published in the *London Review* an imaginary debate between two members of the 'middle rank' called A and B, on *Whether Political Economy is Useful*. The main point of the device is to defend economics against the charge that it is unscientific. As a preliminary to trying to show that it has, contrary to popular opinion, an agreed set of empirically-testable doctrines, the participants explore the nature of utility and welfare. There are, they agree, two parts to human nature, one conducive to the welfare of the body, the other conducive to the welfare of the mind.

> By conducive to welfare, I mean things serving to yield pleasure or ward off pain ... One class of useful things, therefore, are those which serve to produce bodily pleasure, or ward off bodily pain: another, those which produce mental pleasures, or ward off mental pain ... We need not inquire scrupulously into the comparative

value of this pleasure. It is well known how small is the value of all the merely corporeal pleasures ... the purely mental pleasures, those which begin and end in the existence of pleasurable thoughts, hold a high rank among the enjoyments of our nature.[45]

Bentham's equivalence between the utility of pushpin and poetry, and his struggle to measure utility, are left behind. There are higher pleasures, as well as people better placed to exploit them. Even a subject as difficult and important as Political Economy can bring intellectual enjoyment to its (superior) students.

James Mill as a Utilitarian

John Mill records in his *Autobiography* how he was introduced to the writings of Bentham only in the years 1821/23, when he was sent to John Austin for tutoring in the law. His education had previously been classical rather than utilitarian in content. He also records, of course, that his father accepted Bentham's general views on ethics, government and the law. James Mill may have been the 'consummate utilitarian propagandist' and the 'most uncompromising exponent of the utilitarian point of view in the early nineteenth century'.[46] The Benthamism he advocated, however, was very selective. In economics he was clearly a Ricardian first and last, and managed to make very few direct contributions to the development of utilitarian political economy. In ethics, psychology, government and the law, his interpretations of doctrine continue to be influenced by the Scottish philosophers. More specifically, his insistence upon qualitative distinctions in the nature of pleasures and pains came to be a crucial element in his son's revision of utilitarianism.

In the list of 'classical' utilitarian characteristics, James Mill clearly adopts the greatest happiness as the single overriding objective, although he seems to have been uninterested in the problem of how precisely it should be defined for the community as a whole. There is no discussion in his writings of compensation from the gainers to the losers from any change of policy or the law, and no use of Bentham's disappointment-prevention principle. He is also a consequentalist. Bentham's line on ipse dixitism is faithfully followed and clearly explained. Even Mill's concerns with the moral health of society and the search for truth could probably be explained ultimately in terms of their effects on general happiness. As an economist., Mill applies a very strict definition of welfarism, much stricter than that implied by

Bentham. Only the material conditions of life are important and all non-utility information is excluded from consideration. The business of the community, as with the family, is with the consumption and supply of goods and services. There is no room for any concept of economic justice. In ethics, politics and the law, however, his position is more relaxed. Like Bentham, utility is widely interpreted to include many of the features of a the 'good society': democracy, freedoms, rights and liberties.

Mill extols the virtues of economic individualism. Private enterprise is the most efficient method of organising production and consumption. The government has a very limited role. He is perhaps more dogmatic on the subject than most of the other classical economists.

> Every farthing which is spent upon it, beyond the expense necessary for maintaining law and order, is so much dead loss to the nation, contributes so far to keep down the annual produce, and to diminish the happiness of the people. [47]

He certainly has no list of things the government should do to support and supplement the activities of the market as can be found in Bentham's economic writings. In addition, there are the political liberties and freedoms of the individual citizen which have to be protected against the tyrannies, vices, and mischiefs of governments. Yet the importance he attaches to education (moral, technical, and social), for the children of the poor as well as the rich, suggests that the government should be at least interested in the extent and quality of its provision. Education is essential, after all, if individuals are to be the best judges of their own welfare, and understand their responsibilities as electors. Similarly, Mill concentrates on equality of opportunity rather than outcome. Taxpayers should be treated equally. There is no case made out for redistribution from the rich to the poor. Happiness is not a function of the degree of inequality. Nor does Mill investigate the problems of aggregation (apart from a brief digression on the relationship between population size and the standard of living) or the measurement of utility. Bentham's ambition to found the science of society, to develop a calculus of utility, appeals to none of his instincts or prejudices. Literary precision and clarity is Mill's great strength.

Notes

1. *Autobiography of Bertrand Russell, 1872-1914*, (1976). Also *Life of Bertrand Russell*, Ronald Clark (1975).

Notes continued

2. Thomas (1979) p.143. For James Mill on education and the Panopticon see his essay on Education in *Political Writings* ed. Ball (1992).
3. J.S. Mill, *Autobiography*, Mill, John (1981).
4. Bain (1882a).
5. As suggested by Burns (1962).
6. Mill, James (1992), p.174.
7. Quoted in Bain (1882b) pp.180-181.
8. In 1819 after meeting Mill at Bowood, reproduced in Colvin (1971) p.185.
9 Dickens (1989), introduction by Schlicke, p.x.
10. From Mill, James (1992), p. 41.
11. Letter from Hume to Smith, in Smith (1977), p.157.
12. See Chitnis (1976) and (1986), Meek (1976), Skinner and Campbell (1982), and Collini, Winch and Burrow (1983).
13. Haakonsen (1985).
14. From Mill, James (1992), p.11.
15. In Liveley and Rees eds (1978).
16. In Mill, James (1992), p.47.
17. op. cit., p 119.
18. See the interpretation of the late John Rees, in Rees (1986).
19. Mill, James (1992), p.154.
20. op. cit., pp.155-156.
21. op. cit., p.179.
22. In J.S. Mill's introduction to his own edition of James Mill's *Analysis of the Phenomenon of the Human Mind*, Mill, James (1967).
23. op. cit., Vol. II, pp.207-208.
24. op. cit., p.286.
25. op. cit., p.298.
26. op. cit., pp.258-259.
27. Peacock (1968), Vol. VII, p.236.
28. Preface to Vol. 1 of Mill, James (1826).
29. op. cit., Vol. 2, p.134.
30. Mill, James (1992) p.4.
31. Mill, James (1966), chapter 5 on Taxation p.410.
32. From Mill's Evidence to the Select Committee on the Affairs of the East India Company, 1831-1832, in Mill, James (1966) p.424.
33. For Mill's views on these last matters see his Evidence in Mill, James (1966). For the general utilitarian approach to India, and its alternatives, see Stokes (1959) and Barber (1975).
34. Both Essays are in Mill, James (1966).
35. In the *Dictionary of Political Economy*, ed. Palgrave (1900).
36. Quoted in Mill, James (1966), p.192.
37. See the Introduction to Mill, James (1966).
38. Letter from Ricardo to Mill in 1816, Ricardo (1952) Vol. VII, p 194. See also Introduction to Ricardo (1951) Vol. I.
39. Mill, James (1824) Section VIII, Direct Taxes Which Are Destined to Fall Equally on All Incomes, of Chapter IV on Consumption.
40. op. cit., p.264.
41. op. cit., p 269.
42. op. cit., Chapter II, Section II, p.53.
43. op. cit., pp.53-54.
44. op. cit., p.65.

Notes contined

45. *Whether Political Economy is Useful* in Mill, James (1966), pp.371-372.
46. Introduction by Winch to Mill, James (1966), pp.1 & 19.
47. *Commerce Defended* in Mill, James (1966), p.157.

4. John Stuart Mill

Even his fiercest critics granted John Mill exceptional abilities. Stanley Jevons, who turned against the Ricardo/Mill tradition in economics, had to admit the strength of the younger Mill's influence.

> So peculiar was the power exerted over his friends and readers by Mr Mill's zeal, his fearless independence of opinion, his high moral character, and his lucid, persuasive, and apparently logical style of composition, that his works have acted upon his English readers like a spell, which may take many year's to break.[1]

It is the use of words like 'peculiar', 'apparently logical' and 'spell', that reveal the mixture of awe, admiration and suspicion with which he was regarded. Frederick Maurice, an early Christian friend, read him with both growing admiration and apprehension, for he feared that Mill' rapidly expanding, and increasingly speculative thoughts had no centre[2]. Mathew Arnold found him falling just short of 'being a great writer' because he was not 'sufficiently leavened' of the utilitarian school.[3] William Gladstone managed to square high regard for the man and his policies with disapproval of Mill's lack of religious convictions, by calling him the Saint of Rationalism. Much later, Keynes wondered whether, with his special gifts, he had not done more for pedagogy than science. Did he not sit 'like an Old Man of the Sea on the voyaging Sinbads of the next generation'?[4] Maurice Cowling has been even less sympathetic. Behind the coherence, consistency and success of this proselytiser of 'genius', there stood 'a man of sneers and smears and pervading certainty', self-opinionated and self-deluded.[5]

The twenty-five volumes of Mill's works, collected and edited by the Faculty of Arts of the University of Toronto, testify to his energy and the breadth of interests. Books and essays followed articles, reviews and letters, on subjects as diverse as logic, economics, moral and political philosophy, the classics, history, government of the colonies, India and Ireland, the reform of parliament and the rights of women. None of them were facile or light in tone. Perhaps he took himself and his views too seriously. There were times when he became the butt of jokes, and was satirised in newspaper cartoons and popular verse. Although polite and courteous in debate, he could also be brutally frank, in opposing conventional beliefs on sensitive issues like religion, women's suffrage, and birth control. In spite of the ridicule and disapproval, however, he became the undisputed leader of enlightened reform and progressive causes.

His volumes on logic and political economy rapidly became the dominant texts for successive generations of undergraduate. Those on liberty, utilitarianism, and representative government are still on recommended reading lists. His attempts to accommodate individual rights within the framework of the greatest happiness principle continue to fascinate moral and political philosophers. More to the point, his personal version of utilitarianism is enjoying a new life in the hands of modern exponents of welfare economics and social choice theory. One recent exponent of Mill's philosophy calls him one of the highest peaks in 'the central massif of the nineteenth century thought'.[6] He certainly throws a long shadow into the twentieth.

Life's Work

John Mill's famous autobiography was written late in life and published posthumously. It should be approached with caution. A shorter and less controversial account was given by Mill to an American journalist. After expressing surprise that the details would be of interest to the general public, he wrote as follows:

> The only matter which I can furnish is a few dates. Born in London, May 20th 1806. Educated wholly by my father, James Mill, author of History of British India, Analysis of the Phenomenon of the Human Mind, and other works. In 1823 received an appointment in the East India House, and rose progressively to be head of the principal office of correspondence between the home authorities and the local government of India, a post which had been held by my father. Quitted the service in 1858, when the functions of the East India Company were transferred to the Crown. Married in 1851 to Harriet, daughter of Thomas Hardy Esq. of Binksgate, near Huddersfield and widow of John Taylor Esq. merchant of London; who died in 1858. Elected to Parliament for Westminster in 1865; was an unsuccessful candidate for that city in 1868.[7]

To complete the condensed biography it is only necessary to add that he retired to live in Avignon with Harriet's daughter, Helen. He and Harriet had both suffered from tuberculosis and the same disease probably killed two of his brothers. Mill finally succumbed on the 7th

May 1873, and is buried next to his wife in the churchyard of St
Véran.

The difference between this account and the longer version in his
Autobiography are quite revealing. Here he draws no conclusions
about the dominance exerted by his father over his childhood,
education, and subsequent career. The importance of India and the
East India Company to both of them is readily acknowledged. There is
no mention of utilitarianism and no reference to his own publications.
It is written as if he had no mother or other family. Marriage to Harriet
Taylor, and failure to be re-elected as a Member of Parliament, appear
to merit rather more attention. In the longer version, he fills in some of
the gaps and changes the emphasis. His reaction against the
narrowness of his upbringing, his mental crises, his discovery of new
friends and interests, his revision of Benthamite doctrines and
contributions to the theory and practice of utilitarianism in all its
forms, are given at great length. There is still nothing about his mother
and scarcely anything about his brothers and sisters. But there seems
to be a wish to put the influence of his wife above that of his father.

Of the intensity of his studies there can be no doubt: Greek at 3,
Arithmetic and a great wodge of History by the age of 8; then Latin,
elementary Geology, a thorough grounding in Algebra, the Differential
Calculus, more History, and several treatises in Chemistry before he
was 12; and at 13, Logic and Political Economy. For much of the time
he also acted as monitor to his younger brothers and sisters, marking
and correcting their work under the direction of his father. He even
helped to write the first drafts of his father's books! There can be no
doubt, either, about the isolation of this education. The suspicions
James Mill had of the public school system meant that all John's
education was conducted at home. Consequently, he had no friends of
his own age outside the family. Impractical and lacking in manual
dexterity, as he himself admitted, John Mill emerged from the
experience as a superbly engineered thinking and writing machine,
with surprisingly little psychological damage. The mental 'crises'
were to come several years later.

In 1820 Mill spent six months in France, at the invitation of the
family of Bentham's brother, General Sir Samuel Bentham. Travelling
with a companion, he first paid his respects to the economist Jean
Baptiste Say in Paris, and then joined his hosts in the south. For a 14-
year old, it must have been an exciting adventure, and the attractions
of France and French thought stayed with him for the rest of his life.
Apart from improving his French and Mathematics, and becoming
fascinated by the history of the French Revolution, he attended classes

in singing, dancing and fencing. On return to England, a period of self-education along more serious lines followed with studies of the law, of Bentham and Helvetius, and of philosophy, of Hartley, Hume, Dugald Stewart and Reid, among others, guided by two friends of his father, George Grote and John Austin. The production of his father's *Elements of Political Economy* has already been described. Mill also began to make friends with other young men, primarily with those who accepted the appeal of the utility principle, and who were keen to debate radical politics. In 1823, his father obtained a position for him as assistant examiner in the East India Company.

Schumpeter thought that the combination of his interest in current events and his office work, account for the incessant hurry that all his writings display.[8] Or do they? Mill's works are if anything long and verbose, giving the contrary impression that they were the outcome of relaxed and patient enquiry. Keynes credited Mill with powers of 'rapid execution and continuous concentration', which is not quite the same as 'incessant hurry'. By all accounts, Mill was conscientious in attendance at East India House. He managed to complete all his office work within the 10 to 4 day, and still found time to meet with friends and write while on the premises. In his own words, these duties were 'an actual rest from the other mental occupations which I have carried out simultaneously with them.'[9] Of course, most of the other occupations had very little to do with India and the business of the Company.

One of those occupations nearly put him in prison. He was caught handing out birth control leaflets. In those days, they counted as obscene literature. What could have been a serious incident, was evaded in rather mysterious circumstances. His writing was more respectable. None of it had to be issued under a pseudonym. Some of the major works are listed here.

1830	Essays on Unsettled Questions in Political Economy
1833	Remarks on Bentham's Philosophy
1838	Bentham
1840	Coleridge
1843	A System of Logic (2 volumes)
1848	Principles of Political Economy (2 volumes)
1859	On Liberty
1861	Considerations of Representative Government
	Utilitarianism
1865	An Examination of Sir William Hamilton's
	Philosophy

                    Auguste Comte and Positivism
1869   Thornton on Labour and the Its Claims
1873   Autobiography.

Mill claimed that after reading Bentham for the first time in 1821, he
resolved to be a reformer of the world. This was sufficient to fill up a
an 'interesting and animated existence' until the autumn of 1826,
when he awoke 'as from a dream' into 'a dull state of nerves',
'unsusceptible to enjoyment or pleasurable excitement', and began to
question the principles on which his upbringing had been based. Its
'habit of analysis' had convinced him, intellectually, that he should
find pleasure in sympathy with other human beings and the good of
mankind. Unfortunately, the conviction was not strong enough to 'give
me the feeling'. He found himself stranded at the commencement of
life's journey 'with a well-equipped ship and a rudder, but no sail'
There followed a period of re-appraisal: of his acceptance of
utilitarianism, and the neglect of his 'passive susceptibilities'. He
decided that he needed to cultivate the 'internal culture of the
individual', to experience the meaning of art and poetry. By the
autumn of 1828 he was reading Wordsworth and Byron. They opened
the way to an appreciation of the ideas of Samuel Taylor Coleridge
and his followers. Thus Coleridge appeared in the 1838 essay on
Bentham, as one of 'the two great seminal minds of England in their
age'. (The other mind being still that of Bentham.) Whereas the
'Progressive' Bentham discerned the truths 'with which existing
doctrines and institutions were at variance', the 'Conservative'
Coleridge discerned 'the neglected truths which lay in them'.

    It has been suggested that the crisis had been partly brought on by
the Greek loan scandal of 1824.[10] John Bowring and others had been
caught speculating in Greek debt, whilst professing great concern for
Greek freedom. The affair delighted Tory critics and shocked the
liberals. Mill must have been very sensitive to the damage it did to the
reputation of the utilitarian camp. The trouble is that the only evidence
as to cause and effect comes from Mill himself. He makes no
reference to external circumstances, and none of his friends seem to
have noticed any difference in his behaviour. He carried on working as
before. The re-appraisal eventually led forward to a new style of life
and new areas of interest. Recovery of inner health was slow, so he
reports, but steady. By 1828 he had been appointed an Assistant
Examiner at East India House, with a salary of £600 per annum. Soon
after he started to read the works of St Simon and Comte, and he
taught himself German. His circle of friends grew to include the

Unitarians and the Cambridge Apostles around W.J. Fox. Through them he met Mr and Mrs John Taylor.

He was first introduced to Harriet Taylor in 1830, and was supposedly in love with her by 1832. Their relationship of 'strong affection, intimacy of friendship, and no impropriety', continued for almost twenty years before they could be married. They dined regularly together, stayed in the same country houses, and travelled abroad as a pair. John Taylor was usually absent. Victorian England found the circumstances quite scandalous. Carlyle called her Mill's Platonica. The strains imposed upon everyone involved took a heavy toll. Friendships were broken off. Harriet felt ill-used by everyone, including Mill. He became irrational about the legality of their wedding ceremony; and after the marriage quarrelled bitterly with his mother and sisters. Through all these difficulties, Harriet exerted a powerful influence on the direction of his thoughts. No one reading the dedication he wrote for his essay *On Liberty* can fail to be embarrassed by the exceptional strengths and abilities attributed to the lady who was 'the inspirer, and in part the author, of all that is best in my writings'. They discussed 'all subjects of intellectual and moral interest', and she made contributions to his books, starting with the *Principles of Poltical Economy*. The fact that Mill probably exaggerated her role in retrospect, does not mean that her criticisms and suggestions for improvement were confined to feminist subjects.

A second crisis in 1836, 'an obstinate derangement of the brain', may have been related to the tensions of his private life with Harriet Taylor, and guilt about the distance that had opened up between him and his father; but it also had physical symptoms. Mill was recuperating in Brighton, for example, when his father suffered his last illness. In an obituary, he denied that James Mill could be dismissed as 'a mere follower of Bentham'. 'His place was an eminent one in the literary and even political history of the country.' John Mill had also been very busy with work on *Logic* and with a futile attempt to found a new political party for the radicals. Then, in the three years from 1837, much money and energy had been devoted to trying to save the utilitarian journal, the *Westminster Review*. In the end, he was relieved that it passed into other hands, and looked upon 1840 as the start of what he called 'the rest of my life'. Work at the East India House until 1858, the production of major texts in political economy, political theory, and philosophy, and the all too short seven and a half years spent as the husband of Harriet, kept him fully occupied.

M.P. for Westminster

Early in 1865, Mill was approached by some electors in Westminster to stand for Parliament. He showed great reluctance. Why exchange the 'tranquil and retired existence as a writer of books' for the 'less congenial occupation of a member of the House of Commons?' Disclaiming any personal wish for fame, refusing to canvass or incur any expense in the election, and promising to ignore local interests, he nevertheless accepted their nomination as an independent, radical candidate. He enjoyed being a man of action for a brief two and a half years, and was probably hurt more by defeat than he was prepared to admit.

Mill was by then well known as a writer and supporter of progressive causes. He had recently taken the North's side in the American civil war. More significantly to the election, he was seen as a friend of the lower middle and working classes. This was no recent conversion. In 1842, he had written to William Lovett expressing support for Chartist views.[11] He could not accept that 'one class, even if it is dominant in number, should rule', but he would aid their fight for extending the suffrage. Cheap editions of the *Principles of Political Economy* had sold well. Its chapter On the Futurity of the Labouring Classes was more sympathetic to Socialism and the aspirations of trade unions, and other associations of workers, than might have been expected from any restatement of orthodox Ricardian economics. Although he drew back from complete agreement with trade union programmes, there was always enough sympathy expressed to put him well ahead of most members of the Liberal party.

In practice, Mill's attitude to the lower orders was, in spite of his radicalism, ambivalent. Whereas Bentham and his father sometimes gave the impression that they cared little for the majority of less fortunate citizens, John Mill never lost sight of their plight or their threat. (The working class would not, of course, have been much in evidence in the electorate of Westminster in either 1865 or 1868) He wanted them to escape from poverty and despair, but believed they had to do it largely on their own. He was not altogether optimistic about their chances. Rural labourers, for example, came low down in his expectation. Years of exposure to the old poor laws had made them reckless and feckless. Prudential motives were more evident among the middle classes and skilled artisans. Even here education held the key.

None are so illiberal, none so bigoted in their hostility to the improvement, none so superstitiously attached to the stupidest and worst of all forms and usages, as the uneducated.[12]

The 'uncultivated herd' make regular appearances in his political writings. Towards the end of their lives together, he and his wife reflected on their hopes for the future.

We saw clearly that to render any such social transformation either possible or desirable, an equivalent change of character must take place both in the uncultivated herd who now compose the labouring masses, and in the immense majority of their employers.[13]

It would be no easy task. Deep-rooted selfishness, and the institutions that supported it, stood in the way.

Once in Parliament, Mill generally voted with the Liberals and developed a great admiration for Gladstone. As might be expected, he spoke for women's as well as men's suffrage and denounced the mode of Irish government. He argued for municipal government in London: a sound utilitarian position. He was proud of his influence over the labouring classes and claimed, with some evidence, to be the only person able to restrain their violence. Jevons convinced him, as he convinced Gladstone, of the need to pay off the national debt before the nation's coal reserves were exhausted. Pursuit of General Eyre over the Jamaican atrocities made him very unpopular, but confirmed his independent principles and moral earnestness. More surprisingly, he was against the abolition of capital punishment.

India and Ireland

Mill claimed that had been approached several times to stand for Parliament. He had even been offered an Irish seat. Catholic emancipation and the removal of unfair restrictions on Irish commerce had been two of his radical causes. Land reform presented the next and most important test. 'Once at least in every generation', he wrote in 1868, the Irish question, 'rises again to perplex the councils and trouble the conscience of the British nation'. Unfortunately, Ireland was at once too close and too distant. A comparison between her problems and those of India should be instructive. 'When one country falls under the power of another' there are only two possible ways of dealing with it: either it is incorporated 'with the more powerful country, to be placed in a state of equality'; or it is 'to be governed despotically, as a mere province'. India 'was in that stage of advancement at which absolute subjection to a more civilized and more energetic people' resulted in better government than could ever be 'framed out of domestic materials'. By contrast, Ireland was neither sufficiently advanced to be 'treated exactly like Scotland or Yorkshire', nor were the English capable of 'shaking-off insular prejudices' to govern it 'according to its wants'. 'No other civilized nation' (England), is 'so conceited of its own institutions, and of all its modes of public action'.[14]

As long as the East India Company remained responsible for Indian government, all would be well. Its servants had long learnt to throw off their English habits and notions. The reason for the difference was that, 'by fortunate accident, the business of ruling India did not rest with the Houses of Parliament or the offices of Westminster', but with a professional group of dedicated officials who resided in that country. They would never have suggested, for example, turning peasant farmers into hired labourers as a solution to the crisis in Irish agriculture. Permanent tenancies and small-scale cultivation were better suited to the special conditions in Ireland, not the imposition of an English model. Reform of the land law along these lines was the only practical way of increasing production and tackling the problems of famine and mass emigration. A government stands condemned if its citizens are driven to seek a decent living in another country.

There is something very familiar about Mill's position. The superiority of western civilization is taken for granted. No questions are asked about how one country became subject to another. Landlords, rents and population pressures are the main obstacles to the achievement of the greatest happiness. Ricardo and Malthus seem to have a greater relevance to the analysis than Bentham. Finally, government by a local agency is compared favourably to government from the centre. It sounds very much like James Mill on India, and not without an element of special pleading. 'Those Englishmen who know something of India, are even now those who understand Ireland best'. Ireland provides yet another opportunity to defend the East India Company. Indeed, Mill's overall conclusions on the relationship between the two countries was still imperial. In the case of Ireland, and in spite of his genuine sympathy for the sufferings of the Irish people and belief that no other civilized nation was so far apart from Irish history and 'the whole constitution of its social economy' as England, he did not favour separation. England would be dishonoured and Ireland seriously damaged. Geographical proximity and defence against potential enemies like America and France were mentioned as special circumstances. Federal solutions were rejected on the grounds that the constituent parts would be too unequal in size and power. 'A peaceful legislative revolution in the laws and rules affecting the relation of the inhabitants to the soil', would remove most of the causes of Irish resentment against the English. Ireland deserved special treatment, not independence. Like his father, he could not imagine the appeal of pure nationalism.[15]

Political Economy

In his *Essays on Unsettled Questions in Political Economy* Mill had made original contributions first to the theory of international trade in his Laws of Interchange between Nations, secondly to the meaning of Say's Law and its consequences for the role of money in his Of the Influence of Consumption on Production, and thirdly to the epistemology of economics as a social science in his *On the Definition of Political Economy*. In further preparation for his magnum opus, he had also written on the public finances and the working of the monetary system When it was published in 1848, the *Principles of Political Economy* quickly became the dominant text for students of economics of all levels. Broad in coverage, accessible, stimulating, authoritative, and persuasive, it had no equal until Alfred Marshall's *Principles* appeared in 1890. Marshall himself recognised that some of Mill's most ardent admirers had caused resentment by their dogmatic assertion of its virtues. They could not undermine, however, the lasting influence it had on the thoughts of 'the older living economists in England'; and 'what is perhaps even more important' on the attitude which they take with regard to social questions.[16] Marshall's attitude to social questions was certainly strongly influenced by Mill.

There is, therefore, little justification for dismissing Mill the economist as just Ricardo written long. There are of course his injudicious remarks about value theory. The treatment of production and distribution occupies the whole of Volume One of the *Principles*. Exchange appears at the start of Volume Two. Value for a society in which 'the industrial system is entirely founded on purchase and sale', is so important that the 'smallest error' will throw everything else into 'confusion and uncertainty'. Fortunately, 'the theory of the subject is complete'. The only remaining task is to clear up the 'chief perplexities' which occur in its application. In the event, clearing up the perplexities of exchange took Mill nearly 250 pages, with the consolidation of his previous innovations in international trade and money playing a prominent part. This is also where, according to Jevons, Mill helped Ricardo to shunt the engine of economics onto the siding of a cost of production theory of value, when it should have been left to steam along the mainline of subjective utility. Both Sidgwick and Marshall felt that Jevons had been unfair, and they were not convinced that he had could tell the mainline from the siding.

Mill takes value as meaning value in exchange. Value in exchange is command over purchasable commodities, not value in money. For things to have value in exchange, they must satisfy some desire and be scarce. The power to satisfy a desire is for him, as for all the other classical economists, to possess utility, and it underpins demand. Scarcity relates to the conditions of supply and the costs of production. It seems from the start that he is going to explain value in exchange in terms of the twin forces of demand and supply. The upshot of the argument is that utility serves as an upper limit on the demand side.

> the utility of a thing in the estimation of the purchaser, is the extreme limit of its exchange value: higher the value cannot ascend; peculiar circumstances are required to raise it so high.[17]

Things are not normally in such short supply. Most are susceptible of multiplication, and produced either under conditions of constant or increasing, long-run cost. In the former case, demand enters to determine

> the perturbation of value, during a period which cannot exceed the time necessary for altering the supply. While thus ruling the oscillations of value, they themselves obey a superior force which makes value gravitate towards Cost of Production.[18]

In the latter case, although demand and supply govern value, they are subject to a minimum set by a cost of production that includes normal profit under competition. This is what all the fuss is about. There is as much Smith in it as there is Ricardo.

This was no accident. The *Principles of Political Economy* and the *Logic* were the crowning achievements of Mill's intellectual maturity. The former, he claimed, was a different text from those written in England since 1776. It returns to the approach of Adam Smith, which always associated theories with their applications and recognised the close connection between political economy and the other social sciences. In his *Logic* and his essays on the positivist sociology of Comte, as well as in *On the Definitions of Political Economy*, economics is treated as a branch of a much wider study of human relationships. Sometimes the association is with the study of the laws of society, of 'moral man in society', which Mill called Speculative Politics or Social Economy; and sometimes it is with what he called Ethology, or study of the laws which regulate the formation of human character. Understanding of these other disciplines is vital; 'a person is not likely to be a good political economist who is nothing else'.

Books IV and V of the *Principles* fulfil the promise of its sub-title, *with Some of Their Applications to Social Philosophy*. In turning from the statics to the dynamics of political economy, Mill offers a cautious welcome to the onset of the 'stationary state' and delivers a homily on the future prospects of the 'most numerous class of manual labourers'. The change in emphasis from theory to policy is carried further with a study of taxation and the extent of government intervention in the economy. Although the themes are often the same, the conclusions go well beyond the boundaries of Ricardian orthodoxy. The recommendations that workers should explore the advantages of co-operation, that solitude ought to be a pleasure enjoyed by the many, and that middle-class consumption is often un-necessary, are not typical of the members of the Political Economy Club. For Marshall, the merit of Mill was that he moved away from Ricardo in recognising the pliant nature of human motives (a phrase actually used by John Austin). Activities and tastes developed together. It was dangerous to draw conclusions about the way in which people behaved in one state of society and assume they applied to another. In any case, wealth was not the only object of life.

> All know that it is one thing to be rich, another to be enlightened, brave or humane; that the questions how a nation is made wealthy, and how it is made free, or virtuous, or eminent in literature, in fine arts, in arms, or in polity, are totally distinct enquiries.[19]

J.E.Cairnes admired him for his dissent from orthodox positions on policy. Just because he accepted the explanations of economic growth provided by the classical economists, did not mean that Mill had to accept their policies: the sciences should be our servant not our master in such matters.

Mill tries to draw a careful distinction between positive and normative political economy. He rejects the simplification of the subject as just an art, in the sense of a set of recipes for making a nation rich. To turn this trick, the practitioner needs first to understand the limitations of economic science. Political economy is

> The science which traces the laws of such phenomena of society as arise from the
> combined operations of mankind for the production of wealth, in so far as those
> phenomena are not modified by the pursuit of any other object.[20]

Not merely is it a science, but it has to be a deductive and positive
science. In his *Logic* there are two kinds of science: the physical and
the moral. The phenomena studied by the physical sciences conform
to the laws of nature and their conclusions describe what is, not what
ought to be. Unfortunately, he is not sure he can keep to this definition
in economics. Part of the difficulty is that experiments are impossible
in the social sciences. The facts under examination are too
complicated. So the 'Chemical' method is inapplicable. Laws cannot
be derived by a process of induction, from a comparison of details.
There is only one way of proceeding and that is to adopt 'a priori' or
'abstract speculation'. Bentham's application of the principle of utility
to politics was a brilliant exercise in the abstract 'geometric'method.
Political economy needs to be like the more complex models of the
physical sciences, reasoning from assumed premises, 'which might be
totally without foundation in fact'. It is in the application of the
science that facts become important.[21]

Mill still believes that the laws relating to the production of wealth
are similar to physical truths. They are reasonably safe. He did not
want economist to give them up altogether. He takes a different
attitude towards the laws of distribution. Here outcomes are
determined by the institutions of society. They are not immutable.
They are subject to changes in opinions and feelings, in the state of
knowledge, culture, and economic progress. His famous retraction of
the Wages Fund doctrine, which comes in the essay, *Thornton on
Labour and its Claims*, and not in the later editions of the *Principles*,
is a good example. Trade Unions may be able to raise the share of
labour after all, but the right and wrongs of their action,

> becomes a common question of prudence and social duty, not one which is
> peremptorily decided by the unbending necessities of political economy.[22]

The many 'modifying influences of miscellaneous causes', and 'the
general social changes in progress', must not be ignored. Yet it is still
possible to say something about distribution, after careful amendment
to the premises of an argument for changed circumstances. If 'free
competition' stands for one state of society, and the determination of
'the rent, profits and wages, received by landlords, capitalists, and
labourers' as the subject of the laws of distribution, then whoever
masters them

will have no difficulty in determining the very different laws which regulate the distribution of the produce among the classes interested in it, in any of the states of cultivation and landed property set forth.[23]

One of the implications of this statement is that Ireland and India can be usefully studied by a Political Economy written in a society far removed from them in development and culture.

Mill grants that progress can be made by assuming the desire for wealth to be the immediate cause of economic behaviour, and the preferment of a greater to a smaller gain the underlying psychology. Under its influence, mankind can be shown,

> accumulating wealth, and employing that wealth in the production of other wealth; sanctioning by mutual agreement the institution of property; establishing laws to prevent individuals from encroaching upon the property of others by force or fraud; settling the division of the produce by agreement, under the influence of competition (competition itself being governed by certain laws, which laws are therefore the ultimate regulators of the division of the produce); and employing certain expedients (as money, credit, etc) to facilitate the distribution.[24]

Mill is now, of course, using laws in two senses: as human devices, social enactments to control behaviour, and as natural tendencies of the human mind. He believes that both external and internal sanctions influence behaviour. The formation of human character, of which the desire for wealth is one element, has to be deduced from the general laws of the mind, allowance being made for circumstances and self-development. Circumstances can change, and people learn new standards of behaviour, even though their underlying natural tendencies stay the same. Thus the desire for wealth is an important motive, but does not work alone. It might be modified. Economists have to guard against 'mistaking temporary or local phases of human character for human nature itself'. For these reasons, there can be no absolute certainty about the laws of political economy. They will only be true in ideal situations. Nor can political economy make predictions with any accuracy. Not merely is it impossible to foresee all the factors that might determine individual acts,

> even in any given combination of (present) circumstance, no assertion, which is both precise and universally true, can be made respecting the manner in which human beings will think, feel, or act ... because ... the impressions and actions of human beings are not solely the result of present circumstances, but the joint result of those circumstances and the character of the individual: and the agencies which determine human character are so numerous and diversified ... that in the aggregate they are never in any two cases exactly similar.[25]

There must always be room for modest doubt, therefore, in the application of the principles of political economy. An unexpected cause could always disturb confident assertions about the way things are supposed to turn out.

The possibility of development in the human character and in attitudes to moral questions, is taken very seriously by Mill. The labouring classes, for example, will have to rely upon 'their own mental cultivation' to ensure an increase in their standard of living. The economic condition of a class, or of a society to which it belongs, is a function of its moral, intellectual and social condition. These details were not normally the concern of political economy; but 'in more comprehensive inquiries it is impossible to exclude them'. In spite of the fact that the *Principles*, and most of what else he wrote on economics, is not supposed to be part of this more comprehensive inquiry, he has difficulty in keeping the moral, intellectual and social out. Moreover, his eagerness to clarify major issues of issues of public policy inevitably involve the use of value judgements. Political economy in his hands is not always a positive science. Anyone reading his chapter On the Probable Futurity of the Labouring Classes in the *Principles* would be amazed to find it so described. It is more a study in speculative politics and normative social economy than in applied poltical economy. Yet there is an almost complete absence in any of his economics of any reference to utilitarianism or the greatest happiness principle. Mill's moral earnestness shines through, but its source, the foundation of the wider inquiry, the moral science from which it is derived, is never disclosed. Emphasis is placed instead upon the economic, social and moral improvement of human beings.[26]

Utilitarianism

The repeated references in Mill's writings on the nature of economics and the social sciences to the pliability of human nature and the dangers of inferring universal laws, can be derived from his intellectual inheritance. He followed Bentham and his father in being both a reformer in politics and an associationist in psychology. In his *Autobiography*, he remarks that reformers have a natural hostility to those who want to treat feelings and moral facts, as fixed elements in human nature. Those who would oppose change, tend to fall back on notions of what is right for individuals and society, as intuitive truths. Reformers should rather argue for a rational ethics that can be learnt by association and adapted to circumstance. According to Bentham and his father, the utility principle was supposed to provide the key to such an ethics. When Mill begins to turn against the tradition in which he had been educated, one of his objectives was 'to free philosophical radicalism from the reproach of sectarian Benthamism' and 'to show that there was a Radical philosophy better and more complete than Bentham's, while recognising and incorporating all of Bentham's work which is permanently valuable.' Despite all Mill's strictures on the narrowness of the faith, he never becomes an apostate.

As a young man, Mill became conscious of the disdain with which the ideas of Bentham, his father and himself, were often received. Too many of his contemporaries found the principle of utility 'cold calculation', political economy 'hard-hearted', and birth-control 'repulsive'. He thought the critics were generally wrong, and hoped by rational argument to persuade them to accept, as he and his friends had accepted, happiness as a standard of conduct in ethics and politics.

> What we principally thought of, was to alter people's opinions; to make them believe according to evidence, and know what was their real interest, which once they knew they would, we thought, by the instrument of opinion, enforce a regard to it upon one another. While fully recognising the superior excellence of unselfish benevolence and love of justice, we did not expect the regeneration of mankind from any direct action on those sentiments, but from the effect of educated intellect, enlightening the selfish opinions.[27]

It seems a strange mixture of optimism and priggishness, doomed to lead to disappointment. Other people rarely take kindly to be told what their real interests entail. Forty years later, a disillusioned Mill admits that few of his fellow-believers were still relying on educated enlightenment to save the world. In the 1820's, he thought failure was due to the things utilitarianism had left out. It made no appeal to feelings of sentiment, spirituality, or idealism. Sympathy was the only motive relating to other people that Bentham allowed, and even that was not strictly disinterested. There seemed to be no room for duty or obligation, and no foundation for justice.

This growing awareness of the incomplete nature of the intellectual tradition in which he had been brought up, reinforced the doubts and disenchantment Mill had experienced during his first mental crisis. Thus, when he came to write about the principle of utility, he had to re-build the foundations and defend it against alternative theories, in particular intuitionist explanations of virtuous actions and moral rules. He was required to undertake a much more careful and objective reading of the words of Bentham than his father had ever attempted.[28] The outcome was a series of important revisions to the utilitarian position, in economics as well as philosophy and politics. They can be conveniently discussed under the same seven characteristics of 'classical utilitarianism' that were used for Bentham himself; only in Mill's case, it is more logical to change the order. After the Single Objective will come Aggregation and Measurement, then Consequentalism and Welfarism, and lastly Equality and Individualism.

A Single Overriding Objective

Mill never rejects the greatest happiness principle as the ultimate test of conduct for individuals and government. He may criticise Bentham for making it too simple and narrow. Bentham assumes that individuals are always cool and calculating and, worst of all, ignores the effects of their actions upon the formation of human character, or the importance of self-education and training. In the end, Mill comes back to utility because he could find no better foundation for ethics. Moral rules are more important than explanations of behaviour. He is an ethical hedonist first and a psychological hedonist second. But he enlarges the notion of utility to include the whole experience of the good life. 'Higher pleasures' are distinguished from 'lower pleasures' and given more weight. Secondary principles are recognised as often being more effective in achieving the objective of utility than utility itself. Standards of behaviour are, in most cases, better regulated by general rules. The extent of individual liberty and the opportunities for moral improvement are crucial to the assessment of the greater good.

In his *Remarks on Bentham's Philosophy* (1833), Mill begins to come to terms with the Benthamite inheritance. Bentham was guilty of 'insufficient knowledge and appreciation of the thought of others', and needed to be a 'profounder and subtler' metaphysician; but he did for the law what Bacon had done for physical knowledge. To deduce all secondary and intermediate principles from one great axiom, and to resolve the mystery of law into a simple piece of practical business, was a tremendous achievement. By contrast, as an analyst of human nature, Bentham was not ranked very high. He was right to hold that the pursuit of happiness is natural to us. 'Reid and the Stewart School, and the German Metaphysicians' also started with our common nature, the instincts of the species. Where he went wrong was to take happiness as 'the test of all rules of conduct, and the end of life', when many people found it indirectly in the pursuit of some other objective. The happiness of others, for example, should be sought as an ideal end in itself, not as a means. Individuals were never truly happy when only thinking about their own happiness. Aiming at the improvement of mankind brings happiness 'by the way'. Nor are human beings alike in all times and all places. They may not have the same wants or face the same evils, and are not all well served by the same institutions.

Although only a small part of his essay on *Bentham* (1838) is devoted to a discussion of the principle of utility, Mill allows himself to be more generous. Bentham is now one of 'the masters of wisdom, great teachers and permanent intellectual ornaments of the human race'. Very little of what is positive in Bentham deserves to be rejected. It is his one-sided version of human actions that lets him down. Every human act has three aspects:

> its moral aspect, or that of its right and wrong; its aesthetic aspect, or that of its beauty; its sympathetic aspect, or that of its loveableness. The first addresses itself to our reason and conscience; the second, to our imagination; the third to our human fellow-feeling. According to the first, we approve or disapprove; according to the second, we admire or despise; according to the third, we love, pity, or dislike.[29]

Bentham's mistake was to concentrate on the first, to the exclusion of the other two. Mill grants that the morality of the foreseeable consequences of an act might be the most important consideration, but wants to make room, in an overall assessment, for its aesthetic and sympathetic qualities. Some acts can be right, even admirable, and yet remain unlovable. Mill uses the example of Lucius Junius Brutus, who sentenced his sons to death for supporting the restoration of a tyrant. Presumably, other acts can be loveable (showing great kindness to others) and admirable (brave), though wrong (reducing the happiness of the community). Unfortunately, Mill offers no guidance as to how bravery, kindness, and happiness might be compared or weighed.

By the time he wrote *Utilitarianism* (1861), Mill had adopted a more positive and sophisticated defence of the doctrine. He starts with a definition which appears almost identical to Bentham's:

> The creed which accepts as the foundation of morals, Utility, or the Greatest Happiness Principle, holds that actions are right in proportion as they promote happiness, wrong as they tend to produce the reverse of happiness. By happiness is intended pleasure, and the absence of pain; by unhappiness, pain, and the privation of pleasure.[30]

The emphasis is ethical. What is right and wrong becomes the leading question. The implication of his defence of the principle, nevertheless, is that what is right is also natural. Earlier, in his *Remarks on Bentham's Philosophy*, he referred to non-utilitarian philosophers who would have accepted that 'the pursuit of happiness is natural to us; and so is ... the reverence for, and the inclination to square our actions by, certain general laws of morality.' The difference between them and Bentham was about ethics, not psychology. For Mill, 'the ingredients of happiness are very various'. Human beings are constituted to desire either things that are part of happiness itself, or things that are the means to happiness. Desire and pleasantness, aversion and painfulness, are inseparable in the mind. Desire implies that things are pleasant in themselves, or bring some benefit to the person involved or to others for whom that person cares. Music and health, for example, are desired 'in and for themselves; besides being means they are a part of the end'. Money may only be worth what it can purchase, but it too is often wanted for its own sake. Power and fame are strongly attractive because they lead to the attainment of so many of the other wishes of mankind. Music, health, money, power and fame are desired as part of happiness. Virtue, by contrast, is a good for which there was no naturally constituted desire. It has to become associated with pleasure, and protection from pain, and so 'may be felt good in itself'. Unlike money, power and fame, the pursuit of virtue is always a blessing to other members of society.

The purpose of this analysis of the desire for happiness is to find a 'proof' of the principle of utility. Mill accepts that it is not possible to find a proof in the ordinary sense of the word. All first principles, he asserts, suffer from the same incapacity. In the case of sound, the only proof that it is audible is that it is heard. In the case of utility, the only proof that it is desired is that people desire it. Everyone desires their own happiness. Their own happiness is a good to them. Mill's transition from good in this sense to good in the moral sense becomes the crucial stage in the argument. If human nature is, in fact, constructed to desire things either as a means or as part of happiness, then, he believes,

> human happiness is the sole end of human action, and the promotion of it the test by which to judge of all human conduct; by whence it necessarily follows that it must be the criterion of morality, since a part is included in the whole.[31]

Few of Mill's readers have been persuaded by his argument at this point. They do not find the 'proof' very convincing. Sceptics question whether every individual wills pleasure in the moral sense. Mill admits that there are some in whom 'the virtuous will is still feeble'. They have to be made to recognise its strengths by learning to associate it with pleasure, or the absence of pain. To admit that virtue needs to be acquired, he maintains, is consistent with the notion that it is natural. It is naturally acquired. How 'naturally' can be squared with being 'made to recognise' is another question the reader will ask.

Once the idea of a variety in the ingredients of pleasure is accepted, Mill's claim that the principle of utility can accommodate different kinds of pleasure, is less surprising. Some pleasures are more desirable and valuable than others. Following his father once again, he distinguishes between the pleasures of the mind and those of the body. The pleasures of the intellect, of feelings and imagination, and of moral sentiments are higher pleasures. The pleasures of mere physical sensation are the lower pleasures. Instead of attributing the superiority of higher pleasures to their greater 'permanency, safety, uncostliness, etc', he argues that the advantage lies in their 'intrinsic nature'. It is a matter of quality and quantity, not just quantity. Variations in quality are revealed by comparative preference and desire. Taking two pleasures, compared without reference to any moral obligation, if one is

> by those who are competently acquainted with both, placed so far above the other that they prefer it, even though knowing it to be attended with a greater amount of discontent, and would not resign it for any quantity of the other pleasure which their nature is capable of, we are justified is ascribing to the preferred enjoyment a superiority in quality, so far outweighing quantity as to render it, in comparison, of small account.[32]

Mill is confident that those 'competently acquainted' will always prefer the 'manner of existence which employs the higher faculties'. Only a few will choose the lower pleasures, and allow quantity to outweigh quality.

Mill's conclusion that 'it is better to be a human being dissatisfied than a pig satisfied', is of little help in comparisons where quantities and qualities are more evenly balanced. He is insistent that higher and lower pleasures are heterogeneous, that they differ in kind, but equally sure that human beings are aware of both sides of the question. A capacity for 'nobler feelings' can be developed. But it is a 'tender plant' and needs careful cultivation, by self-examination and observation. Alternatively, lower pleasures could become addictive if they are the only pleasures available. If higher and lower pleasures are to be compared, and a judgement made between them, therefore, Mill is forced to rely on those who have experienced both. The implication is that they will have been convinced of the superiority of nobler feelings. In the event that these judges disagree, a majority among them must make the final decision. This leads to a restatement of the Greatest Happiness Principle, for which the aim is to provide, an existence exempt as fast as possible from pain and as rich as possible in enjoyments, both in point of quantity and quality; the test of quality, and the rule for measuring it against quantity, being the preference felt by those who, in their opportunities of experience, to which must be added their habits of self-consciousness and self-observation, are best furnished with the means of comparison.[33]

This definition provides the ethical standard for human conduct and its benefits should be extended to include, not merely the whole of mankind, but also, 'so far as the nature of things admits', the 'whole sentient creation'. The satisfaction of the pleasures of beasts should count for something.

Aggregation

Mill's preoccupation with the problems of personal ethics does not prevent him from applying the happiness of all as the ultimate test. On the contrary, his 'proof' of utility is supposed to show that the Greatest Happiness Principle is as natural a good to the 'aggregate of all persons' as it is to the individual. In discussing the standards of justice as they apply to taxation, for example, he uses the term 'social utility'. Good government is a means to the end, and the end is happiness. Happiness is a function, among other things, of the wealth of a country and the standard of living its citizens can afford. The one element missing from all these statements, is aggregation in the sense of adding-up utility across individuals. Mill spends no time worrying, as Bentham worried, about the meaning of the greatest happiness of the 'greatest number'. Individuals might be expected to sacrifice their immediate happiness for the general happiness, but no attempt is made to ensure that their loss is sufficiently compensated by gains elsewhere. General happiness is a rather vague concept.

Mill readily acknowledges that the 'aggregate interests of society' is a 'complex object', made up of several disparate elements. They can be summarised under two heads: those determining the virtue and intelligence of the members of the community; and those determining the quality of the community's legal and administrative structures. In *Utilitarianism* he stresses the requirement that the standard of the greatest happiness principle is the greatest amount of happiness altogether, for all and not just the agent's own happiness. This simple objective is repeated, when he defends utilitarians against the charge that they deny the power of individual sacrifice for the good of others. All they deny, says Mill, is that the sacrifice is itself a good. On the contrary, they strongly believe that every actor should be concerned with the happiness of all concerned.

> As between his own happiness and that of others, utilitarians require him to be as strictly impartial as a disinterested and impartial spectator ... As a means of making the nearest approach to this ideal, utility would enjoin, first, that laws and social arrangements should place the happiness, or (as speaking practically it may be called) the interest, of every individual, as nearly as possible in harmony with the interests of the whole.[34]

The reference to a disinterested and impartial spectator is strongly reminiscent of Adam Smith, and that to laws and social arrangements of Bentham. The combination is peculiarly Mill's own.

Mill, however, is much more interested in providing an explanation for including the happiness of all, in his proof of utility. His previously quoted comments on the kind of proof to be expected, are followed by a famous claim that it is easy to move from the individual to the aggregate good.

> No reason can be given why the general happiness is desirable, except that each person, so far as he believes it to be attainable, desires his own happiness. This, however, being a fact, we have not only all the proof which the case admits of, but all which is possible to require, that happiness is a good; that each person's happiness is a good to that person, and the general happiness, therefore, a good to the aggregate of all persons.[35]

No one else has found it so easy to dismiss the need for any other reason. Leaving the concept of aggregate happiness vague is obviously a help. Mill has no properly defined utility maximand. In a letter to George Grote, written several years later, he accepts that the general happiness can be looked upon as 'composed of as many different units as there are persons'.[36] But in terms of the analysis in *Utilitarianism*, each 'unit' can also enjoy higher and lower pleasures in varying proportions, and with varying intensities. Why should each unit's perceptions of the general good be the same, or, if not the same, mutually compatible?

Mill relies for the defence of his version of the general good on natural sentiments of social co-operation. The argument is dense and confusing. Human beings, he affirms, have a desire to be in unity with each other. This feeling has always been present in their natures, but grows with advances in civilization. Political progress encourages the removal of privileges and the reduction in inequalities of status and power. Economic progress draws more of humanity above subsistence level and into the realms of happiness.

The social state is at once so natural, so necessary, and so habitual to man, that, except in some unusual circumstances or by an effort of voluntary abstraction, he never conceives of himself otherwise than as a member of a body ... So long as they are co-operating, their ends are identified with those of others; there is at least a temporary feeling that the interests of others are their own interests. Not only does all strengthening of social ties, and all healthy growth of society, give to each individual a stronger personal interest in practically consulting the welfare of others; it also leads him to identify his feelings more and more with their good.[37]

Every person learns that they must take some account of other people's interests, and the advantages of taking joint action to meet common interests grow familiar. It all sounds very idealistic.

In the same passages, Mill also says something very different. The binding force of utilitarian morality may take time to develop. Even in an advanced country like mid-nineteenth century Britain, most people have a weaker desire to promote the welfare of others than the welfare of themselves, and 'it is often wanting altogether'. Individuals have to be made conscious of the fact that their needs do not necessarily conflict with the needs of other. Education helps by nourishing feelings of sympathy. It cannot succeed alone. Behaviour has to be constrained by the powerful agencies of moral sanction and the law. For those (few) who have been (voluntarily) convinced of the validity of the greatest happiness principle, it becomes a natural feeling.

It does not present itself to their minds as a superstition of education, or a law despotically imposed by the power of society, but an attribute which it would not be well for them to be without.[38]

Mill clearly wishes that everyone could escape from superstition and despotism. He worried about the manipulation of minds that are 'moral blanks' Public opinion can take on a repressive form. Religion, whether of the traditional kind, or of Auguste Comte's organised version of social humanism, might so exaggerate the duty of giving service to the community that 'human freedom and individuality' would be threatened. There is a contradiction between these two versions of the moral being.

One of the important problems facing the community was, for Mill and other utilitarians, the size of the population. He repeatedly warns against the dangers of over-population and not just because there would be too many mouths to feed. Space, solitude, and privacy, are, for him, important aspects of the quality of life. The labouring classes, in particular, cannot expect any permanent improvement in their living standards until they reduce the number of children they bring into the

world. The decision to become a parent should never be taken lightly.
It involves serious moral responsibilities.

> Every one has a right to live. We will suppose this granted. But no one has a right
> to bring creatures into life.[39]

Not, that is, until they can provide these 'creatures' with the means to
a comfortable existence. General happiness, therefore, must be a
function of the number of people as well as the wealth in a
community. The challenge is to determine how these factors relate to
each other. Is greater wealth always to be associated with smaller
numbers of people? Are not the most humble and poor of families
capable of generating some happiness? Will not sheer numbers
outweigh the greater happiness of the few?

In spite of the underlying priority Mill gave to the subject, he fails
to give very specific answers to this kind of question. Life can be
worth living. There is so much to enjoy, and anyone born in a civilized
country will inherit enough moral and intellectual culture to be
capable of an enviable existence. Provided, that is, the positive evils of
sickness, mental incapacity, and lack of kindness, or objects of
affection, can be avoided. Then general happiness will increase when
the number of persons who can obtain, 'by their bodily and mental
exertions a comfortable existence' increases. It is better for there to be
more people at this level than fewer people at a higher level. It is
worse for there to be more people at a lower level. A sophisticated
interpretation of the position is that he believed a larger population
was desirable only if average utility rose. The dimensions of happiness
or utility being so varied, and details of the way in which they might
be measured so scarce, it is difficult to be sure. Mill seemed anxious
not to commit himself.

Measurement

In ethics, Mill precludes the use of quantitative measurement by
making utility a 'subjective feeling of the mind'. Only those who have
experienced both 'higher' and 'lower pleasures' can properly judge
them. Only they can fully appreciate the superiority of quality over
quantity. By contrast, in a science which studies the pursuit of wealth,
where 'greater gains are preferred to smaller', he could surely afford
to adopt a more objective approach. Instead, he takes a step back from
the lead given by Bentham. Economics is not allowed to become a

calculus of utility. Bentham's 'clear quantitative notions' never translate into 'exact quantitative statements'.

The description of pleasures contained in *Utilitarianism* stresses the difference in kind between pleasures derived from the higher faculties and those susceptible to 'the animal nature'. If those competent to judge, place one kind above another (in spite of suffering associated 'discontents', and rejecting other pleasures in exchange[40]), Mill has little doubt that they will 'knowingly and calmly' prefer quality over quantity. By observing the behaviour of 'connoisseurs' of pleasure, across extended choices, he could have gone on to develop a process for the measurement of individual utility. The quantities of pains they could bear, or quantities of pleasure they could forbear, rather than lose the pleasure in question, would be a test for the strength of their preferences. Mill always expects quality to outweigh quantity, and now he would know by how much. In fact, he fails to exploit the opportunity. He wants to see aggregate happiness increasing, but is uninterested in deriving numbers for either levels of utility or differences in utility. His concern is rather to defend his 'proof' of utility, and show that quality is superior, and different, to quantity. Judgements by the educated and experienced about the happiness of themselves and the uneducated or uninitiated, are almost the only source of utility information in which Mill has confidence. He will expect them to be based on as much empirical data as there is available, covering the whole range of personal and community circumstance. They will emerge, nevertheless, in the form of statements like this person, or this community, is enjoying more or less happiness, rather than this person or community is enjoying twice as much or half as much happiness. The fact that the judges are supposed to settle their differences (and it is significant that he admits there might be differences) by majority decision, supports the view that he is thinking of ordinal rather than cardinal comparisons of utility.

Matters are no more advanced when Mill is writing about economics. The subject cannot be confined to the lower pleasures, where quantitative measurement might appear to be easier. Progress means that a larger proportion of humanity can be raised above mere subsistence and begin to enjoy some superior happiness. They will then gradually learn how to develop their higher faculties. The pursuit of wealth, therefore, is for the enjoyment of utility in the widest sense, quality gradually winning-out over sheer quantity. It has to be admitted that most of Mill's *Principles of Political Economy* concerned the satisfaction of material wants. He may have been optimistic in the long term about finding a solution to the problem of poverty, but for now most people had to struggle for survival. Their 'animal needs' must be satisfied first. Thus, when he came to issues of economic policy, he addressed the lower pleasures of the mass of the population as well as the higher pleasures of the minority.

Taxation presents a major policy issue and an opportunity to attempt the measurement of total and marginal utility. The payment of compulsory levies to the government, on whatever basis, represents the sacrifice of utility by the citizen. In order to derive utilitarian recommendations about the system of taxation, it is necessary to decide on the correct utilitarian principles of sacrifice. The two candidates are equal individual sacrifice and minimum aggregate sacrifice. (Under very special circumstances, they amount to the same thing). Mill in one place advocates equality of sacrifice, and in another, that 'social utility alone should decide the preference' between alternative definitions of justice in taxation. As far as measurement is concerned, his clearest statement occurs when he is arguing the case for proportional as against progressive taxation. He questions (what are in effect) Benthamite presumptions about the relationship between utility and income.

> It may be said, indeed, that to take £100 from £1,000 ... is a heavier impost than £1,000 taken from £10,000 ... But this doctrine seem to me too disputable altogether, and even if true at all, not true to a sufficient extent, to be made the foundation of any rule of taxation. Whether the person with £10,000 a year cares less for £1,000 than the person with only £1,000 cares for £100, and if so, how much less, does not appear to me capable of being decided with the degree of certainty on which a legislator or a financier ought to act.[41]

The final sentence implies that he is not willing to accept, as an indisputable fact, that the marginal utility of income declines (the pain of marginal sacrifice is less the larger the income which is being taxed); and even if it were undisputed, he denies that it can be precisely measured.

Individualism

Mill was a famous champion of individual liberty. Human originality is a precious asset to be protected against the tyranny of public opinion and conventional morality. The only justification for the exercise of power over individuals is when their actions threatened harm to others. They are the persons most interested in their own happiness, and, almost always, the best judges of their own happiness.

Government interference is usually incompetent and misdirected. This did not mean that human beings are solitary creatures. They are naturally gregarious and voluntary collective action is an excellent way of satisfying their joint interests. A civilised society is based on compromise and co-operation, between free and independent people.

In his *Logic* Mill lays down a clear commitment to what is called Methodological Individualism. The whole (the collective or aggregate outcome), is nothing more that the sum of the parts. Social science studies a whole of this kind.

> The laws of the phenomenon of society are, and can be nothing but the laws of the actions and passions of human beings united together in the social state. Men, however, in a state of society, are still men ... are not, when brought together, converted into another kind of substance, with different properties ... Human beings in society have no properties but those which are derived from, and may be resolved into, the laws of the nature of individual man. In social phenomena the composition of causes is the universal law.[42]

The happiness of the community is, therefore, simply the sum of the happiness of the members of the community. Collective interests must be part of the interests of individual units. They cannot exist on a separate plane of their own. The cultivation of the individual is also supposed to strengthen society. Mill's concept of self-development and self-improvement is designed to avoid the opposite extremes of self-assertion and self-denial. As each person comes to be of more value to themselves, so they come to be of more value to others: when there is more life in the units there is more in the mass of which they are composed. The principle that individuals should be free to follow their own interests, as long as the interests of others are not harmed, is far from being used as an argument for private isolation.

> It would be a great misunderstanding of this doctrine to suppose that it is one of selfish indifference which pretends that human beings have no business with each other's conduct of life, and that they should not concern themselves about the well-doing or well-being of one another, unless their own interest is involved.[43]

The advance of civilization is an object lesson in co-operation, compromise and combination. It always involves a sacrifice of some individual welfare for the common good. When voluntarily made, the sacrifice presents no problems.

All those who have reached the years of maturity, and are of a sound mind, are entitled to enjoy the freedoms of individual liberty. The only reason for the exercise of state power over them is to prevent harm to others. In fact, Mill sees dangers in any corporate body or agency having authority. The precious assets of individual genius and eccentricity can be so easily worn down into dull uniformity by public opinion and conventional morality. He insists that these freedom should not be regarded as an abstract right, but derived from the principle of utility. Utility remains the ultimate appeal in ethics; only now it is utility defined 'in the largest sense, grounded on the permanent interests of man as a progressive being'. These permanent interests include the common good. Interference can only be justified if it corrects the bad consequences for the common good, of both positive and negative acts. Individuals might do those things that harm others, and not do those things that benefit others.

Mill devotes a whole chapter of the *Principles of Political Economy* to a consideration of the case for government intervention in the sphere of wealth creation. The case for individualism is repeated.

> Whatever theory we adopt respecting the foundation of the social union, and under whatever political institutions we live, there is a circle around every individual human being, which no government ... ought to be permitted to overstep: there is a part of life of every person who has come to the years of discretion, within which the individuality of that person ought to reign uncontrolled either by any other individual or by the public collectively.[44]

That is a moral argument. There are also practical grounds for the economist to hesitate before advocating public action.

> We have observed, that as a general rule, the business of life is better performed when those who have an immediate interest in it are left to take their own course, uncontrolled by the mandate of the law or by the meddling of any public functionary.[45]

When governments restrain private conduct in the pursuit of wealth, or impose taxes so that they can provide goods and services on behalf of their citizens, compulsion is involved and individual liberty infringed. Every increase in government responsibility increases the opportunity for the expression of arbitrary power, and imposes yet another function upon 'a body already overcharged with duties'. Most things are more efficiently done by the individuals directly involved. However talented and informed, a government still suffers one great disadvantage: 'an inferior interest in the result'. Above all else, government intervention should be avoided because it is a substitute for the collective action of the people. The cultivation of spontaneous action for the common good is an essential part of a healthy society. Intelligence and talent should not be confined within the government.

A democratic constitution at the centre needs to supported by democratic institutions at every level below.

All this is about the production or supply of goods and services. What about consumption or distribution? The general presumption having been stated, Mill then asks if those who do the work are always the best judges of the end, as well as of the means, of the business of life.

> can it be affirmed with the same universality, that the consumer, or person served, is the most competent judge of the end? Is the buyer always qualified to judge of the commodity? If not, the presumption in favour of the competition of the market does not apply to the case; and if the commodity be one, in the quality of which society has much at stake, the balance of advantages may be in favour of some mode and degree of intervention, by the authorized representatives of the collective interest of the state.[46]

Six (Mill calls them large) exceptions to laisser faire are then examined. The first concerns education. The uncultivated cannot be competent judges, and education is one of the things that, in principle, the government should provide. Mill is inclined to follow Smith and have the government require parents to obtain the necessary instruction for their children, rather than have the government do the actual providing. Where the labouring classes clearly cannot afford to pay the full cost, then the government has to intervene. Even then, there are dangers of having a public education monopoly. The solution is to encourage schools of the voluntary charities to operate side by side with those of the state.

The second exception concerns the effects of long-term contracts. Mill doubts whether individuals can judge what will be in their interests 'at some future and distant time'. Any presumption that they will have entered, even voluntarily, into an irrevocable contract knowing for sure what their needs and circumstances will be, is false. The law should discourage such pre-commitment, and allow cancellation or recontracting. Strangely in a book on political economy, the only example he gives is of marriage: 'the most important of all cases of engagement in life'. The reader can only speculate on the kind of economic contract Mill would have included in this censure. The third exception could have, at first sight, very extensive implications. It concerns those activities which can only be organised through a private, voluntary organisation, as distinct from those conducted by self-employed individuals. Private firms may suffer from the same defects as government.

> Whatever, if left to spontaneous agency, can only be done by joint-stock associations, will often be as well, and sometimes better done, by the state. Government management is, indeed, proverbially jobbing, careless, and ineffective, but so likewise has been joint-stock management. The directors of a joint-stock company, it is true, are always shareholders; but also the members of a government are invariably taxpayers.[47]

Having breached a large hole in the defences of private enterprise, Mill quickly closes it up again. Most of these activities should, nevertheless, be left to private agencies because of the dangers of overloading the functionaries of the state, and of creating an oppressive, national bureaucracy. The outcome will be tolerable provided the community has powers to regulate those which are 'practical monopolies' (water, railways, roads and canals), or else it will have to municipalise them. The self-interest of private managers will not provide sufficient security against the abuse of such market power.

The fourth exception is quite different. Instead of overruling the judgements or preferences of individuals, the government may have to give effect to them. Mill gives an early version of group coercion. If, for example, it were true that a reduction in the hours of labour, with wages remaining the same, would be to the benefit of all workers (and the community), that happy event could not come out of voluntary action.

> A workman who refused to work more than nine hours while there were others who worked ten, would either not be employed at all, or if employed, must submit to lose one tenth of his wages. However convinced, therefore, he may be that it is the interest of the class to work short time, it is contrary to his own interests to set the example, unless he is assured that all or most of the others will follow it. But suppose a general agreement of the whole class: might not this be effectual without the sanction of law? Not unless enforced by opinion with a rigour practically equal to that of law.[48]

Mill stops short of actually recommending legislation to limit the hours of adult workers. He is content to use the analysis as an illustration of situations in which compulsion might be needed to realise deliberate collective actions. As Mill remarks at the conclusion of this section, penal laws exist to punish those who rob or defraud, because 'though it is in the interest of each that nobody should rob or cheat, it is not in any one's interest to refrain from robbing and cheating when all others are permitted to rob and cheat him'. Carried to its logical extreme, the principle that individuals are the best judges of their own welfare, will prove that governments ought not to exist at all.

Exception number five deals with those cases in which acts are not done for selfish reasons but in the interests of others. Should there be public arrangements to help people in need, or should the support be left to voluntary charities? Mill follows the utilitarian and classical economist's tradition in Poor Law reform of wanting to restrict relief to a standard just below that which would be earned at work. The incentive for finding a job and becoming self-dependent must be maintained.

> if assistance given in such a manner that the condition of the person helped is as desirable as that of the person who succeeds in doing the same thing without help, the assistance ... is mischievous.[49]

Subject to this limit, the public authorities should provide relief for the able-bodied destitute because, (a) voluntary charity is uncertain and inconsistent in its coverage, always doing too much and too little, (b) the state gives subsistence to prisoners and if it were to deny the same level of relief to the honest poor, there would be a premium on crime, and (c) the state must act on general rules and not, like private charities, try to discriminate between the deserving and undeserving poor. Once again, the state is left to provide the 'minimum which is due even to the worst'.

Surprisingly, Mill associates with the problem of the poor relief, those acts which, though intended for private benefit, have long-term and extensive public consequences. He turns to colonization as the example. A 'bridge' has to be built from over-populated countries like Britain to the empty continents. The movement of labour and capital from old to new countries, from where productivity is low to where it will be high, on a large scale, is a business which only governments can perform. Migration has to be subsidised, otherwise only a small number of relatively prosperous workers and farmers will take the risk. Private capitalists have an interest in advancing the necessary sums, but will not be in a position to enforce repayment from the migrants. Only governments can raise the necessary taxes. Once established, the colonies can be encouraged to become self-sufficient. The benefits of such a policy are not confined to a single country, and should not be measured simply in terms of relieving the pressures on the labour market. 'The collective interests of the human race' are served by 'the most efficient employment of the productive sources of the world'.

Finally, under the sixth exception, Mill groups together a number of services which are not in the interests of any individual to perform, for which no adequate return would naturally arise, or rather, for which no marketable revenue could be appropriated. The list includes voyages of geographical exploration, lighthouses, scientific research, the maintenance of a learned class to cultivate speculative knowledge in literature and philosophy (which require 'a long and continuous devotion of time', and 'engross and fatigue the mental faculties'), and the conferring of Professorships (though not like those in England which are 'little more than nominal'). Before embarking on their provision, however, the government should ensure itself they cannot be left to voluntary agencies, and the 'zeal and liberality of individuals'.

Of course, all six exceptions apply to civilized and democratic nations, with well-read and educated citizens following the ordinary business of life in a system of competitive markets. Where those conditions are not met, the exceptions may become the rule.

> It is, however, necessary to add, that the intervention of government cannot always practically stop short of the limit which defines the cases intrinsically suitable for it. In the particular circumstances of a given age or nation, there is scarcely anything really important to the general interest, which it may not be desirable, or even necessary, that the government should take upon itself, not because private individuals cannot effectively perform it, but because they will not ... roads, docks, harbours, canals, works of irrigation, hospitals, schools, colleges, printing-presses.[50]

Even then, he government should have as its aim the gradual elimination of the need for intervention. People need instruction in how to do these things for themselves, to learn the benefits of 'individual energy and voluntary co-operation'.

Equality

Mill follows Bentham in believing that each person's happiness is to receive equal treatment: each should count for one and not more than one. Justice and general utility require impartiality to be shown between different people. It does not follow that each person's happiness should be the same. Equality of opportunity to obtain the means to happiness is the proper object of policy. While attempts to equalise post-tax earned income are wrong, and the correct formula to apply is proportional rather than progressive, the limitation of inherited wealth is justified. Mill stays clear of the Benthamite connection between complete equality in the distribution of income and the maximum sum of happiness.

In his letter to George Grote which has alreday been quoted, Mill defines general happiness as made up of the individual happinesses of the members of the community, 'all equal in value, except in so far as the amount of happiness itself differs'. Human beings cannot be treated as identical in their tastes or in their capacities for feeling of pleasure and pain. When examining the utilitarian notion of justice, he insists that the standard of right conduct requires agents to be strictly impartial between their own happiness and the happiness of others, to be impartial spectators. Such an idealistic motive for individuals makes more sense as part of the notion of justice, as a matter of social policy and social utility. Even then, it is not to be construed as a blanket treatment for all citizens. They have to be virtuous: society should treat equally with those who have deserved to be treated equally. In reply to the criticism of Herbert Spencer, Mill protests that the principle of greatest happiness itself implies an equal claim to all the means of happiness, and that equal amounts of pleasure are equally desirable, whoever enjoyed them. Unless, that is, 'the inevitable conditions of human life, and the general interest', set limits. As long as these limits are clearly stated, there is no problem. Therefore, social inequalities which cannot be defended on grounds of general utility, should be denounced as unjust.[51]

Taxation offers several examples of those which Mill was prepared to accept on grounds of expediency and social utility. After reciting the four canons, or guides to good practice, laid down by Adam Smith (equality of treatment, certainty, convenience, and efficiency), he feels the need to discuss the meaning of equality. Smith had apparently confused the principle that citizens ought to contribute to the expenses of government in 'proportion to their respective abilities', with the principle that they ought to contribute in 'proportion to the revenue they respectively enjoy under the protection of the state'. The two have since become known as the 'ability to pay' and the 'benefit' approaches to taxation. Mill came down on the side of ability to pay.

> Equality of taxation ... as a maxim of politics, means equality of sacrifice. It means apportioning the contribution of each person towards the expenses of government, so that he shall feel neither more nor less inconvenience from his share of the payment than every other person experiences from his.[52]

That would be the perfect standard. Reality will only produce an approximation. It is important to note that Mill is confining the comparison of sacrifice to individual (dis)utilities. At this stage in his argument, he makes no appeal to aggregate sacrifice.

Benefit, or 'quid pro quo' taxation is rejected because, in Mill's opinion, what governments provide is the concern of all, and fairness dictates that its citizens pay according to their means. Those who enjoy most protection may also be those who can least afford to protect themselves. If there are citizens who receive nothing back from the government, something is wrong with its pattern of expenditure, not its system of taxation. One suggestion he considers is that they should pay a lump sum for the common services and a variable sum, in proportion to their property, for the protection services. In answer, he both denies that the sole function of government is to protect property, and insists that, even if it were, the costs of protection would not be proportional to the value of property. The discussion also prompts him to make further observations about the dangers of looking for too much accuracy in policy matters.

> There is in this adjustment a false air of nice adaptation, very acceptable to some minds ... the practice of setting definite values on things essentially indefinite, and making them a ground of practical conclusions, is peculiarly fertile in false views of social questions.[53]

The weakness he saw in the discussion of benefit taxation, he could neither accept in ability-to-pay taxation, nor in any other practical application of utilitarianism.

Mill favours a tax structure which leaves a minimum of income for subsistence untaxed (after Bentham), a proportional rate on the surplus of income above that level, and the exemption of savings. He grants that there is some force in the case for a graduated tax. Equal sacrifice might be better served by taking a rising proportion from the higher incomes. The case, however, is not strong enough. Taking £5 from a person whose income is £50 involves a sacrifice greater than taking £1,000 from a person with an income of £10,000, but the two are 'inconmeasurable'. It is sufficient to tax the 'luxuries' of richer persons at a constant rate. As they are restricted to exactly the same deduction (tax credit) for the basic 'necessities' of life as the poor, they will have larger surpluses to tax. Mill seems close to realise that the combination of a proportional tax with a minimum of tax-free income, fixed in absolute amount, will produce a mildly progressive tax structure overall.

He is in favour of reducing the inequities of wealth, but against using a graduated tax to redistribute earned income. In one place, he describes it as 'graduated robbery'. In another, he spells out the consequences for incentives to work and to save.

> To tax the largest incomes at a higher percentage than the smaller, is to lay a tax on industry and economy; to impose a penalty on people for having worked harder and saved more than their neighbours. It is not the fortunes which are earned, but those which are unearned, that it is for the public good to place under limitation.[54]

Nor is there any justification for treating perpetual and terminable incomes on a different basis. To hold that it is fairer to tax incomes on their capitalised value rather than on their annual value, is mistaken. Both income receipts and tax payment need to be capitalized. A permanent income of £100 p.a. may be worth £3,000, and a temporary (life-time) income of £100 p.a. only £1,500. It does not follow that the temporary should pay half the (annual) tax of the permanent. Supposing the tax rate to be 10%, both should pay £100 p.a., not the first £10 and the second £5. When properly capitalised, the value of their tax payments will be £300 and £150 respectively. Mill only admits that those who have no way of providing for their old age, or for their families in case of death, other than by saving, should have that portion of their incomes exempt from taxation.

The inequities of inheritance can be tackled by placing an upper limit on the amount any one person may receive, by transferring to the state the wealth of those dying without close heirs (a favourite proposal of Bentham), and by subjecting very large legacies to a tax, even of a graduated kind. Coupled with the support Mill would give to the education of the poor, the way is cleared for an acceptance of remaining inequalities in earned income.

> if all were done which it would be in the power of a good government to do, by instruction and by legislation, to diminish the inequality of opportunities, the differences of fortune arising from people's earnings could not justify giving umbrage.[55]

He is very much against the double taxation of savings, and in an ideal world would find expenditure more attractive and fairer than income as a basis for the taxation of persons. In reality, neither can be perfectly applied because of the problems of assessment. Their practical injustice would be as great as in any other form of taxation. Thus, in spite of all his theoretical arguments in their favour, direct taxes should be 'reserved as an extraordinary resource for great national emergencies, in which the necessity of a large additional revenue overrules all objections'.

Consequentalism

Mill acknowledges the connection between utilitarianism and consequentalism in several places. Indeed, he believes that the consideration of the consequences of actions is the rational test for all schools of moral philosophy. It is in the examination of what those consequences are that he begins to make changes to received opinion. Indirect consequences are distinguished from direct consequences. The effects of an act upon the character and habits of the actor may have been neglected. Pains and pleasures that precede the moment of an act are distinguished from those that are looked forward to, in prospect of an act. The former could have important consequences for the cultivation of social virtues. Finally, instead of concentrating on the consequences of each act, it may be more sensible to pursue human happiness by observing general rules of conduct.

Bentham is criticised for keeping too close to the expediency of William Paley, who judged the morality of actions solely by their probable consequences for happiness. Dispositions and habits of mind are important consequences that precede actions. These dispositions and habits may damage the character of the individual, even though the acts themselves are not expected to increase the unhappiness of the actor or others. Damage to the human character tends to reduce 'general happiness'. In the extreme case of crime, an individual may weigh the probable consequences of being found out and punished, or of remorse for the victim, against the probable gains. It would be a decision based on personal expediency. Mill wants the individual

> to recoil from the very thought of committing the act; the idea of placing himself in such a position is so painful, ... but by a pain that precedes that act, not by one that is supposed to follow it. Not only may this be so, but unless it be so, the man is not really virtuous. The fear of pain consequent upon the act, cannot arise unless their be deliberation.[56]

He then quotes with approval the suggestion that anyone who stops to deliberate (about committing a crime) is 'in imminent danger of being lost'. True utilitarians will, consequently, often apply their principle through secondary objectives: to nobility of character, to sympathy for others, to telling the truth (perhaps even to increased national wealth) rather than relate them directly to happiness. Opponents of utilitarianism tend to elevate the secondary objectives into primary objectives. A strong advantage of having one single end, general happiness, is that it can be used to settle ties and conflicts between several objectives.

Provided consequences are defined in this broad sense, Mill is content for their measurement to be at the centre of the doctrine of utility. Often they are thought of as what would follow from an act 'if practised generally'. In matters of law, and for many social arrangements that reconcile the individual with the collective interest, general rules are more efficient. In the by now familiar letter to George Grote, Mill spells outthe argument.

> human happiness, even one's own, is in general more successfully pursued by acting on general rules, than by measuring the consequences of each act.[57]

There could be 'incessant quarrelling' and 'uncertainty' about each act's consequences in the absence of such guidelines. Individual rights and obligations had to be established so that people knew how they were expected to behave towards one another. In particular, the sacrifice of personal interest for the wider good, smething which Mill was anxious to justify as utilitarian, neded to be set within clear limits.

> people must .. not be required to sacrifice even their own less good to another's greater, when no general rule has given the right to the sacrifice; while when the right has been recognised, they must, in most cases, yield to that right, even at the sacrifice, in the particular case, of their own greater good to another's less.[58]

This does not mean that someone who 'has charge of' (a parent?) another person and knows more about their needs and welfare, should be stopped from sacrificing much for them.

On other occasions, the moral rule may appear to overrule simple utility calculations. Mill wrote to William Thornton in 1863[59] on the example of the Carthaginians who were required to sacrifice a distinguished citizen under threat of group extermination. In spite of the fact that the survival of the community seems to guarantee a larger sum of utility than the loss of one individual, Mill says they should resist. He gives two reasons. The first is the relationship of the community and each of its members to the victim, who happens to be their great benefactor. They have a special obligation to honour. The second is the general obligation to resist tyranny. Even the weak can make a tyrant pay dearly. General utility requires that both claims be upheld against the other consequences. Yet Mill is not always a rule utilitarian. There may still be exceptions. Circumstances can vary so much that some acts may have to be assessed on their own merits.[60] Less extreme sacrifices, and less serious breaches of moral obligations, might not allow direct utility benefits to outweighed indirect utility costs. General utility might be satisfied by telling some lies and breaking some promises.

Welfarism

Given Mill's wide definition of consequences, and his willingness to elevate general utility considerations above those of sums of particular utilities, it is difficult to place him the 'classical' welfarist camp. All kinds of information are considered relevant to judgements of what is good for individuals and the community. The utility of consumption, and even its distribution between persons, is only a small part of social welfare. The cultivation of individual potential, and the protection of individual rights, are both ultimately of greater significance. Nor can it be justified to describe as a narrow welfarist, someone who finds explanations in economics to a large extent dependent on moral, psychological, and institutional factors and, therefore, belonging to 'moral or social science' rather then the 'physical'.[61] On the other hand, Mill always ends these discursions with a return to the single guiding principle of general utility. Rights, liberties, freedoms, justice, equity and fairness, serve no other ultimate purpose than general utility. Whether such a broad definiton of the term can serve any operational purpose, is another matter.

Notes

1. Letter to H.S.Foxwell, 1875, in Jevons (1977) Vol. IV, p.77.
2. Quoted in Maurice (1884) p.252.
3. From an Essay *Marcus Aurelius,* quoted in Alexander (1965).
4. In *Marshall,* Keynes (1972e), p.174.
5. Cowling (1990) p.93.
6. Skorupski (1989) p.xi.
7. Mill, John (1986) Vol. XXII, p.39.
8. Schumpeter (1954), pp.527-534.
9. Mill, John (1981), p.85
10. In Thomas (1979)
11. In 1842, Mill, John (1963),Vol. XIII, p.533.
12. From *Thoughts on Parliamentary Reform,* in Mill, John (1977), Vol. XIX, p.327.
13. Mill, John (1981), Vol I, pp 231-232.
14. See Mill, John (1982) Vol. VI.
15. op.cit., pp. 216 and 219.
16. In a footnote that appeared only in the 1st ed. of the *Principles.* See the Guillebaud ed. of the *Principles,* Vol. 2, p.759.
17. Mill, John (1965) Vol. III, p.462.
18. op. cit. p.476.
19. Mill, John (1965) Vol II., p.3.

Notes continued

20. op. cit., p 140. See also his discussion in *On the Definition of Political Econonomy* in Mill, John (1967) Vol. IV, pp.316-317.
21. Mill, John (1974) Vols VII and VIII, particularly Book VI Chapter V. Similar ground is covered in *On the Definition of Political Economy*, (1967) Vol. IV, pp.317-320.
22. *Thornton on Labour and Its Claims*, in (1967) Vol V., p.646.
23. Mill, John (1974), Book V Chapter IX, p.904.
24. Mill, John (1965) Vol. III, p.322.
25. Mill, John (1974) Vol VIII., pp.846-847.
26. For a discussion of the role of this objective see Kurer (1991).
27. Mill, John (1981) Vol. II., p.113.
28. Even then there are large gaps. Mill, for example, never semed to be aware of Bentham's work on monetary economics.
29. Mill, John (1969) Vol X., p.112.
30. op. cit., p.210.
31. op. cit., p.234.
32. op. cit., p.211.
33. op. cit., p.214.
34. op. cit., p.218.
35. op. cit., p.234.
36. In 1862. Mill, John (1972) Vol. XV, pp.761-764.
37. op. cit., p.218.
38. op. cit., p 234.
39. Mill, John (1965) Vol. III, p.358. See also Mill, John (1986) Vol. XXII., p.249.
40. Mill, John (1969) Vol. X, p.211
41. Mill, John (1965) Vol. III, p.810.
42. Mill, John (1974) Vol. VIII, p.879
43. *Liberty*, in (1977) Vol. XIX, pp.276-277.
44. Mill, John (1965) Vol. III, pp.937-938.
45. op. cit., p.946.
46. op. cit., p.947.
47. op. cit., p.954.
48. op. cit., p.957.
49. op. cit., p.961.
50. op. cit., p.970.
51. *Utilitarianism*, (1969) Vol. X, Chapter IV.
52. *Principles of Political Economy*, (1965) Vol. III, p.807.
53. op. cit., p.807.
54. op. cit., pp.810-811.
55. op. cit., p.811.
56. *Remarks on Bentham's Philosophy*, (1969), Vol. X, p.12.
57. Mill, John (1972) Vo.l XV, pp.761-764.
58 The same letter.
59. Mill, John (1972) Vol. XV, pp.853-854.
60. For an example see his letter in 1867 to Henry Brandreth. op. cit., p.1234.
61. *Principles of Political Economy*, (1965) Vol II, p.21.

5. William Stanley Jevons

While 'Marshall knits in wool', wrote Keynes, Jevons is 'simple, lucid, unfaltering, chiselled in stone'.[1] Perhaps Marshall's knitting showed a greater appreciation of the difficulties of economics. Whatever the merits of the case, Keynes was right to credit Jevons with a peculiarly original and enquiring cast of mind. The first British economist to present 'in finished form' a theory of value based upon subjective utility and the application of the calculus, showing 'the now familiar technique of algebra and diagrams', Jevons can claim to be one of the founders of neo-classical economics. Together with Carl Menger and Leon Walras, he independently launched what has become known as the marginal revolution. Though he appears to have had no contact with Menger, he corresponded with Leon Walras and looked upon him as an ally in the fight to introduce 'the mathematical theory of economy, believing it to be the only basis upon which an ultimate reform of the science of political economy can be founded'. His own work on statistical inference, particularly with regard to the investigation of cyclical fluctuations, was another pioneering venture of great promise. He deserves equal credit for discovering, and publicising, the contribution of others to the mathematical foundations of economics, particularly the French.

Jevons is less well known as a utilitarian economist. A lack of personal or family connections, not to mention his rather obsessive dislike of John Stuart Mill, would seem to count him out. His *Theory of Political Economy* is, nevertheless, dedicated to treat the subject as a 'calculus of pleasure and pain', and by the time of the second edition (1879) Bentham's ideas have become 'the starting-point' of its analysis. Jevons may not have been brought up with a thorough grounding in Benthamism, being first persuaded to adopt hedonistic philosophy by lectures he attended in Australia, but he developed a keen interest in the writings of the master, and strong opinions on the development of his ideas. By the time Jevons had finished his academic studies back in Britain, he thought of himself as a utilitarian, but of a special kind. Mill was taken to task for criticising and revising Bentham too much. Bentham and Paley had more sensible ways of describing utilitarian ethics, and Herbert Spencer's theory of social evolution offered a grim but realistic way of looking at society. It is difficult to understand the subsequent development of utilitarian economics by ignoring Jevons's contribution. Those who came after certainly thought him one of theirs. Sidgwick was rather wary of the direction he took; Edgeworth warmly appreciative.

Life

William Stanley Jevons was born in Liverpool on 1st September 1835, the ninth child of prosperous, middle-class unitarians. His father was an iron merchant and his mother a member of a family of bankers and lawyers. (Her father, William Roscoe, had been a Member of Parliament, reformer, opponent of slavery, and philanthropist.) Tragedy struck the family when Stanley Jevons was a young boy. His mother died in 1845, and three years later the Jevons firm went bankrupt with the collapse of the railway boom. Financial stringency and non-conformity help to explain Jevons's education and early choice of occupation. After private tutoring at home and attendance at local schools, including the Liverpool Mechanics Institute, he was sent to University College School in London. There he was prepared for entry to the 'godless institution', University College itself, which had been opened in 1828 (with much Benthamite support) for those excluded from Oxford and Cambridge by the religious tests of the established Church. Towards the end of his first year as an undergraduate (the 1852/53 session), he decided that the family could not afford to support his studies any longer and accepted the offer of a post as Assayer to the Royal Mint in Sydney.

In the event, he did not sail until 1854, and even then arrived in Australia nine months before the work of the Mint started. At University College he had studied Chemistry (he lodged with Henry Enfield Roscoe, a cousin who was to become a distinguished Professor of Chemistry), Mathematics, Logic and Scientific Method, and came under the influence of Augustus De Morgan, whose work on Probability and the Differential Calculus was to be important for Jevons's later development. Employment at the Mint was neither well paid nor particularly demanding, and he had time to study the climate, geography, geology, topology and flora of the continent. In 1855 he started to take daily meteorological observations, and in the following years became well known in the scientific and philosophic community of Sydney and its new University.

A contemporary dispute on the funding of railway investment in Australia started an interest in economics. He read the *Wealth of Nations* in 1856, Mill's *Principles* and *Logic*, and Dionysius Lardner's *Railway Economics* in the following year. The impact of the growth of railway on land values turned his attention to the concepts of capital and time, and they were to be subject of some of his most original ideas. It was also a period of self-examination. His father had died in 1855. The time had come to make a decision about the direction of his future life. In a letter to his sister of the same year, he described ambitious objectives.

My whole second nature consists of one wish, or one intention viz to be a powerful good to the world ... To be powerfully good, that is good, not towards one or a dozen, or a hundred, but towards a nation or the world.[2]

The trouble was that while he was confident in his own abilities, he was not sure how this good could be done. So many things caught his attention; and yet he still lacked academic qualifications in anything.

This last obstacle was overcome when he returned to London in 1859. He took a first class B.A. at University College the following year. In addition to the subjects he had started seven years before, he took Latin, History, and Animal Physiology; and although only coming third in the College's Political Economy examinations, won the Ricardo scholarship. The M.A. followed in 1862, with Jevons being awarded the gold medal for the best candidate in the branch which included Logic, Philosophy and Political Economy. It was here that he was introduced to the mathematical logic of George Boole. Although he became increasingly involved with the application of new methods to economic analysis, he never lost his interest in Chemistry or Climatology. Vowing to make his living as an independent writer, he found that others were slow to appreciate the originality of his offerings. Apart from the money he had saved in Australia, he had no other sources of income until, in 1863 he became a tutor at Owens College in Manchester, another place that employed non-conformists. In 1865 and 1866 he lectured in Political Economy there, and was a part-time Professor of Logic, Moral Philosophy and Political Economy at Queen's College, Liverpool. Finally, after several setbacks, he was appointed Professor of Logic and Philosophy at Owens College in 1866. He was 31.

Manchester had its compensations. By one of those strange coincidences that seem to abound in the history of utilitarianism, Jevons married another Harriet Taylor; this Harriet a daughter of the founder of the Manchester Guardian. No scandal attached to their courtship. Ten years later, in 1876, they moved to London where he had been made Professor of Political Economy at University College. In the same year he was elected a Fellow of the Royal Society. Music, walking, swimming, and 'hunting' for books were his favourite relaxations. He rarely went out for other reasons, and disliked lecturing. Henry Sidgwick became one of his close friends. Faith in a kind of Unitarianism[3] was restored to him, along with a reluctant acceptance of Darwinian evolution and Spencerian sociology. God was manifest in creation.

> Creation is not yet concluded, and there is not one of us who may not become conscious in his heart that he is no Automaton, no mere lump of Protoplasm, but the Creation of a Creator.[4]

He never enjoyed good health and was forced to retire in 1880. In spite of warnings from doctors, he still insisted on swimming and was drowned in the sea in 1882. He left a library of several thousand volumes, and according to Keynes, such a large stock of paper (of all kinds), fearing a world-wide shortage, that even fifty years after his death his children were still drawing on it for their own needs.[5]

Utilitarian and Economist

Jevons utilitarianism was largely expressed in his economics. He wrote no separate treatise on ethics. As the list of his major publications shows, however, logic was almost as important to him as economics, and he grew proficient at producing very readable introductory texts and exercises.

1862 Two papers sent to the British Association meeting at Oxford: Notice of a General Mathematical Theory of Political Economy, and On the Study of Periodic Commercial Fluctuations (with five diagrams).

1863 A Serious Fall in the Value of Gold.
Pure Logic (logic of quality apart from quantity, with remarks on Boole's system).

1865 The Coal Question.

1870 Elementary Lessons in Logic.

1871 The Theory of Political Economy.

1874 Principles of Science.

1875 Money and the Mechanism of Exchange.

1876   Primer of Logic.
1879   Four essays on John Stuart Mill's Philosophy Tested.
1880   Studies in Deductive Logic.
1882   The State in Relation to Labour.

Posthumously:
1883   Methods of Social Reform.
1884   Investigations in Currency and Finance.
1870   Pure Logic and other Minor Works.
1905   Principles of Economics.

The two papers sent to the British Association and read at its Oxford meeting in 1862 were remarkably prescient. The first contained an outline of all the major changes Jevons wished to introduce into economics, namely mathematical methods and subjective utility, whilst the second was really a study of seasonal fluctuations in prices rather than of the trade cycle. Both were to become the dominant themes of his economics (his use of sun-spot activity to explain the periodicity of agricultural trade booms and slumps only being published in the 1870's). Unfortunately, no one seemed interest in these new ideas in the 1860's, and Jevons became depressed about his chances of ever making an impact on the academic world.

Writing the *Coal Question* turned out to have a significant impact on his career and influence. After quoting Adam Smith on the progressive state being 'cheerful', the stationary state 'dull'and the declining state 'melancholy', Jevons warns that 'we cannot long continue our present state of progress' because when coal is used up 'no powerful substitute will be forthcoming'. Coal is the key to Britain's industrial success. Population pressures and the advance in energy requirements mean that demand is soon set to exceed supply. Unless something is done to discourage the present rate of consumption, when coal is cheap, future generations will face the melancholy of economic decline.[6] The promise of imminent disaster sells books and brings authors fame. The *Coal Question* sold well and Jevons was to meet Gladstone and be quoted favourably by Mill in the House of Commons.

It is a strange book. As the dire consequences of the coal crisis gradually emerge, the reader is led to expect some radical solutions. When the end comes, however, Jevons rejects the obvious remedies of a prohibition on coal exports or a tax on coal consumption. He is too much of a believer in the virtues of free-trade. The real surprise is that someone with those convictions has so little confidence in markets, at home and abroad, to solve the problem of allocating an increasingly scarce commodity. Instead, he falls back on the device of an increase in legacy and succession duties to help pay back the National Debt. In this way, future generations will have one less burden to carry when they face the exhaustion of energy supplies. This was the policy prescription that Gladstone and Mill found so attractive, for reasons which had little to do with the question of coal as such. They were more worried about the size of the National Debt.

Utilitarianism makes no appearance in his economic writings until the first edition of the *Theory of Political Economy* in 1871. In its preface Jevons connects 'the calculus of pleasure and pain' to the 'endeavour of arriving at accurate quantitative notions of utility, labour, capital etc.', and 'especially the most puzzling of notions, value'. By the second edition in 1879, Bentham's ideas are specifically mentioned.as the inspiration of the whole work. In the long introduction that follows, he quotes Bentham's *Principles of Morals and Legislation* and *Table of the Springs of Action* as examples of a quantitative theory of morals. Pains and pleasures are summed-up and compared.

> I have no hesitation in accepting the utilitarian theory of morals which does uphold the effect upon the happiness of mankind as the criterion of what is right and wrong. But I have never felt that there is anything in the theory to prevent our putting the widest and highest interpretation upon the terms used.[7]

In economics the object is to 'maximise happiness by purchasing pleasure, as it were, at the lowest cost of pain'. It is never clear whether he fully adopts, even on the widest and highest interpretations, the greatest happiness principle. Being largely concerned to explain individual behaviour, the sum of the net pleasures of the community is never given much attention. Yet he appears to maintain qualitative distinctions in the interpretation of happiness in contradiction to the views of Paley and Bain, who, Jevons thinks, go too far in arguing that all pleasures and pains are of the same kind. He suspects that the issue may 'turn upon the language used', and then uses some language of his own which adds only further confusion. Motives and feelings can be high and low, and of the same kind 'to the extent that we are able to weight them against each other'. On the other hand, 'they are, nevertheless almost incomparable in power and authority'.[8] (Some Marshallian knitting might have been prefereable at this point)

According to Jevons's own testimony, he was converted to hedonism while working for the Royal Mint in Sydney. In 1856 he had attended a course of lectures given by the Rev. Dr John Wooley, Principal and Professor of Classics at the new University of Sydney, on 'The Selfish Theory of Morals'. Reflecting on the alternative forms of benevolence and selfishness, Jevons felt he must reject moral theories that rely on benevolence as a duty. He wanted to accept the strength of self-interest, but reserve the highest pleasures to benevolence. Benevolence was itself a form of selfishness.

> I regard man in reality as essentially selfish, and that is as doing everything with a view to gain enjoyment or avoid pain ... But he is not necessarily what we should call an avaricious ... in its full sense a selfish man. It is by the quality of those pleasures which he is continually seeking and by the causes of pain that he is equally fleeing from that he is to be judged. It is quite possible that one of his chief pleasures may be to see another person happy, or that he may have a friend connected to him by such intimacy, similarity of feelings, and in short complete sympathy, that pain to the friend is pain to himself.[9]

Jevons tries to apply the analogy of a railway engine to this 'moral man', following the curves and turns of the 'line', with selfishness as the 'steam power' or the prime mover, and the curves and turns being the result of the pulls of sympathy.

In his *Theory of Political Economy*, a chapter on Pleasure and Pain precedes those on Utility and Exchange. In the first, Bentham is quoted again on utility, on its intensity, duration, certainty and remoteness of pleasure and pain. These circumstances are an acceptable part of the analysis of utility. When Bentham goes on to list fecundity (the chance that the feeling be followed by a another of the same kind), purity (the chance that the feeling will not be followed by one of the opposite kind), and extent (the number of people who are affected by the feeling), Jevons insists they are part of the theory of morals and not of the 'simple and restricted' problems of economics. In the latter enquiry (i.e. the study of utility and exchange), intensity and duration are the two crucial dimensions of pain and pleasure, just like length and breadth of the 'superficies'. The anticipation of feelings must also be taken into account.

> The intensity of present anticipated feeling must, to use a mathematical expression, be some function of the future actual feeling and of the intervening time, and it must increase as we approach the moment of realization.[10]

The power of anticipation affects decisions about the accumulation of stocks for future consumption. Provision for the future is the main incentive to savings and investment. Similarly, the existence of uncertainty affects the present value of future pleasures and pains.

In selecting a course of action which depends on uncertain events, as, in fact, does everything in life, I should multiply the quantity of feeling attaching to every future event by the fraction denoting its probability. A great casualty, which is very unlikely to happen, may not be so important as a slight casualty which is nearly sure to happen.[11]

Jevons is at his most stimulating in these speculations. They are not developed any further, however, except for some remarks on the link between uncertainty and decisions about capital investment, which appear in a later chapter.

Total utility, variation of utility, and degrees of utility are analysed in terms of the maximisation of pleasure by consumer and owner of the factors of production. Exchange between individuals becomes the focus of attention. The consumer is in equilibrium when further exchange of an infinitely small amount of a commodity will bring neither gain nor loss of utility. The worker is in equilibrium when the pleasure received from the earnings of labour just exceeds the pain of its exertion. Two further terms are introduced: disutility and discommodity, as the opposite or negative of utility. For example, the exertion of effort produces the disutility of work, and unpleasant substances like ash and sewage, which most people dispose of rather than desire, become discommodities. The analysis almost amounts (almost because it is nowhere worked out properly) to an early use of the modern concept of 'bads' or negative externalities.

Jevons, who did so much to discover the contributions of many continental economists to the mathematical analysis of value (including Cournot, Dupuit and Gossen), is also anxious to extend his knowledge of the writings of Bentham and the utilitarians. A postcard to Henry Sidgwick in 1879 asks for a reference to the place where Bentham used the term 'utilitarian'[12]; and there is evidence that he read Bentham's *Manual of Political Economy* some time after. Between 1877 and 1879 he had produced a set of four essays, John Stuart Mill's Philosophy Tested, for the *Contemporary Review*. The distance between the two had not diminished since Jevons's early misgivings about Mill's impact on economics. Now his criticism extends to Mill's interpretation of utilitarianism. Back to Bentham, not forward with Mill, is Jevons's slogan.

Jevons and Mill

Jevons's dislike of Mill went beyond the normal bounds of academic disagreement. It had started with the feeling that Ricardo and Mill stood in the way of the new subjective utility theory of value, and thus 'put as much error into the Science as they had truth'. It grew into an obsession with the dominance that Mill was supposed exert in economics, politics and philosophy. After studying him for twenty years, Jevons expressed the confident belief that Mill's writings 'would be allowed to consist to a large extent of a series of ingenious sophisms'. Mill had no idea of what capital was, and his *Principles* contained much that was erroneous, although 'not the maze of self-contradictions which his *Logic* undoubtedly is'. Mill's reaction to Jevons was equally critical, but less emotional. Publicly, he found Jevons's writings 'give evidence of decided originality, much knowledge and mental vigour', and his work on logic showed an 'extra-ordinary familiarity with and power over Formal Logic'. If there was a fault it lay in his tendency to employ a 'power greater than any result to be obtained' might justify. Privately, he found Jevons to 'have a mania for encumbering questions with useless complications and notation implying the existence of a greater precision in the data' than actually exists. By the time *The Theory of Political Economy* appeared, he was living in retirement at Avignon, and what he might have thought of it can only be guessed.[13]

Like Mathew Arnold and Mill, Jevons and Mill had more in common than these comments might indicate. On the virtues of private enterprise, competition, free trade, individual liberty and democracy, they are in close harmony. If Mill goes further than Jevons in the exceptions he would grant to government intervention in the economy, Jevons completes the abandonment of the wages fund doctrine that Mill had begun. On the application of logic and scientific method to economics, Jevons tries to make a quarrel, but it is very difficult to discover any fundamental difference in their approach. He agrees with Mill's classification of economics as a 'physical or concrete deductive' science. He accepts that the verification of its laws is difficult because the circumstances surrounding the events to be explained are so 'infinitely complicated'. Then he introduces induction as the inverse operation to deduction. What his 'complete method' means for economics is simply described.

Possessing certain facts of observation, we frame a hypothesis as the laws governing those facts; we reason from the hypothesis deductively to the results to

> be expected; and we then examine these results in connexion with the facts in question; coincidence confirms the whole reasoning; conflict obliges us either to seek for disturbing cause, or else to abandon our hypothesis.[14]

Mill would have been pushed to disagree with much in the statement. Nor will anything very different or more sophisticated be found in the methodological sections of most modern introductory economic textbooks.

In the article Jevons wrote on Mill's *Utilitarianism* a more substantive dispute arises. He is at first very complimentary about Mill's style and powers of persuasion. As the argument develops, however, he sees a lack of consistency and 'a wide gulf' between what Mill intends and what he actually achieves. This discrepancy is regarded as having a serious implications. Jevons suddenly becomes quite severe.

> These Essays may be very agreeable reading; they may make readers congratulate themselves on so easily becoming moral philosophers; but they cannot really advance moral science if they represent one thing as being another thing. I make it my business therefore in this article to show that Mill was intellectually unfitted to decide what was utilitarian and what was not.[15]

Other contemporary critics had taken a similar line on Mill's alleged contradictions and confusions; yet not all of them went so far as Jevons. Sidwick, for example, whom Jevons acknowledges as one of the forerunners of his own denunciations, did not believe that Mill had 'thrown ethical philosophy into confusion as far as could well be done in ninety-six pages' (a reference to Mill's *Utilitarianism.*). In fact, Jevons only examines parts of these 'ninety-six pages' in any detail, largely confining himself to Chapter II on What Utilitarianism Is. There he comes up against Mill's distinction between higher and lower pleasures. Whatever he may have thought before, this version of the dual nature of utility now causes him great distress, and it alone forms the basis of his denunciation of Mill.

In 1871, in the introduction to his *Theory*, Jevons had noted that there were various 'grades of feeling'. A single higher pleasure will sometimes 'neutralise a vast extent and continuance of lower pains'. Economics being concerned with 'supplying ordinary wants at the least cost of labour', only treats with the lowest rank of feelings. Until the question of how to use wealth for the benefit of others is reached, economics can proceed with this lower calculus of utility and ignore any possible concern for judgements of right and wrong. In the essay of 1879 this rather confused story of the relationship between economics and ethics had hardened into a full acceptance of Paley's position that there was no difference between pleasures except 'in continuance and intensity'. Jevons claims, moreover, to find no evidence that Bentham believed in 'the intrinsic superiority of one pleasure to another'. Morality becomes a question of the 'ledger and balance sheet of utility'.

Mill was wrong, therefore, to try substituting quality for quantity. His attempt to give utilitarianism a more 'genial character' is flawed. Aggregate happiness is made up of the happiness of the individual units of the community. Individuals must pursue their own happiness. The vast majority of them will have only a small chance of achieving happiness through the development of their higher faculties.

> Mill's scheme of morality, is to aim high; it is equivalent to going into a life-lottery, in which there are no doubt high prizes to be gained, but few and far between. It is simply gambling with hedonic stakes.[16]

His conclusion in favour of the higher pleasures is arrived at by 'a packed jury': as vegetarians would be in favour of a vegetable diet, so those who enjoy the higher pleasures say they are the best. Jevons insists that he is not denying the moral superiority of some pleasures. He is denying, instead, that Mill can reconcile his treatment of them with utilitarianism. Bentham has already shown how higher pleasures can be dealt with in the calculus of utility. Jevons offers his own version.

> It is a higher pleasure to build a Free Library than to establish a Race Course; not because there is a Free-Library-building emotion, which is essentially better than a Race-Course-establishing emotion ...; but because we may, after the model of inquiry given by Bentham, resolve into its elements the effect of one action and the other upon the happiness of the community.[17]

Pleasures have attributes of intensity, length, certainty, fruitfulness and purity. They may even be altruistic. A Free Library could, presumably, give long lasting and fruitful pleasures to its users, and still reward its donors. If when added together they create a larger surplus of pleasure over pain, the outcome is higher (than that of a Race-course) but not morally superior.

Jevons concludes with a dismissal of Mill's notion that moral feelings are acquired rather than innate, and yet remain somehow natural. Human nature is no more pliable than the body. Where Marshall finds gold in Mill, Jevons finds dross. The trouble is traced to Mill being 'the last great philosophic writer conspicuous for his ignorance of the principles of evolution'. Herbert Spencer shows the way to reconcile the greatest happiness with a realistic and evolutionary theory of moral sense. Darwin's theory of evolution had, of course, been accepted by Mill (except he refused it the mark of a final proof), and the application of its alleged lessons to the social sciences was being pressed hard by Spencer. Sidgwick, for one, is not persuaded of the need to prefer him to Mill on these subjects. Jevons has no such doubts.

> According to Mill, we are little self-dependent gods, fighting with a malignant and murderous power called Nature, sure, one would think to be worsted in the struggle. According to Spencer, as I venture to interpret his theory, we are the last manifestation of an all-prevailing tendency towards the good - the happy.[18]

Apart from being, at times, a grossly unfair description of Mill's philosophy, the essay reveals the extent to which Jevons had deviated from the mainstream utilitarian position. None of the other classical utilitarians believed, not even Edgeworth, that their philosophy could completely reconciled with Spencerism.

Jevons as a Classical Utilitarian

As with Mill, it seems more logical to examine the evidence of classical utilitarianism in the writings of Jevons using a different order for the characteristics. In so doing, it has to be recognised that many more of them are missing altogether.

Measurement

There are several approving references to Bentham in Jevons's *Contemporary Review* article. He is 'old Mr Jeremy', who would have taken a dim view of Mill's revisions to his doctrine of utility. The original calculus of pains and pleasures may have been 'dry', but it offers a sound and sensible basis for practical action. The one area of utilitarian economics, therefore, to which Jevons attempts to make a positive contribution is measurement. He regards it as an integral part of the introduction of mathematical methods to economics. Where the requirements of a theory of value and exchange end and those of aggregate utility begin is not so clear. All the analysis is to be found in the first two editions of the *Theory*, which, unlike Mill's *Principles*, has very little to say about policy issues.

Jevons takes a line in advocating the use of mathematical methods in economics which has a very familiar ring. Those who despair at ever being able to quantify 'feelings of the mind, units of labour, or suffering, or enjoyment', are reminded of progress made in other areas of scientific enquiry. Pascal is quoted on doubt and belief; and the theory of probabilities, and the examples of electricity, of temperature, and of weight paraded as instances where exact data have been established where once 'uninquiring and unhoping spirits' thought that all attempts would fail. Particular emphasis is given to De Morgan's views on the measurement of weight where balance and differences, equalities and inequalities, are used to fix a 'magnitude' and 'ascertain how many times the greater contains the less'. Jevons immediately claims the prospect of similar progress for economics.

> Now there can be no doubt that pleasure, pain, labour, utility, value, wealth, money capital, etc., are all notions admitting of quantity; nay, the whole of our actions in industry and trade certainly depend upon comparing quantities of advantage or disadvantage.[19]

He admits that the statistical evidence on 'wealth, money, capital, etc.' is abundant, while that on 'pleasure and pain' is more difficult to obtain. They cannot be measured directly. The comparative amounts of 'feelings' have to be inferred by observing the 'decisions of the human mind'.

To prepare the reader for what comes after, Jevons begins to retract some of his claims for exactness. In the theory of value and exchange it is the balance between pleasures, and the avoidance of pain, that is measured, and small changes that are compared.

> We can seldom or never affirm that one pleasure is an exact multiple of another ... it seldom involves the comparison of quantities of feeling differing much in amount ... Similarly, the whole amount of pleasure that a man gains by a day's labour hardly enters into the question; it is when a man is doubtful whether to increase his hours of labour or not, that we discover an equality between the pain of that extension and the pleasure of the increase of possessions derived from it.[20]

The reader is also warned that no attempt will be made to get inside minds. The susceptibility of one mind to derive feelings from external circumstances can be very different from that of another. Amounts of feelings in minds cannot be compared. Even if they were, it would not matter because no one could be sure how these feelings would effect motives.

Nevertheless, when Jevons comes to analyse pleasures and pains, and their intensity and duration, he tries to present Bentham's

quantities on a diagram with time measured along the horizontal axis
and intensity on the vertical. The quantity of pleasure during each
minute is indicated by the (thin) rectangle 'whose base is supposed to
correspond to the duration of one minute, and whose height is
proportional to the intensity of the feeling during the minute in
question'. Time can be measured in seconds, minutes and hours.
Intensity of feeling is something that, apparently, can be thought of in
proportion to height. This something has no units, unless it makes
sense to talk about inches of pleasure. Intensity of feeling gradually
declines as the time for enjoyment is extended. With the intervals of
time becoming 'infinitely shorter', the intensity of feeling will 'vary
continuously', and the relationship can properly be represented by a
downward sloping curve.[21]

When Jevons comes to utility as such it is defined as 'the abstract
quality' whereby an object serves as a commodity. Commodities are
objects, substances, actions and services that 'can afford pleasure or
ward off pain'. Although utility is the property of an object, it is not
fixed in direct proportion to the amount of the object. It varies
according to circumstances, to scarcity and demand, and to the will
and inclination of the person using it. Bread, for example, to a starving
person has the 'highest conceivable utility'. A diamond lying
undiscovered, in contrast, has no utility at all. On closer examination,
the relation between commodities and utility shows that,

> Utility must be considered as measured by, or even as actually identical with, the
> addition made to a person's happiness. It is a convenient name for the aggregate
> of the favourable balance of feeling produced, the sum of the pleasures created
> and the pain prevented.[22]

In the new diagram, the horizontal axis measures the quantity of the
commodity and the vertical axis measures its utility. Jevons uses the
example of food consumed during a twenty-four hour period, so the
dimension of time can be suppressed. Each (thin) rectangle represents
the utility of the (small) increment of food consumed. At least, its area
can be presumed to be in proportion to the utility of the increment of
food.

Up to subsistence level, increments of food will yield infinite and,
therefore, indefinable utility. Above that level, the utility of
increments of (a single commodity of) food will become finite and
start to decline as the total intake increases. With the increments
themselves becoming smaller and smaller, their utility will vary
continuously and the relationship between units of utility units of the
commodity can be represented by a downwards sloping curve. Jevons

has arrived at the concept of diminishing marginal utility (to a single commodity and of one person); what he calls the final degree of utility in consumer equilibrium. The total utility of the food consumed is the sum of all the rectangles, or the area beneath the curve. There are still no units of utility, so this may not mean very much; unless, again, it makes sense to talk of square inches of utility. Jevons is not worried because,

> To be able to estimate the total enjoyment of a person would be an interesting thing, but it would not really be so important as to be able to estimate the additions and subtractions to his enjoyments, which circumstances occasion. In the same way a very wealthy person may be quite unable to form any accurate statement of his aggregate wealth; but he may nevertheless have exact accounts of income and expenditure, that is, of additions and subtractions.[23]

Utilitarians, it might be thought, would be very interested in estimating the total enjoyment of a person. Even if they were content with additions and subtractions, however, they still lack exact units of measurement like money.

In his chapter on the Theory of Exchange in *The Theory of Political Economy*, attempts are made to remedy this deficiency in the utilitarian armoury. The progress of economics, he contends, is dependent upon 'acquiring more accurate notions of variable quantities', in particular of 'the laws of the variation of utility numerically'.

> The price of a commodity is the only test we have of the utility of the commodity to the purchaser; and if we could tell exactly how much people reduce their consumption of each important article when the price rises, we could determine, at least approximately, the variations in the final degree of utility, the all important element in economics.[24]

If it can be assumed that the 'general utility' of the consumer's income is unaffected by changes in the price of the commodity, that the utility of money is constant, then what the consumer is willing to pay for an increment of the commodity in question will approximately measure its utility to that consumer. Economics can be as exact as 'meteorology is likely to be for a very long time'. Of course, Jevons acknowledges that for many commodities, and bread is an obvious example, these conditions will not be met. Changes in price are bound to affect the utility of money income. With the accumulation of suitable statistics on the proportions of income spent on different commodities, he has faith in the ability of economic science to disentangle their respective marginal utility schedules. Unfortunately,

the 'vast differences in the condition of persons' and the complicated
ways 'in which one commodity replaces or serves instead another'
provide further obstacles. These are the passages to which Marshall
objected with such force. He thought that Jevons should have dropped
the quest for utilitarian measurement. Laws of demand were there to
be discovered, not laws of utility. Jevons had promised much and
delivered very little.

Aggregation

Measurement of the utility of individuals naturally leads on to the
possibility of aggregation. Jevons mentions the aggregate of
individuals in the Measurement of Feeling and Emotion section of his
Introduction to *The Theory of Political Economy*. Individuals are not
identical in mind or motive and their reactions to economic stimuli
often have the appearance of caprice. If the laws of economics take the
same form for individuals or nations, in practice they are forced to
treat the behaviour of groups of individuals as an average. They
depend upon the 'high probability that accidental and disturbing
causes will operate, in the long run, as often in one direction as the
other, so as to neutralise each other'. Thus what might seem to be
quite indeterminate at the individual level, has a regularity and
exactness in the whole. While this may be a very sensible way of
dealing with tendencies and averages in behaviour, it has no bearing
on aggregation in the sense of adding-up the feelings or utilities of
different people. Jevons manages to avoid the issue, just as he avoids
tackling the utilitarian implications of the doctrine of population. He
holds it to be no direct problem of economics. Economics is
concerned with maximising the happpiness of a fixed population, with
a given technology and resources. Changing the variable changes the
problem. Even here there is no examination of the meaning of
aggregate happiness. It is true that a brief mention can be found in
towards the end of his life in *The State in Relation to Labour*, where
he is largely concerned with policy matters. Laws are described as
being enacted (and made away with) to achieve a larger 'sum total of
happiness'.[25] That is all. Jevons is then more anxious to draw attention
to the dangers of public interference which benefits a section of the
community, not the community as a whole.

Individualism

Jevons had always opposed any great extension to the role of government in economic affairs. Competition and free enterprise are generally recommended in the interests of efficiency. In most cases, individuals are the best judges of their own interests. Back in Australia, he argued for a commercial fare structure to enable the railways to break even. There was no need to assume they generated indirect benefits and no case for subsidising their investment. At home, and much later, he came round to the view that the state had certain responsibilities towards labour. The subtitle for *The State in Relation to Labour* was *The English Citizen: His Rights & Responsibilities*. Liberty has to be defended for it is a necessary condition for the free development of individuals and contributes to their happiness. In social matters, nevertheless, there are no abstract rights, absolute principles, or unalterable and inflexible laws or rules. Absolute principles ignore the reality of a labour market in which labourers are 'free' to accept dangerous conditions of employment.

> The difficult question thus arises whether, out of respect to some supposed principle of individual liberty, the State ought to allow men to go on working and living in the midst of needless risk.[26]

Jevons's answer is that, in certain circumstances, they have to be protected against themselves. Similarly, there is no absolute right in private property. The very existence of taxation serves to make the point. It is a necessary evil.

In the *Principles of Economics* published after his death, Jevons also notes how some things (public libraries, museums, markets, weighing machines) are used jointly and successively. In this way their utility is multiplied.[27] Evidently, he developed a more pragmatic approach to both government restrictions and government initiatives. When there can be a definite improvement in the condition of some class of people, without injury to others, the state should promote it. This does mean, however, that there will be a debate even among those who think they know what the ultimate test of government interference should be.

> We cannot expect to agree in our utilitarian estimates ... we must consent to advance cautiously ... We must neither maximise the functions of the government at the beck of quasi-military officials, nor minimize them according to the very best philosophers ... Tolerance therefore is indispensable.[28]

Compared to the late 'socialist' phase of Mill, these observations are relatively mild. They are, nevertheless, a step away from crude interpretations of laisser faire, favoured by many non-economists at the time, and a step towards the more balanced views of Sidgwick and Marshall. The admission that utilitarians cannot expect to agree on their estimates of the balance of pleasure and pain on every issue of policy, is more disturbing.

Equality

Jevons appears not to take any great interest in the subject of distribution and equity in taxation. He certainly fails to make the link between maximising happiness and the distribution of personal incomes. In his *Principles*, least sacrifice is acknowledged to be the only rough and realistic guide to 'a sounder state of things' for taxation, but there is no explanation of why this should be, or what it really means. In an essay called On the Pressures of Taxation, dated 1869, and published in the same posthumous volume as the *Principles*, Jevons concludes that there is no case for equal taxation in the sense of taxation proportional to income. He gives two reasons. First, the available information is insufficient to prove that there is great inequality in the existing system of taxation (which is not really the point). Second, there is insufficient evidence to tell whether any particular class of citizen suffers from excessive pressure of taxation. No other utilitarian economist, not even James Mill, finds it so easy to avoid such awkward problems.

A Single Overriding Objective

There can be no doubt that Jevons accepted general happiness as the end of private and public actions, but he has little to say by way of elaboration. It is also reasonable to infer that he was a consequentalist and a welfarist in economics. Again, he felt no need to justify such positions.

Notes

1. Keynes (1972c).
2. 18th November 1857. Quoted in Jevons (1972) Vol. I, p.30.
3. There has always been a unitarian connection with utilitarianism. The Rev. Southwood Smith, for example. But it is too much to conclude that the unitarian church was utilitarianism at prayer.

Notes continued

4. Jevons in his *John Stuart Mill's Philosophy Tested*, (1879), p.538.
5. Apart from Keynes's essay, see Könekamp in Jevons (1972) Vol. I, Black (1972), Huthchison (1953) and (1982), Bostaph (1989) for the Australian background, and Schabas (1990) for the mathematical.
6. Jevons (1906).
7. Jevons (1970) p.91.
8. Introduction to op. cit., pp.93-93.
9. Jevons's Journal, in Jevons (1972) Vol.1, p.133.
10. op. cit., p.98.
11. op. cit., p.99.
12. Jevons (1977) Vol. V, 13th October 1879.
13. For Jevons's views on Mill see Letters to Henry Foxwell, 7th February 1875 and 16th November 1875, Jevons (1977) Vol. IV, and his *Progress of the Mathematical Theory of Political Economy* in op.cit, Vol. VII, (1981) p.77. For Mill's views on Jevons, see his testimonial of 4th May 1866 in Jevons (1973) Vol. III, p.120, and Mill, John (1972) Vol. VII.
14. Introduction to 2nd ed of *The Theory of Political Economy*, Jevons (1970), p. 87.
15. Jevons (1879), p.523.
16. op cit., p.531.
17. op. cit., p.533.
18. op. cit.,p.538.
19. Jevons (1970), Introduction, p.83.
20. op. cit., p.84.
21. op. cit., Chapter II.
22. op. cit., p.106.
23. op. cit., p.111.
24. op. cit., p.174.
25. Jevons (1882), p.165. This is the book Hayek describes as marking the end of the liberal era.
26. op. cit., p.5.
27. Jevons (1905), Chapter VI.
28. Jevons (1882), pp.165-166.

6. Henry Sidgwick

Henry Sidgwick never claimed to be anything more than a re-interpreter of the works of other economists and no one can quarrel with Schumpeter's judgement that his 'rendering' of classical theory was competent if unoriginal. With no time to deal properly with Sidgwick's ethical and political doctrines, Schumpeter nevertheless sketches a pen portrait of great perception.

> But he was one of the greatest English university men all the same: milieu-creating, milieu-leading, soul-shaping to an extraordinary degree ... Of all the Cambridge leaders, he was, with his anti metaphysical mind that was so lucid and so wingless, the one most favourably disposed to accept utilitarian starting points. Nevertheless, his ethics cannot be called straight utilitarianism, and this is the test, for it is here that a utilitarian creed, *qua* philosophy, would have to assert its sway.[1]

Sidgwick was primarily a philosopher: the first 'academic' or 'professional' philosopher among the Benthamites, and the last to combine philosophy with a serious commitment to economic and political theory. He believed that by drawing on the intuitionist tradition and paying respectful attention to the guidance of common sense, he had found a better way for utilitarianism to reconcile self-interest with duty. Friend to Jevons, Edgeworth and Marshall, member of the Apostles, married to the sister of a future Prime Minister (Arthur Balfour), and with his own sister married to a future Archbishop of Canterbury, Sidgwick was nothing if not well connected. The nature of his influence, however, was exclusively intellectual. That is not to say that it was insignificant. Much of what now passes for utilitarian doctrine in philosophy, politics and economics, is as much Sidgwickian as it is Benthamite. It was he who, with Edgeworth, laid down the foundations of modern welfare economics.

A Cambridge Man

Sidgwick was born in Skipton, Yorkshire, on the 31st May 1838, one year after Queen Victoria had come to the throne. His father, the Reverend William Sidgwick, was master of the local grammar school. Grandfather Sidgwick had been a prosperous cotton spinner. Money was not a problem. When the Reverend William died in 1841, the family settled in Bristol. Edward White Benson, the future Archbishop, was a cousin of Sidgwick's father and it was he who persuaded Mrs Sidgwick to send her son to Rugby (where Edward was to teach) in 1852. In the following year, she moved the household to Rugby, so that Henry could live at home. (Edward became a lodger. Henry's sister Mary, who later married Edward, was only 12 when he joined the family.) In 1855 Sidgwick went up to Trinity College Cambridge (his father's College),and remained there, with only one term's absence, for the rest of his life.

He won scholarships and prizes, graduated with first class honours in Classics and Mathematics, and was elected a Fellow of Trinity in 1859. The two great influences in his early life were Edward Benson and John Stuart Mill. Benson had guided him from school to university in Christian ethics and the religious view of life. Only in 1861 did Sidgwick finally decide not to take holy orders. However painful the break, it was made on matters of principle rather than on any objection to the value of the Church as a social institution. He continued to hover between the belief that the tenets of Christianity were 'true and final' or 'not true and temporary'. In either case, he could not accept the formal doctrines required of members of the Church of England, in particular the Apostles creed. As a man of principle, he resigned his fellowship in 1869, which carried with it such an obligation, and was not re-elected until 1885. The episode had little effect on his academic career, and he was soon found a College lectureship.

Sidgwick later said that the years between 1859 to 1869 had been his years of 'storm and stress'. The justification of religious beliefs was a constant preoccupation and he spent much time on an historical investigation of Christianity. He had also become interested in supernormal phenomenon and psychical research, and it was to be at a séance in the house of Arthur Balfour (a one time pupil) that he would meet his future wife, Balfour's sister, Eleanor Mildred (Nora). Above all else, this period marked the start of his quest for answers to fundamental questions of philosophy: the determination of truth and error, of right and wrong, and the discovery of the basis for a practical morality that would direct science and human progress. First he found inspiration in Mill, and then in Comte. Like Mill, he drew inspiration from poetry. Like Mill he read Kant with great interest; but with a greater sympathy for Germany and German culture, he read him with more respect and attention. Membership of the Apostles (Sidgwick was a 'joiner', unlike Marshall, although they both were active in the discussions of the Grote Club) brought him in touch with those who been early admirers of the radical Mill. It was, however, the latter's version of ethical hedonism which proved the strongest attraction. Sidgwick claimed to have left both Mill and Comte behind in 1866. It has been suggested that this was because he found their agnosticism unacceptable. A more likely explanation is that he rejected their notion of limiting the view of the universe to positive knowledge. Sidgwick wanted to leave room for spiritual and metaphysical theories.

He was promoted as Praelector in Moral Philosophy by his College in 1875, married in 1876, and appointed to the Knightsbridge Chair of Philosophy in 1883. Sidgwick was a reformer within the University, pressing for more efficient administration and encouraging both the addition of new subjects to the curriculum and the education of women. He was, for example, responsible for the introduction of the Moral Sciences as a separate route to graduation. On women he is supposed to have been more progressive than Marshall. Sidgwick had, after all, been largely responsible for the establishment of Newnham College, and Mrs Sidgwick was its second Principal. Marshall had opposed the completely equal treatment of women in the University, while Mrs Marshall had been only a student at Newnham. Yet even Sidgwick was not prepared to follow John Stuart Mill all the way on female emancipation. He could not accept, in keeping with common opinion, that 'women generally' are the 'safest guardians of their own pecuniary interests'. There was a tendency towards the orthodox in all his opinions. Charming, courteous, wistful. uncertain, disinterested, and delicately humorous, were some of the adjectives used to describe his character. Balfour, as his student, found the absence of dogma and the love of truth more than victory in his teaching, rather attractive. He had to admit that the approach may not have been the best for filling lecture theatres or enthusing disciples. G.E. Moore, who was a student in Sidgwick's last years, found his lectures dull and his books provoking.

Others sometimes complained of the 'ceaselessly changing complexity of his mind', of being exasperated by 'his inability to commit himself, his elusiveness'. To the outsider he seemed always to be thinking of leaving Cambridge and never making the move, always trying to reconcile religion and science and never succeeding. Sidgwick himself thought that he was 'fearfully impulsive and unstable'. There is his famous statement about faith: 'I believe in God, while sometimes I can say no more than I hope this belief is true and I must and will act as if it was'. Marshall provides evidence of a different side to his character: Sidgwick refused to sign any report on selected books for the Moral Sciences Tripos unless Mill and Bentham were included, so strong was his belief in the value of a training in utilitarianism. He and his wife became increasingly involved in activities of the Society for Psychic Research. He served as its President twice, and as President of the 1888 Congress of Experimental Psychologists in Paris. He was also closely involved with the establishment of the British Association. Sidgwick died, soon after a major operation, on the 28th October 1900, six months before Queen Victoria.[2]

The Victorian Scholar

Sidgwick was no less productive than the other utilitarians. He published more than 160 articles over a period of 40 years, in addition to ten books, (six of them printed posthumously). The books are listed below.

1874 The Methods of Ethics (seven editions)
1883 The Principles of Political Economy (three editions)
1886 Outline of the History of Ethics for English Readers (five
        editions)
1891 The Elements of Politics (four editions)
1898 Practical Ethics: a Collection of Addresses and Reviews (two
        editions)
1902 Philosophy, Its Scope and Relations (edited by James Ward)
1902 Lectures on the Ethics of T.H. Green, H. Spencer, and J
        Martineau (edited by E.E. Constance Jones)
1903 The Development of European Polity (edited by Eleanor
        Mildred Sidgwick)
1904 Miscellaneous Essays and Addresses (edited by Eleanor
        Mildred Sidgwick and Arthur Sidgwick)
1905 Lectures on the Philosophy of Kant and others (edited by James
        Ward)

More significantly, three of his books have had a lasting impact on the development of the subjects they studied: Ethics, Political Economy, and Politics. Utilitarianism plays a part in all of them.

The Methods of Ethics is Sidgwick's masterpiece. An 'expository and critical' examination of the 'different methods of obtaining reasoned convictions as to what ought to be done', starts from the premise that what is right can be known and is to be found, implicitly or explicitly, in 'the moral consciousness of mankind'. As such it seems to be an exercise in pure philosophy, concerned with individual acts, and with no direct relevance to political economy or politics. One of the crucial questions of ethics, however, concerns the 'the grounds and limits of obedience to the state'. What is right conduct towards the laws and commands of the government? Answers to this question would seem to be related to another: what are the legitimate functions of government, the limits to its power? There can be right and wrong for the conduct of institutions as well as for individuals.

In Sidgwick's *Principles of Political Economy*, the purpose of government interference, or of its non-interference in economic matters, is to attain a result desirable for 'a political community (or aggregate of such communities)'. In his *Elements of Politics*, the concern is to construct 'the system of relations which ought to be established among the persons governing, and between them and the governed'. In addition, citizens will have moral opinions about the social order within which they live and work; about the fairness of the system of private property, for example, or the extent of the suffrage. The power of an 'enlightened government' in a 'civilized' country is bound to be constrained by their views. Indirectly, then, an examination of the basis of moral convictions can be relevant to Politics (for Sidgwick, the Art of Political Economy is part of Politics).

The Philosophy of Ethics.

Sidgwick's own account of the development of his ethical thought[3], starts with John Mill's psychological hedonism (universal pleasure seeking) and ethical hedonism (each ought to seek the general happiness). The 'frank naturalism' of pleasure seeking allied with the apparent 'dictate of absolute self-sacrifice' proved very attractive. The reconciliation of the two was the problem. Why should individuals choose a moral duty to others over their personal interests? Mill's solution of a moral disposition towards duty was unacceptable. Kant's golden rule (that we must be able to will that a maxim of our action should become a universal law) was not the 'grotesque failure' that Mill thought, but it was still inadequate as an explanation of the subordination self-interest to duty. Thomas Hobbes, the Scottish philosophers (Adam Smith in the *Theory of Moral Sentiments*, as well as Hutcheson and Hume), Bishop Butler, Aristotle and Socrates are all studied for the light they could shine on this dualism in human nature. Sidgwick comes to believe that the aim of general happiness must rest on a fundamental moral intuition.

The first chapter of *Ethics* mentions, almost as an aside, that utilitarians take the general happiness as the ultimate end of all conduct. The reader then has to follow a long trail through the different varieties of Hedonism, and its alternatives of Intuitionism, Rational Benevolence and the Morality of Common Sense, before reaching the conclusion that Universalistic Hedonism is the only reasonable and rational concept of the good. At least, that seems to be where the argument is leading. So careful and balanced is his treatment, so thorough is the assessment of every possible objection, that it is difficult to find a final and confident assertion of the Sidgwickian truth. Even at the end of the last chapter in the book, he is still wondering whether 'ethical nihilism' or 'universal scepticism' can really be avoided. He prefers Psychological to Egoistical Hedonism because while the former holds that 'volition is always determined by pleasures and pains, actual or prospective', the latter holds that only my own pleasures and pains are to count and 'a different end cannot be prescribed for me by reason'. Pleasures and pains are not determined independently of moral judgements: moral pleasure is one of our ends. He thinks Bishop Butler went too far in suggesting that many of our impulses are disinterested, that we could not pursue pleasure at all unless we had desires for something other than pleasure. Virtue, for example, might be desired for its own sake. Sidgwick kept closer to Mill in taking these desires to be exceptional, but he accepted that there are both self-regarding and extra-regarding impulses in the human consciousness. Extra-regarding means that they are not just about pleasures and pains, or about our own pleasures and pains. The two impulses may alternate, or, what is more significant, come into conflict and prompt opposite courses of action. It is not possible, therefore, to accept the pure doctrine of Psychological Hedonism. Introspection and observation tell us something rather different.

Universalistic Hedonism is Benthamism. It shares with Egoistical Hedonism the belief that all actions are a means to an end, and that the ultimate end is pleasure (over pain). In opposition, as he thinks, to Bentham and Mill, Sidgwick wants to separate the two doctrines. To call hedonism universalistic implies that the ultimate end is general happiness. To show how individuals in pursuit of their own happiness somehow also desire the happiness of all, is the difficult part of the exercise. Mill's proof is not complete.

> For an aggregate of actual desires, each directed towards a different part of general happiness, does not constitute an actual desire for the general happiness, existing in any individual.[4]

The gap can be filled by the intuitions of Rational Benevolence. These relate to the concept of the Ultimate Good. When the Ultimate Good has been defined carefully, Rational Benevolence can become Utilitarianism.

The Ultimate Good is resolved into the 'desirable consciousness of all sentient beings', or 'Universal Happiness'. Virtuous actions are one of its constituents. Most of the principles that guide virtuous actions are intuitively clear and certain because they contribute to (1)'one's own good on the whole' (Prudence), and (2) 'others good no less than one's own' provided there is 'no undue preference' for any particular person or good (Benevolence). Usually, it is objective goodness, and actual virtuous conduct, not subjective volition or virtuous character, that is desirable. Sidgwick admits there might be apparent exceptions to the goodness of happiness. For example, sentient individuals may prefer a life of freedom and penury to one of luxurious servitude because they have an aversion to being subjected to some one else's will. He nevertheless wants the reader to agree that, after calm consideration, objects like liberty and justice are desired only for the happiness they will bring, one way or another.

> it is paradoxical to maintain that any degree of Freedom, or any form of social order, would still be commonly regarded as desirable even if we are certain that it had no tendency to promote the general happiness.[5]

Justice and Virtue can be similarly subordinated, although to a lesser degree; and an appeal to general happiness is the obvious way to resolve conflicts between them. No other method has this ability to reduce to a common measure the different dimensions of a moral problem.

Unlike Bentham, who was fierce in his denunciation of ipse-dixitism, Sidgwick attempts to bridge the divide between intuitionism and utilitarianism. Those who would judge the morality of actions by 'their conformity to certainties or dictates of Duty unconditionally prescribed' and those who would judge them according to their likelihood of producing 'the greatest happiness of the whole', need not be opposed.

> I am finally led to the conclusion ... that the Intuitional method rigorously applied yields as its final result the doctrine of pure Universalistic Hedonism, which it is convenient to denote by the single word, Utilitarianism.[6]

Like Mill he points to long human experience as to the effects of action, but goes further than Mill in accepting the merit of an intuitionism which seeks to find 'a philosophic basis for general rules implicit in the moral reasoning of ordinary persons'. According to Sidgwick, Mill thought that the rules of the multitude were only acceptable until something better came along. Sidgwick wants to study the morality of common sense with more respect and patience.

Utilitarians cannot construct a complete set of rules. Nor can they assume that they are dealing with an ideal society made up of perfect human beings. Every member of society ought to be included in the calculation of the greatest happiness, but it is impossible for utilitarian philosophers to know (by putting themselves into the position of) the circumstances of everyone else. They have to turn, instead, to

> the moral judgements, and especially the spontaneous unreflected judgements on particular cases, which are sometimes called moral intuitions, of the persons to be found in all walks and stations of life, whose earnest and predominant aim is to do their duty.[7]

'Plain men's consciences' were unreliable guides in the absence of a sense of duty to others; but those whose judgements were so directed, often 'intuitively enunciated General happiness as the end'. Even then, utilitarians have a duty to make a thorough review of these judgements. They cannot be assumed to represent a consensus, and they may suffer from a limited sympathy for others; but if common sense morality needs to be reinforced by reflective utilitarian arguments, and occasionally amended to allow for exceptions; it will be rarely displaced by new utilitarian rules. Common sense should only be overruled, Sidgwick warns, when there was a strong probability that the alternative promised a larger surplus of pleasures over pains.

He takes the balance between self-love and sympathy to be the key to any successful morality. General happiness is not served if each person looks to the happiness of others as much as to their own. Self-love must come first: it stimulates the 'active interest' and ensures that the individual's own needs are efficiently met. Close feelings of affection for family come next: otherwise every kind of sympathy would be reduced to what Aristotle described as a 'watery kindness'. General happiness is equally damaged by a total absence of any wider concern for others, even of the watery kind.

> whether it is true or not that the whole of morality has sprung from the root of sympathy, it is certain that self-love and sympathy combined are sufficiently strong in average men to dispose them to grateful admiration of any exceptional efforts to promote the common good.[8]

Sidgwick seems later to have doubts about whether it is so certain. The cultivation of benevolence has to be encouraged, and its coincidence with prudence cannot be empirically proved. Persuading people to sacrifice for a general and remote general good is often very difficult. His Kantian-like statement of utilitarianism as Rational Benevolence,

> I certainly could will it to be a universal law that men should act in such a way as to promote universal happiness,[9]

is a philosopher's hope. In the end, he is unable to decide whether the reconciliation of self-interest with duty is a 'self-evident premise' or a hypothesis we have a 'strong disposition to accept'.

The Science and Art of Political Economy

Sidgwick wrote *The Principles of Political Economy* in an attempt to restore confidence and respect for the version of classical economics handed down by Mill.

> My primary aim, then, has been to eliminate unnecessary controversy, by stating these results in a more guarded manner, and with due attention to the criticisms and suggestions of recent writers.[10]

Between the publication of Mill's own Principles in 1848 and his retraction of the wages fund doctrine in 1871, there was little dispute about the theory of economics and its practical applications among 'the great majority of educated persons in England'. The undermining of what was supposed to be one of the fundamental principles of economic orthodoxy caused great consternation. It was not the only shock to be suffered by persons educated in Ricardian political economy. By 1870 Cliff Leslie had introduced the German historical school's criticism of Ricardian a priori methodology, and further challenges to the basic assumptions of classical economics were to come with the publication of Jevons's *Theory* in 1871, and to a lesser extent from John Cairnes's *Leading Principles of Political Economy* in 1874. At about the same time, economists began to accept that there was a long-term industrial problem: economic growth and free trade had yet to cure the evils of mass poverty, and some feared that strife between labour and capital would threaten social harmony.

While his admiration for Mill (whom he called the most influential writer since Locke and the most suggestive since Bacon) as economist never faltered, Sidgwick openly attacked Mill's interpretation of utilitarianism at several crucial points. On economics, Sidgwick simply felt that Mill had followed the wrong strategy. He should have told his readers exactly where and how he, Mill, differed from Ricardo. The result was that Jevons could launch an unfair attack on an apparently united set of Ricardo-Mill doctrines. The interesting omission from Sidgwick's discussion is any reference to Jevons as a utilitarian. He must have been aware of Jevon's criticisms of Mill's *Utilitarianism*. The implication is, and there are some hints to this effect, that if Jevons misunderstood Mill on economics, he could also misunderstand Mill on Bentham and philosophy.

Sidgwick applies the terms 'utility' and 'useful' interchangeably, to mean the power to satisfy or prevent some want or desire. This power is not confined to situations of exchange. Even a Robinson Crusoe would give up something to gain useful things or prevent their destruction. Then, in a long footnote, he rejects Jevons's development of subjective utility into the realms of pleasure. It is not 'convenient', he says, to measure utility in a Benthamite way as the balance of pleasure over pain. In the first place, some things are desired (alcohol and opium, for example) even though those who desire them know they will produce more pain than pleasure. In the second place, economists are interested in the desire or demand for things, measured by what people are willing to give for them, including their labour, rather than in these painful consequences. The theory of value is about supply and demand. Ricardo's labour theory becomes a cost of production theory of supply, as it does in the hands of Mill. Demand is the desire for useful things, but the desire is only indirectly a function of pleasures and pains. Jevons's final degree of utility is assumed to equate with market value. When it comes to the question of wealth, in the sense of a total of resources available to persons, Sidgwick again prefers economists to use exchange value as the measure. There is an imperfect correspondence between lumps of wealth and lumps of utility. Such difficulties are made worse by the real possibility that needs increase as well as the means to satisfy them.

Apart from putting the record straight as far as Mill's distance from Ricardo is concerned, Sidgwick offers a detailed examination of the inadequacies of the wages fund doctrine, and of the confusions and erroneous notions which surround it. In passing, he notes that labour is not always painful. Some people may actually derive pleasure from their work. He also takes Jevons to task for describing economics as a 'mathematical science'. Although naturally quantitative, it requires an approach mid-way between the two extremes of verbal simplicity and mathematical complexity. In many applications, the mathematical symbols and diagrams are 'not indispensable'. On the contrary, they can be 'troublesome to the non-mathematical reader'. Yet this scepticism does not prevent him from quoting Antoine Cournot on exchange value and monopoly. Although his value judgements about the end of economic activity are simiular to those of Jevons, Sidgwick spends much more time in trying to justify them. Following Mill, he treats the methodology and philosophy of political economy very seriously (he is proudly described as the author of *The Method of Ethics* on the frontispiece of the *Principles of Political Economy*). Sidgwick believes conditions are still not right for the emergence of a general science of society. Controversy between sociologists and economists on who should conduct this kind of investigation is likened to disputes between 'those wanting to occupy territory, where the territory is neither effectively occupied or cultivated by either science'. In the meantime, Sidgwick was anxious to address the wider issues of methodology and policy that had been raised by other critics.

Misunderstandings about the correct use of the concept of 'economic man', about limits to the superiority of 'the system of natural liberty', and about the consequences of inequalities in the distribution of income and wealth, had to be clarified. A clear and consistent distinction must be drawn between what is and what ought to be in economics. There is, says Sidgwick, a popular tendency to confound the assumptions and conclusions of the theory and practice of economics. For convenience sake, they can be called the Science and Art of political economy. (Leon Walras made a similar distinction, only he introduced a third branch called ethics.) It is difficult, nonetheless, to confine positive statements to the Science and normative to the Art. Effects and causes are not exclusively economic. Just as in the practical world, non-economic effects have to be included in the over-all assessment of economic policies, so in the theoretical world, non-economic causes cannot be ignored. Sidgwick claims that the transition from art to science is easier in the production than in the distribution branches of economics. It partly depends on what is meant by distribution. There is, after all, a positive theory of distribution.

> It must be obvious ... that the investigation of the laws that determine actual prices, wages, and profits, so far as these depend on the free competition of individuals, is essentially distinct from the enquiry how far it is desirable that the actions of free competition should be restrained or modified, whether by the steadying force of custom, the remedial intervention of philanthropy, the legislation or administrative control of government, or the voluntary combination of masters and workmen.[11]

The effects of the working of free competition, in terms of inequalities in the distribution of personal incomes, immediately spring to mind as subjects for correction. Custom, philanthropy, and combination, on the other hand, are not among the usual list of remedies.

Sidgwick attributes much of the confusion about value judgements in economics to the misuse of the word 'natural'. Adam Smith started the trend by sometimes equating natural as meaning 'what would be without interference' with natural as meaning 'what ought to be or what a benevolent Providence intended'. Ricardo had a more scientific approach, using natural in the neutral sense of market or competitive outcome. The issue relates to the use of two central propositions in economics, which come originally from Adam Smith. The way in which Sidgwick expresses them, however, owes much to Mill. The first claims that 'economic man', the 'normal' human being for political economy,

> always prefers a greater apparent gain to a less, and prefers to attain any desired result with the least possible apparent expenditure.

The second claims that

> the best possible result will be attained, so far as the production and distribution of wealth are concerned, if the individual is left free to regulate his own activities for the supply of his own wants, within the limits necessary to secure a like freedom to all other individuals.[12]

Sidgwick then argues that although there is a 'close affinity' between the two propositions, they have no logical connection. Both are true under certain conditions, and the conditions differ. The second does not follow from the first: economic man may be confused by appearances; and the interests of the individual may clash with those of the community. The first is an important premise in the logical reasoning of science and gives information about what actually happens, whether good or bad. The second is a maxim of policy which judges that what would happen under certain circumstances is the best that could happen. It may be reasonable to assume that people will prefer a greater gain to a less, other things being equal. It is unreasonable to draw any conclusions from that assumption until all the other facts affecting behaviour have been examined. It could be affirmed that competitive markets will produce acceptable prices, but only a study of the facts will show whether such markets exist. Inductive as well as deductive methods are required in economics.

It is interesting that Sidgwick should precede the section of his *Principles* on the Art of Political Economy with a chapter on Custom. The main reason, he says, why economic man differs from an ordinary member of a civilized community is that the latter does some things out of habit (how they were done before) and other things out of custom (how others do them). Non-economic behaviour is not necessarily moral, but it is often socially acceptable. Private morality also has implications for the working of the System of Natural Liberty. Concepts of justice and fairness underlie most exchanges in civilized communities. A 'really free' contract between traders must exclude fraud and undue pressure. Advantage should not be taken of those in desperate need or those denied access to knowledge of market conditions and opportunities. There is a danger of taking too much for granted. The System of Natural Liberty may not even deliver all that is expected of it in the realm of production.

This conception of the single force of self-interest, creating and keeping in true economic order the vast and complex fabric of social industry is very fascinating; and it is not surprising that, in the first glow of the enthusiasm excited by its revelation, it should have been unhesitatingly accepted as presenting the ideal condition of social relations, and the final goal of political progress.[13]

Abstract economic science can have a very different view of the effects of free markets than a political economy seeking to justify the superiority of a system based on free markets. Monopolists, for example, rarely have an incentive to consider the interests of the community; solicitors sometimes encourage litigation; workers take action against the introduction of machinery. Self-interest will not remedy all the evils in the system of 'laisser faire'.

Sidgwick still insists that government intervention will be limited to qualifications and exceptions to the general rule of self-interest. He is no advocate of socialism. The possibilities for administrative and legislative control are discussed under the heads of production and industry; the role of government expenditure and taxation under the heads of distributive justice and public finance. Both divisions have regard to questions of efficiency and equity. Taxes, for example, can discourage the supply of labour and capital as well as create a fairer distribution of income. Public education can increase opportunities for the children of the poorer classes and improve the skills of the labour force. The answers Sidgwick gives to these questions about government intervention reveal the underlying utilitarian assumptions of his approach. Aggregate utility or happiness is now the guide and final arbitrator. What is true of economics is also true of politics. His art of political economy and many of the chapters in his *Elements of Politics* follow the same logic and reach the same policy conclusions.

Utilitarianism

Sidgwick's application of the greatest happiness principle owes much to Mill. His arguments for government intervention and his principles of equitable taxation develop rather than amend those already set down. In spite of this general agreement, he is prepared to part company with Mill on some fundamental points of interpretation. He cannot accept the qualitative distinction between different kinds of pleasure, the belief that attempts to measure utility are doomed to failure, or that there should be a protected area of purely private behaviour. In addition, he pushes the notion of happiness further away from desire to states of mind or consciousness. It is a careful and scholarly account. In many ways he is *the* classical utilitarian. But his utilitarianism somehow lacks the warmth and breadth of Mill's concerns.

A Single Overriding Objective

For Sidgwick, utilitarianism is primarily an ethical theory which takes universal good as the object to be attained. Universal good is 'happiness', 'pleasure' and the 'greatest possible surplus of pleasure over pain'.

the pain being conceived as balanced against an equal amount of pleasure, so that
the two contrasted amounts annihilate each other for purposes of ethical
calculation.[14]

All sentient beings should be included in the calculation, however
difficult the measurement, and 'the interests of posterity' given equal
attention. The only reason why the happiness of future sentient beings
might be given less weight is the uncertainty that attaches both to their
existence and the effect of present actions upon their lives.

Realistically, happiness is the standard, not necessarily the motive
of individual conduct. Common sense prefers motives like reason or
conscience. It may be sensible to encourage people to aim at
subsidiary ends, to apply other immediate criteria of rightness, as long
as utility remains the final test. Similarly, common sense dislikes pure
egoism. Enlightened self-interest should lead individuals to develop
feelings of sympathy towards others. 'If my happiness is desirable and
a good, the equal happiness of any other person must be equally
desirable'.[15] But it is difficult to persuade people to sacrifice for a
general and remote good. The harmony between prudence and
benevolence may have to be demonstrated in more practical ways.
Nevertheless, the individual can distinguish between self-interest and
the interests of the larger whole, and even accept that, on particular
occasions, his interests should be subordinated to those of the whole.

'The aggregate of utilities', in the sense of the sum of enjoyments
arising from economic activity, makes a brief appearance. Increases in
'happiness', or the 'greatest aggregate happiness', or 'the greatest
happiness on the whole' are the targets for economic and political
interventions. The true standard of 'right' legislation is the same as it
is for 'right' individual conduct. The only difference is that the
community has a role to play in the calculations. The welfare of the
community, means, in the last analysis, the happiness of the members
of the community.[16] If each state is concerned with the happiness of
all those affected by its action, there is even room for a reference to
the 'general interests of the community of nations'. Free trade is
simply the application of laisser faire on a 'cosmopolitan' scale. The
pursuit of a state's own interests is justified provided the interests of
other states are not harmed, or the common (global) good enlarged. As
with individual conduct, a concentration of effort on limited ends is
often the best way to reach general happiness.[17]

When dealing with Egoism and Self-love,[18] Sidgwick suddenly
announces that pleasures and pains are mixed up and subject to
qualitative differences. The same activity can bring both good and bad
feelings. Some activities appear to generate feelings of a higher degree

of intensity. Instead of concluding, as Mill concluded, that this means they cannot be meaningfully compared, Sidgwick insists that these differences must be 'resolved into quantities'. All pleasures (and presumably all pains) have a common property, and, therefore, a basis for comparison. He cannot accept that some pleasures should be called 'noble and elevated', and thus intrinsically different. Such distinctions introduce a 'non-hedonistic ground' for calculation. It is a more logical and tidier analysis than Mill's, but lacks one important corollary. There are no instructions as to how these differences are to be resolved into quantities. This is made all the more difficult when he proceeds to argue that pleasure is a state of mind, and then that 'desirable consciousness' is what all human beings seek. Human beings make choices over things that they believe will bring them good mental feelings. What if they are mistaken? What if preferences are not an accurate reflection of utility?

Consequentalism

Sidgwick's ethical theory is concerned with the effects of conduct on utility, private and public. He claims to find inspiration in the rules of common sense and to embrace the strengths of intuitive morality, but always come back to judging actions by their outcomes. His utilitarianism means that,

> the conduct which, under any given circumstance, is objectively right, is that which will produce the greatest amount of happiness on the whole; that is taking into account all whose happiness is affected by the conduct.[19]

Empirical hedonism is the obvious method to apply, but it has to be supplemented by other forms of guidance. Observations of our own and others experience should be used to estimate 'the probable degree of our future pleasure or pain' in any given circumstance. Anticipation and uncertainty cloud the issue. This form of 'scientific reasoning', from the point of view of personal ethics, tries

> to compare all the pleasures and pains that can be foreseen as probable results of the different alternatives of conduct presented to us, and to adopt the alternative which seems likely to lead to the greatest happiness on the whole.[20]

Unfortunately, he does not believe that such clarity and certainty is available. Too many errors can creep into the analysis. It would be easier to estimate results for the conduct of human beings in general (the law of averages) than for any one person in particular. Individuals may be better advised to stay with rules that have grown, largely unconsciously, out of the wealth of human experience on the effects of actions. Yet he is not persuaded to give up the methodology altogether. Even these rules can be confusing to the ordinary person and lacking in unanimous support among competent judges. They need to be carefully tested and occasionally replaced. Only empirical hedonism offers a standard against which they can be measured.

The rules of conduct for the government are fixed by legislators and interpreted by judges. They should be guided by

> the same kind of forecast of consequences as will be used in settling all questions of private morality: we shall endeavor to estimate and balance against each other the effects of such rules on the general happiness.[21]

Sidgwick makes it clear, however, that the method is not confined to rules. Governments have a responsibility to formulate policies for dealing with particular problems. Sometimes their effects may give contradictory signals. For example, the evidence from economics is that a policy will probably increase the wealth of the nation, and from medical science that it will probably reduce the health of the nation. The utilitarian, in his eyes, has the advantage of being able to compare their respective effects on the greatest happiness, and decide whether the policy is justified on the whole. In other words, the dimensions of wealth and health can be converted into common units of utility.

Not all personal rules are universal in the sense that, to be successful, they should be followed by all. Sidgwick accepts that there can be exceptions here as well. Telling the truth may not always lead to the greater happiness. Determination of those circumstances in which telling lies is justified, on the other hand, would be equivalent to constructing a more complicated general rule. Other exceptions are more serious, and what would be right for one person to do might be wrong for another. It is important to recognise that for the utilitarian goodness of disposition or motive is not the same as rightness of conduct. A good person can do harm, for example, by being over-zealous. Some actions for a good cause can damage the character of the person performing them. In the final judgement, the felicific consequences of one must be weighed against the felicific consequences of the other. Thus a large disaster should be averted even though this requires the moral deterioration of those individuals who save the community, because their utility loss is smaller than the utility gain to the rest.

Welfarism

Sidgwick is ambiguous about general happiness being simply the sum of individual happinesses, in all their various forms. When dealing with the subject of distribution in the *Methods of Ethics*, he argues that utilitarianism can give no guidance 'on its own'. A supplementary principle of justice is required. Otherwise, non utility information, that which does not show up in the sum of happiness, has no meaning or application. In the *Principles of Political Economy* and the *Elements of Politics*, Benthamite notions of equality and of the relationship between income or wealth and utility appear to fill this particular gap. But Sidgwick is aware of the potential conflict between equal and aggregate happiness.

> To aim at equality in the distribution of happiness may obviously be incompatible with aiming at the greatest happiness on the whole, if the happiness of one person can ever be increased by diminishing to a lesser extent the happiness of a another already less happy.[22]

What is not clear is how he would resolve the incompatibility. Most of the time he takes maximising aggregate utility to be the correct and strictly utilitarian objective. The argument for reducing inequalities runs from more equal distribution to greater happiness, not from justice or fairness to more equal distribution. But there are occasions when he comes to rather different conclusions. Writing on distributive justice, for example, he claims that economists are concerned with 'actual human beings' and 'actual human beings will not permanently acquiesce in a social order that common moral opinion condemns as unjust'.[23] The danger for utilitarians is that some interpretations of 'the largest sum of happiness' will be regarded as unjust.

The treatment of other kinds of non-utility is less ambiguous. Sidgwick has much to say about the importance of individual liberty, the right to personal security, and the protection of private property. Legislation should take freedom as an end, but not as an absolute end.

> It requires for its justification an individualistic maxim definitely understood as a subordinate principle or 'middle axiom' of utilitarianism: i.e. that individuals are to be protected from deception, breach of engagements, annoyance, coercion, or other conduct tending to impede them in the pursuit of their ends, so far as such protection seems to be conducive to the general happiness.[24]

Although these strictures are relaxed to some extent when he examines the role of government in taxation and industry, the implication remains that the existence of deception, annoyance and coercion is not, in itself, utility information. If the loss of liberty can be shown to have no affect on the happiness, of either individuals or the community, it can be ignored. Sidgwick, of course, believes that it is a crucial part of a person's happiness.

Individualism

He stresses the importance of distinguishing between the individual and the community. The larger whole is the sum of the parts. Whilst human beings are conscious of their own needs, have strong feelings for their close kin, and weaker feelings for those more distant, and come to understand the requirements of the larger whole, there is no sense in which the community can rationally and consciously feel or comprehend them. If sacrifices are to be made, they must be made for some individuals, now, or in the future, not for an abstract community. He makes a strong commitment to the notion that human beings are the best judges of their own needs, and better able to provide for themselves than governments or public agencies (that is, sane, adult members of the community). Self-interest is not to be feared. It provides a stimulus to self-development and to the growth in the awareness of others. Only later, when he comes to the problems of economic production, is any exception allowed. The expectation that adult members of the community will have to rely on their own resources to meet their material need, promotes economic efficiency. Unfortunately, some people are unable to 'insure' themselves against unforeseen disasters. Consumers may not always have enough information to decide on their personal interests. Life in a modern industrial society is complicated and technical, and citizens will require advice and support in emergencies.

Freedom means the absence of physical and moral coercion. It is negative rather than positive. There are no 'constitutional' rights, only rules laid down by the community for the protection of property and persons. The utilitarian interpretation of the individualistic principle

> requires us to conceive, as the general aim of law and government, not the prevention among the governed of mutual interference in the ordinary sense, but the prevention of mutual interference with each one's pursuit of happiness for himself and his family.[25]

Individual liberty is to be curbed only when government coercion prevents worse private coercion. The exclusive use of private property is defended on the grounds that individuals have to be offered sufficient incentives to wealth creation. Provided this exclusivity does not reduce opportunities available to other persons (and there is supposed to be a 'natural abundance' of these around), general happiness will increase. To personal security and the protection of private property is added the ability to freely transfer property by gift, sale or bequest, and to fulfil all contracts, freely negotiated. The potential clash between the freedoms of the old to determine what shall become of their wealth when they die, and the freedoms of their inheritors to make the best use of it as they see fit, can only be solved by practical compromise. Taxation is a separate problem.

Thus far, Sidgwick is following Mill quite closely. The central importance of self-interest, private property, and personal freedom are common themes. They both take the task of improving the moral order of an 'admittedly imperfect world' very seriously. Differences emerge when this improvement touches upon private acts. Sidgwick thinks that it is 'practically futile' for Mill to draw a line between individual acts which are of no concern to ethics and those which are. There are a very few aspects of conduct which can be kept entirely private. Decisions on what profession to follow, how to educate one's children, or where to live, affect others. Mill was wrong to dismiss 'secondary injury. The risk of evil (that is to say damage to happiness in general) from ignoring these inter-personal injuries, is greater than the evil from the suppression of individuality.[26] In fact, the disagreement runs deeper than the externalities of personal choices, like where to live. Sidgwick suggests that Mill is asking for exemption from the normal (common sense) rules of behaviour for persons in very special circumstances, or for a class of person with special qualities of intellect, temperament, and character. They should be allowed to recommend what it would not be right to advocate openly; to teach to a sub-set of the community what it would not be right to teach to all; and to do in secret what it would wrong to do in the face of the world. Sexual morality is an obvious item on this hidden agenda. Regardless of whether Mill actually made these claims in quite this form, Sidgwick is clearly alarmed by the possibility. He contents himself with the remark that 'esoteric morality should be kept esoteric'. The implication is that almost all kinds of (literally) private behaviour can affect the happiness of others, and through them the general happiness.[27]

Even in a society composed of 'economic men', laisser faire will not guarantee the maximisation of aggregate utility. Sidgwick explains what he calls the classical connection between Natural Liberty and Production:

For (1) the regard for self-interest on the part of consumers will lead always to the effectual demand for the things that are most useful to society; and (2) regard for self-interest on the part of producers will lead to their production at the least cost.[28]

The existence of competitive markets is not mentioned as an explicit requirement, but he makes references to freedom of transfer, on terms 'freely arranged', and to labour markets in which any excess of labourers will be 'corrected' by a fall in the price of their services. The point of the explanation, however, is not to extol the virtues of the system. In spite of containing 'a very large element of truth', it is too optimistic and should not be applied without noting the qualifications and exceptions of the real world.

Although Sidgwick's list is similar to that of Mill, his arguments can be less persuasive. For example, the fact that individuals want repose, leisure, and reputation as well as goods and services, may explain why less material wealth is produced but not why less happiness is enjoyed. Even if it is true that the ability to exercise power over another might bring utility gains quite distinct from the benefit of any labour services rendered, it is strange that he worries so much about the freedom to contract oneself into slavery. On the other hand, the difficulties of privately appropriating the returns on enterprises such as the building of lighthouses, investment in forests (equalising the rainfall and ameliorating the climate on surrounding lands), and scientific discoveries, are clearly set out. He fears the waste of railway duplication. He understands how private markets can lead to over-fishing, the neglect of flood protection, the failure to take proper precautions against diseases that attack plants and animals, and the under-provision of technical and professional education. He believes that market prices place a lower value on the utilities of the poor than those of the rich. He attacks the inefficiencies of monopolies of both labour and capital, whilst acknowledging that low wages can reduce the performance of the labour force. Sidgwick prepares the way for a sophisticated analysis of the divergencies between private and public gain, for an Economics of Welfare.

He starts with a description of the 'individualistic minimum' state which provides defence, law and order, enforcement of contracts, prevention of deception and fraud, and aid for those who 'through age or mental disorder' cannot look after themselves. From what he has already said about the failures of private enterprise, it is not surprising to find him then justifying a state with wider responsibilities. Where production is concerned, the main guides to action are (1) that the activity is on too large a scale for private provision except as a private monopoly, and (2) that the advantages of the activity to the public exceed the benefit to private enterprise. In the *Principles of Political Economy*, the provision of roads, bridges, (tolls are expensive to collect), railway infra-structure, harbours, lighthouses, the letter post and telegraphs are all included, along with the need to promote the movement of people away from over-populated areas, and to settlements overseas. Nor does he miss the opportunity to emphasis the importance of stability in the value of money and the government's role in the regulation of the currency and the banking system.[29] In *Politics* he looks beyond production. Anything which individuals cannot provide at all, or which they cannot afford to buy on their own, or which it is not worthwhile for private interests to pursue or appropriate, become candidates for state action. The German experiment in social insurance legislation impressed him, but he is not prepared to countenance full 'Socialistic' interference in pensions, health, and unemployment benefit. The protection of the poor and the equalisation of opportunities for labour are best served by some combination of 'regulated private almsgiving, public relief, and compulsory insurance'. Perhaps the government should help the poor with their insurance. It is after all 'peculiarly adapted' to provide them with the credit guarantees and banking facilities they cannot obtain on their own.[30]

Like Mill, he believes the ownership of land to be a special problem. The private appropriation of natural resources (in commons, seas, and mines) is not justified if it restricted other people's opportunities. Public provision, however, is not the only solution. Governments may achieve the same result more effectively by the regulation and encouragement of private initiatives. Ultimately, the test will be whatever generates the greatest happiness. Sidgwick is anxious to keep the balance of argument in favour of laisser faire. Those advocating government intervention must always guard against the dangers of corruption, of allowing special and sectional interests to dominate the common good, and of pandering to popular and transient sentiments. The machinery of government is not designed to perform these tasks and cannot find suitable incentives for its employees.

> we are not justified in concluding that government interference is always expedient, even where laisser faire leads to a manifestly unsatisfactory result; its expediency has to be decided in any particular case by a careful estimate of advantages and drawbacks, requiring data obtained from special experience.[31]

Among the drawbacks will be the costs imposed by the taxes required to finance the interference, whatever its form. Sidgwick and Mill have similar reservations about state power. It is Mill, however, who places the greater emphasis on the benefits of (strictly individualistic) private enterprise and voluntary cooperation.

Equality

When Sidgwick argues that the utilitarian formula has to be supplemented by some principle of Justice before it can answer questions about the distribution of a given sum of happiness, he quotes Bentham's slogan 'everybody to count for one, and nobody for more then one'. In *Political Economy*, there is extensive treatment of equality under the heading of taxation as well as a separate chapter on Distributive Justice. *Politics* contains observations on democracy which repeat Bentham's definition of public welfare as general happiness. The legislator should count each person's happiness as the same. It does not follow that there should be complete equality in post-tax incomes. The maximization of aggregate utility may not even require a move in that direction. Most governments are, nevertheless, engaged in 'the mitigation of the harshest inequalities in the present distribution of incomes', but in order to realise equality of opportunity rather than of outcome. Taxation is not the only means. Expenditure on education, for example, can have the same effect.

Political economy has room for an Art of Distribution which attempts to discover that apportionment of the product of the economy which will maximise total happiness or utility. Distribution is a matter of equity and efficiency: what seems just and fair, and what will make the best use of given resources. For the utilitarian, equal treatment only implies equal shares if it can be shown that equal shares makes the best use of given resources. Sidgwick's next step is to claim, on grounds of common sense, support for Bentham's axioms (1) that an increase in wealth normally brings an increase in happiness to the possessor, and (2) that the resulting increase in happiness 'stands in a decreasing ratio' to the increase in wealth. Adam Smith is supposed to have rejected the first axiom on the grounds that happiness is as great in the cottage as it is in the palace. Such 'sentimental optimism' having largely disappeared, and with few doubting the second axiom, utilitarians are driven to the

> obvious conclusion is that the more any society approximates to equality in the
> distribution of wealth among its members, the greater on the whole is the
> aggregate of satisfactions which the society in question derives from the wealth
> that it possesses.[32]

An earlier remark on the measurement of utility makes the same point. If on average, each increment in wealth yields diminishing utility, then total utility will depend, in part, on how wealth is distributed. The trouble is that the relationship is not straightforward. Not all individuals are the same.

Sidgwick seems to realise how fragile the argument for equality is for a consistent utilitarian when he explores the confusions of what he calls 'idealised democracy'. In footnotes towards the end of *Politics*, Bentham is called in to show how equality in the distribution of happiness can conflict with greatest aggregate happiness.

> I do not think ... that Bentham intended to deny (1) that one person may be more capable of happiness than another; or (2) that, if so, the former's happiness is more important than the latter's as an element of general happiness.[33]

Bentham may been as explicit in his denials as Sidgwick suggests (no references are given), but he did not spell out all the consequences. Sidgwick only hints at the the possibility of a case for taking away income or wealth from someone who has a relatively low capacity for happiness and giving it to someone who has a relatively high capacity. Given that the latter might already be enjoying a higher income than the former, maximizing aggregate utility might even require greater inequality.

In *Political Economy*, however, the theoretical connection between equality and general happiness stands unchallenged. There Sidgwick is more interested in practical concerns. What happens if the number of people in the community, and the total amount of wealth to be divided among them, are affected by the move to greater equality? Are there side-effects of redistribution that are not related to wealth? Socialism repels Sidgwick not because of its equalising tendencies as such, but because there is a strong likelihood that the size of the 'cake' to be distributed will be smaller. The incentives to produce wealth will be undermined by complete equality. Those who benefit from moves to greater equality will prefer to take more leisure (human beings overvalue leisure anyway), and the generous provisions made by the rich against calamities will disappear. Less saving and a general discouragement to capital accumulation will reduce the efficiency of the labour force. Population will increase. Inequalities in wealth and income may also have a social function. It is necessary to balance the happiness of the rich cultured person against the happiness of the better-off poor. The latter's enjoyment of culture depends on high standards maintained by the rich. Prospects of adding to the happiness of the many through the gradual diffusion of culture downwards, could be endangered by the destruction of its base among the few. Sidgwick can persuade himself that, taken together, these factors make a strong, if not decisive, practical reason for accepting 'present inequalities'.[34]

He keeps close to Mill on taxation. Wherever feasible, publicly provided services should be financed by charges to those who use them. The rest (expenditure which has no divisible or apportionable benefits), has to be financed from general taxation, direct and indirect. Redistribution has arbitrary limits because there is no clear way of determining how much greater should be the burden born by the rich. Should it be twice as much as the burden of the poor, or three times as much, and so on? Statesmen are advised to fall back upon the principle of equal sacrifice. A minimum income for the purchase of basic necessities should be exempt from all taxation, and above that level high marginal rates avoided. Each person should then pay in the same proportion to their 'superfluous consumption'.

> we may assume generally that if poor and rich alike are deprived of a certain proportion of their resources available for non-necessary expenditure, the loss thus incurred of purchasable satisfaction will be at least as great to the poorest class that will be taxed at all, as it will be to any other class.[35]

Anticipating the objection that this might seem unfair to the poor and that equal sacrifice ought instead to lead to progressive taxation, he uses all the previous practical arguments against complete equality (i.e. of incentives and efficiency) and one new difficulty, that of measuring and comparing the sacrifices of the rich and the poor.

A more effective method of approaching equality of sacrifice is to exempt savings, whether for protection against sickness and unemployment or for investment in industry. Exemptions should be extended to include the expenses of education and the transmission of culture. In any case, the really poor should not be paying income tax; and provided indirect taxes are confined to luxuries (roughly defined), they can try to avoid them. Where through failure of will or special circumstances they still buy non-necessities (drink and tobacco), the consequence is that their sacrifice will be greater. The taxation of inherited property and wealth falls outside the normal rules. It leaves the incentive to produce and accumulate wealth on the part of the inheritors untouched, and has a smaller effect on the benefactors than would a straight income tax with the same yield. For those not closely related to the previous owners, a higher imposition is justified. What is missing from the analysis is the severity of Mill's strictures on inherited wealth, and on the difference between earned and unearned income.

Aggregation and Measurement

Sidgwick is another utilitarian who attaches great importance to the measurement, comparison and aggregation of utility, and then fails to deliver much substance. Even when discussing empirical hedonism, he admits that the positive and negative degree of feeling can only be known approximately. Each pleasure ought to be compared quantitatively as it occurs, or recalled in imagination, with other pleasures (and pains). Unfortunately, these comparisons are subjective and any method will yield only rough approximations, particularly when comparing future pleasures. Under the heading of The Meaning of Utilitarianism he is strong for measuring the constituents of general happiness.

> all pleasures included in our calculations are capable of being compared quantitatively with one another and with all pains; that every such feeling has a certain intensive quantity, positive or negative (or, perhaps, zero), in respect of its desirableness, and that this quantity may be to some extent known: so that each may at least be roughly weighed in ideal scales against each other. This assumption is involved in the very notion of Maximum Happiness; as the attempt to make as great as possible a sum of elements not quantitatively commensurable would be a mathematical absurdity.[36]

It is rather strange to offer quantitative measurement in terms of imperfectly known units, roughly weighed, and on an ideal scale. General happiness, or the happiness of the whole, may be the proper objective, but in Sidgwick's hands it lacks all precision.

Population is one topic on which his approach can be put to the test. In the same chapter of *Ethics* he assumes that life, on average, is worth living (at this stage 'average' means on balance, life gives a positive balance of pleasures over pains, for most people). He also contends that the time at which a human being lives cannot affect the value placed upon their happiness; the interests of posterity must be taken into account. If the positive balance remains unchanged, then the utilitarian should want to make the number of people enjoying it as large as possible. He is anxious to correct political economists of the Malthusian persuasion whose population policy is to maximize average happiness (now 'average' means total happiness divided by the number of people). Their policy would restrict numbers whenever average happiness looks likely to fall. The correct utilitarian attitude,

he believes, is to encourage population to increase up to the point at
which

> the product formed by multiplying the number of persons living into the amount
> of average happiness reaches its maximum.[37]

It is not clear why Sidgwick chooses such a roundabout way of
defining total happiness. The implication is that numbers of people
should be allowed to increase as long as average happiness is positive.
(Here Sidgwick is not concerned with how this total happiness is
distributed between members of the community.) He does, however,
seem to have doubts about the exactness of the conclusion and the
prospect of an increasing total being the product of a falling average.
Dealing with the same problem in *Politics*, he warns the statesman
against aiming simply at a growth in numbers as a means of increasing
total happiness. They might threaten the average 'quality of life'. It
would be equally wrong to check the increase in 'civilized humanity'
if through emigration and colonisation, the 'average condition' in the
colony and the mother country together could be improved.

Nowhere is there any indication of how this happiness, quality of
life, or condition is to be measured. Indeed, the other topic which
seems to be an obvious candidate for the exercise of quantitative
commensurability, taxation, brings out a defeatist attitude on
Sidgwick's part. In *Political Economy* his rejection of a progressively
increasing tax on the luxurious expenditure of the rich is based not on
its fairness or unfairness but on the practical objection that

> the progression if once admitted would be very difficult to limit, owing to the
> impossibility of establishing any definite quantitative comparison between the
> pecuniary sacrifices of the rich and those of the poor.[38]

This is almost identical with Mill's views on the subject and far away
from scientific utilitarianism. Sidgwick continues in much the same
vein, and concludes that any attempt to devise a system of taxation
that exactly equalises burdens is practically unattainable because of

> the vagueness of the distinction between necessaries and luxuries and the great
> difference in the needs of different persons and of the same person at different
> times.[39]

What hope is there then of measuring with any precision the utilities
they derive from these necessaries and luxuries?

Notes

1. Schumpeter (1954), ftn p.408.
2. For biographical details see Balfour (1930), Harvard (1959), James (1970), and Schneewind (1977).
3. In the Preface to 7th edition of Sidgwick (1967).
4. op. cit., p.388.
5. op. cit., p.401.
6. op. cit., pp. 406-407.
7. op. cit., pp.36-37.
8. op. cit., p.495.
9. op. cit., Preface.
10. Sidgwick (1969), p.7.
11. op. cit., p.23.
12. op. cit., pp.35-36
13. op. cit., p.402.
14. Sidgwick (1967) p.413.
15. op. cit., p.403.
16. Sidgwick (1919), p.38.
17. op. cit., pp.299-303.
18. Sidgwick (1967), pp.94-95.
19. op. cit., p.411.
20. op. cit., p.460.
21. op. cit., p.457.
22. Sidgwick (1919), p.609.
23. Sidgwick (1969), p.499.
24. Sidgwick (1919), p.55.
25. op. cit., p.45.
26. Sidgwick (1967), pp.477-478.
27. op. cit., p.480.
28. Sidgwick (1969), p.401.
29. op. cit., Book III.
30. Sidgwick (1919), Chapter X.
31. op. cit., pp.167-168.
32. Sidgwick (1969), p.519.
33. Sidgwick (1919), p.609.
34. Sidgwick (1969), Book III, Chapter VII.
35. op. cit., p.586.
36. Sidgwick (1967), p.413.
37. op. cit. p.415. See also Sidgwick (1919), pp.317-318.
38. Sidgwick (1969), p.66.
39. op. cit., p.568.

7. Francis Ysidro Edgeworth

The Maria Edgeworth who met Bentham and corresponded with Ricardo on the subject of the potato, and whose novels and works of education are said to be imbued with utilitarian ideas, was Francis Edgeworth's aunt. There cannot have been any direct influence. He would have been only four when she died (the grandfather, Richard Lovell Edgeworth had four families, with Maria Edgeworth coming from the first and Francis's father, Frank Edgeworth, coming from the last). But it was 'a notable link' between the last of the classical utilitarians and the founder of the faith. Edgeworth was perhaps the purest, most precise and mathematical among them. These attributes served him well as he attempted to take the measurement utility and its application in the moral and economic sciences to their logical conclusions. He was, however, more than a utilitarian. Neither Bentham, nor the Mills, nor Sidgwick come close to the originality of his contributions to abstract economic theory. If Jevons is famous for being one of the leaders of the marginal revolution, then Edgeworth deserves equal credit for pioneering the analysis of contract and the core in bargaining equilibria, and for the application of a priori probabilities to problems of uncertainty. The obscurity of his treatment led to its neglect, and the extremes into which he sometimes allowed his utilitarian arguments to run repelled rather than attracted sympathy. Full recognition came slowly and often grudgingly.

The Edge

Edgeworth was born on the 8th February 1845 at Edgworthstown, Co. Longford, the family estate in Ireland, part of the Protestant Ascendancy. His father Francis Beaufort Edgeworth, had married a Catalan refugee, Rosa Florentina Eroles, hence the Ysidro. In fact, he was christened Ysidro Francis. Educated at home by tutors, he entered Trinity College, Dublin in 1862, and moved, without a degree, to Balliol College, Oxford in 1867. At this stage he was a student of Classics and took first class honours in 1869, although the degree was not awarded until 1873. Mathematics, or rather mathematicians, were an early and additional influence. William Rowan Hamilton, the 'Irish Lagrange', was a friend of his father. After a meeting at Trinity, Hamilton became something of a hero to Edgeworth. Called to the Bar in 1877, he, like Bentham, never practised. Instead he taught himself mathematics at home in London, wrote articles and papers, and 'made his way up through the margins of Victorian academic life'. There did not seem to be any hurry. He had sufficient private income to live as he chose.

There followed a series of appointments at King's College, London: a lectureship in Logic in 1880, a Professorship of Political Economy in 1888, and the Tooke Chair of Economic Science and Statistics in 1890. His career may have started at the margins, and in the wrong London College for a utilitarian; it ended with the Drummond Chair at Oxford in 1891, and a Fellowship at All Souls, where he stayed for the rest of his life. Oxford economics was at the time not too keen on having him, and his concentration on matters theoretical, and reluctance to commit himself on issues of policy, caused his new colleagues to call him 'The Edge'. A climber of mountains, bather in ice-cold waters, generous host (Keynes mentions breakfasts of champagne and pheasant), kind and courteous in conversation, absent-minded, diffident, elusive and contradictory in argument, formal and exact in phraseology, he had few personal possessions, not even books, and though there was a brief courtship with Beatrice Potter (later Mrs Webb, who owned that the prospect of matrimony with him bored her intolerably), he remained a bachelor.[1]

Friendship with Jevons was responsible for his interest in economics, and both Sidgwick and Marshall were held in genuine affection and respect. Academic success brought formal distinctions: a Fellow of the British Academy, first President of the Royal Statistical Society, and, like Sidgwick, a President of Section F of the British Association. It also brought new responsibilities. He edited the *Economic Journal*, from its inception in 1891 to 1911; and again, jointly with Keynes, from 1919 until his death in 1926. In 1925, he published three volumes of his own articles and reviews which had appeared in the *Journal* in the first thirty years of its existence. Extremely hard-working, cosmopolitan in outlook, able to read in more foreign languages than his English contemporaries, Edgeworth drew inspiration from a wide variety of sources, but especially when they applied mathematical and statistical techniques to economic problems. His main publications are now difficult to find.

1877 New and Old Methods of Ethics
1881 Mathematical Psychics
1887 Metretike or the Method of Measuring Probability and Utility
1925 Papers Relating to Political Economy (3 Volumes)

New and Old Ethics, more a pamphlet than a book, concentrated on utilitarianism in economics; *Mathematical Psychics*, by which he is most widely known, dealt with both utilitarianism and contract; whilst *Metretike* included his mathematical papers. They all read more like a collection of long essays than continuous narrative. There being no complete bibliography, all that can be safely said is that he also produced at least 172 articles, pamphlets and notes, and 173 book reviews.

A Peculiar Style

The style of Edgeworth's writing varies enormously. He could explain even the most technical of subjects with great clarity, as anyone who opens the 1925 volumes of essays will quickly discover. Probability, index numbers, statistical testing, and theories of sacrifice under taxation, are tackled in a manner that balances the appropriate mathematical rigour with helpful verbal discussion. On the other hand, it is difficult to find 'better' examples of the impenetrable combination of advanced mathematics and esoteric prose that has come to dominate modern economics than in his theoretical work on contract and utility. Most economists have agreed with Keynes that the clumsiness and awkwardness are more than balanced by technical brilliance and originality. The 'philistine reader', Keynes admits, may never be sure 'it is a line from Homer or a mathematical abstraction which is in the course of integration'. Hard luck, then, that they will find the quotations in Greek untranslated, the diagrams which they are instructed to draw never drawn, and great chunks of algebra left unexplained.

Mathematical Psychics (which contained parts of earlier work) is where 'the full flavour and peculiarity of Edgeworth's mind and art are exhibited without reserve'. In examining the combined effects of diminishing utility to income and increasing disutility to work on the net sum of the pleasures of consumption and the pains of production, he introduces terms like a 'megisthdone', a 'brachistophone', and branches of mathematics like the Calculus of Variations (followed by a set of equations in the Integral Calculus)[2], as if they were as familiar to the reader as cricket scores or football league tables. His language is often imprecise and has to be read several times before the meaning emerges. For example:

> To illustrate the economical problem of exchange, the maze of many dealers contracting and competing with each other, it is possible to imagine a mechanism of many parts where the law of motion, which particular part moves off with which, is not precisely given, (with symbols, arbitrary functions, representing not merely not numerical knowledge but ignorance) where, though the mode of motion towards equilibrium is indeterminate, the position of equilibrium is mathematically determined.[3]

Why this 'eccentricity and openness to mockery' should have afflicted him when he was at his most original in economics, remains a puzzle. Pigou had a very generous way of putting the problem of Edgeworth's style into perspective. When he reviewed the *Collected Papers* he summed up the impact that Edgeworth had made on his fellow economists, both in these essays and in earlier work, with a mountaineering analogy.

> Very few economists are equipped to take an equal part with Professor Edgeworth in his lofty climb: not many are even qualified to follow on the rope behind him. But, standing by the telescope on the terrace of our hotel, the least venturesome among us can watch and admire and congratulate. We can place upon ourselves with gratitude this record of high expedition brilliantly conceived and gallantly carried out.[4]

The highest point of the expedition may now look to have been his theory of contract. His theory of utility is still out of focus.

Mathematics as the Master Key

Edgeworth describes the differential calculus as 'the master key' that would 'unlock the treasure chamber' of pure economic theory. His *Mathematical Psychics* is subtitled, An Essay on the Application of Mathematics to the Moral Sciences, and much of its analysis is formally structured with 'definitions', 'postulates', and 'axioms' preceding 'demonstrations' and 'corollaries'. Several questions of social policy, it is suggested, can only be properly answered by the mathematical method. In particular (and it is a problem to which he constantly returns), how to find the distribution of income that will maximise aggregate happiness. Utilitarianism is the 'economical calculus'. Its economical part relates to competition and contract, in perfect and imperfect markets. Its utilitarian part relates to the greatest possible happiness, and the discovery of those 'middle axioms' which will be the means to that end. When applying these method to problems between landlords and tenants in Irish agriculture, he finds a general justification in the fact that

> human affairs have now reached a state of regular complexity necessitating the aid of mathematical analysis; and that the light of unaided reason (though sparkling with eloquence and glowing with public spirit), are but a precarious guide unless a sterner science fortify the way.[5]

Thus, the common sense rules, upon which Sidgwick rightly placed so much reliance, must be verified by mathematical as well as deductive reasoning. Mill is again an obvious target. Full of eloquence and public spirit, he would go on using unmathematical language to study mathematical subjects.

Edgeworth's faith in the ability of mathematics to solve problems that are beyond ordinary 'elephantine' deductive reasoning, is combined with a fascination for the charms of mathematical elegance. He regards mathematical theorems as naturally and philosophically superior. No other utilitarian, not even Jevons, feels so comfortable with the application of advanced mathematics. Nor is his interest confined to pure mathematics. He makes important contributions to the development of statistical analysis. A philosopher rather than a practitioner of both subjects, he believes that an element of the unknown resides in all problems of mathematical chance and places great reliance on the calculation of a priori probabilities. Fascinated by regularities, averages and aggregates in nature, and the subject matter of economics, he continues the work of Jevons on index numbers and, along with Karl Pearson, pioneers the application of correlation techniques where there is an interplay of independent causes. He is truly one of the first econometricians.[6]

Such commitment and exhibitionistic expertise was not enough to save him from the wrath of Walras. The founder of general equilibrium analysis also considered the foundation of a science of mathematical economics a prime responsibility, but eventually rejected Edgeworth as a worthy collaborator. Edgeworth's approach was counterproductive and discouraging to those wishing to understand new methods. His economic foundations could not support the mathematical edifice he attempts to build upon them.

> I have been particularly impressed by one thing, and that is that economists who are mediocre mathematicians, like Jevons, have produced excellent economic

theory, whereas some mathematicians who have an inadequate knowledge of economics, like Edgeworth, Auspitz and Leiben, talk a lot of nonsense.[7]

Allowance has to be made for the fact that Walras was notoriously quarrelsome and hated (almost) everything coming out of England. Edgeworth dared to criticise Walras's tatonnement process in the establishment of equilibrium. (Auspitz and Leiben displayed an unaccountable lack of faith in general equilibrium analysis.) As a consequence, Walras failed to appreciate the significance of Edgeworth's treatment of re-contracting and the emphasis he attached to imperfect competition.

It is unfair, nevertheless, to put all the blame on Walras. Edgeworth's teasing style may have been at fault again. Marshall also wished that the author of *Mathematical Psychics*, who shows real signs of genius, could have worked out his ideas 'more fully' and obtained the 'simplicity which comes only through long labour'.[8] The real issue for Marshall, however, was not whether mathematical reasoning is possible in the moral sciences, but whether it is profitable. Perhaps the most surprising feature of the debate is that Edgeworth appears to have come round to Marshall's side. Much later, in a review of Pigou's *Wealth and Welfare*, he tries to make the case for a very narrow field of application.

> Mathematical economics are certainly useful to some extent; but does the further elaboration which that study has received in this treatise imply a corresponding contribution to the Art of Political Economy? The analogy of mathematical physics does not help us to answer this question; the calculus of utility and probability is something so peculiar and unique.[9]

To single out Pigou for such an attack is rather odd: there was very little advanced mathematics in *Wealth and Welfare*. Even odder is the fact that the criticism comes from someone who had, hitherto, little interest in the Art of Political Economy unless the calculus of probability and utility could be applied. All the same, it is not the only sign of a change of attitude in later life.

The Utilitarian Tack

There is another link between Edgeworth's economics and his utilitarianism. In the essay, On the Present Crisis in Ireland, his theory of the contract curve is described as a way of understanding 'the mysterious process by which a crowd of jostling agents settle down into utilitarian arrangements'. In other words, the solution to the indeterminacy of bargaining outcomes is to find an arbitration that leads to the greatest sum-total of advantage for all concerned. Indeterminacy arises in imperfect markets, and imperfect markets arise when the number of competitors is limited, they are organised into unions and trade associations, or the goods and services being exchanged are not completely divisible. The landlord and tenant dispute in Ireland is one example.

The story is continued in *Mathematical Psychics* proper. Pursuit of self-interest, what he calls impure utilitarianism, may put the parties into a trading equilibrium. Starting from an initial endowment of goods and services (their relative economic power), they may agree to move to a position of mutual advantage, where each is at least as well off they were before. Unfortunately, there is unlikely to be just one such trading equilibria. Instead there will be a range of possible outcomes, with the difference now that one side can only gain at the expense of the other. There is no natural harmony. The contract curve is really a conflict curve. Within the limits of selfish behaviour, they have reached an impasse. Edgeworth offers what are, in effect, two methods of escape. The first is by arbitration. An external authority could perhaps persuade the parties to accept 'splitting the difference' as a rudimentary concept of justice. He hopes it might 'blossom' into a 'qualitative mean of utilitarian equity': a solution which produces the greatest sum-total of happiness. The maximum of pleasure is described as the mean between two minima.

The second solution is more sophisticated and idealistic. The parties themselves might start to take account of each others' interests in addition to their own. As the role of sympathy increases, the contract curve would narrow down to the utilitarian point, where aggregate utility is maximised.

> we might say that in the neighbourhood of the contract curve the forces of self-interest being neutralised, the tender power of sympathy and right would become appreciable; as the gentler forces of the magnetic field are made manifest when terrestial magnetism, by being opposed to itself, is eliminated.[10]

A voluntary contract of pure utilitarianism would seem to be based on a form of rational benevolence. Why feelings should become more tender as the balance of forces becomes more equal, is not obvious. Perhaps the warring parties become so exhausted that they turn to consideration of the greater good with relief. Or, recognising that an impasse is mutually damaging, they seek some other way out. Of course, at the limit of his argument, at the ideal point where the welfare of others is indistinguishable from your own, there is nothing left to argue about.

As Edgeworth himself acknowledges, the two sides in a conflict are rarely equal. The most powerful, in 'strength, ability, and capacity to co-operate', will only accept a settlement as final when they are sure that they cannot do better under another. The final contract will be biased in their favour. This contrast between the pure and the impure versions of utilitarianism is never resolved. Edgeworth is always extolling the virtues of abstract science and dreaming of what might be achieved in an ideal world. Rather reluctantly, and however briefly, he is forced to consider what is reasonable in the real world. Practical limitations on the applications of theory have to be accepted. He is helped by the observation that it is as difficult to be a pure egoist as to be a pure utilitarian. Most people are mixed utilitarians, and the general good need not always be always uppermost in their minds for it to be served.

Thus when Edgeworth comes to the end of *Mathematical Psychics*, the ideal, vague and abstract nature of pure utilitarianism has to be faced. There is danger in assuming that it becomes more persuasive just because its triumphs are so remote. It merely indicates a general direction. On the other hand, the suggestion made by a Mr Barrat[11] that imperfections in human society force the utilitarians to completely abandon Universal for Egoistical Hedonism, is firmly rejected. A Sidgwickian line is recommended. The realistic utilitarian,

> while constant to his life's star he should tack (in the present state of the storm at least) more considerably than the inexperienced voyager might advise.[12]

Compromise and approximation, the harnessing of selfishness, common sense, and existing institutions to serve the common good, are his policy recommendations, not radical change. When dealing with the crisis in Ireland, he is even more cautious. Theory has 'some bearing' on the 'general drift' of politics. Mathematical method 'makes no ridiculous pretensions to authority in practical politics', it remains in the 'philosophical sphere'. But that is where Edgeworth wants to be. The remarkable feature of his essay on Ireland is that it has very little to say about Ireland, or the practicalities of the dispute between landlords and tenants, and a great deal to say about theory of utilitarianism.

Like Jevons, Edgeworth was also impressed by Herbert Spencer. Whilst Mill accused Spencer of being anti-utilitarian and Sidgwick took pains to counter many of Spencer's arguments, Jevons and

Edgeworth seem to have been more susceptible to his ideas. Spencer combined a form of Social Darwinism and extreme individualism with the acceptance of aggregate pleasure as the ultimate standard of value. His interpretation, however, omitted most of what was radical in the programme of the utilitarians. The state is limited to the administration of justice and the provision of a safety net of poor relief. Laisser-faire in almost everything else, becomes an ideological commitment. Scientific laws of evolution are supposed to apply to the development of society and its morals. When fully evolved, for example, the perfect human being will always act to produce the maximum of pleasure and the minimum of pain. Environment and its variation, influences the race rather than the individual. Thus Edgeworth's references to 'the quality of population' rising with 'evolution', and to society as a 'vast composite flexible organism' whose members are 'by degrees advancing up the line of evolution', reveal the extent to which he had absorbed the language of Spencerism, if not all its doctrines. Another contemporary Social Darwinist who he quotes with favour is Francis Galton. Galton believed in racial improvement almost as a religious vocation, and once divided the civic worth of the population into ten classes, five above mediocre, and five below.[13]

A Single Overriding Objective

Edgeworth defines the central concept of the 'utilitarian calculus' as the 'Greatest Happiness, the greatest possible sum-total of pleasure summed through all time and over all sentients', and the discovery of the distribution of wealth, allocation of labour, and quality and size of the population, as its major task. The rate of increase of pleasure decreases as its means increases, and the rate of increase of the fatigue from labour increases as the work done increases. In other words, there is diminishing marginal utility to income and increasing marginal disutility to work. Individuals have different capacities for enjoying income and performing work. These capacities rise with evolution, but it cannot be assumed that the improvement is uniform across all sections of the community. Put very crudely, those with the highest capacity for pleasure should enjoy more income, those with the highest capacity to suffer fatigue should do more work, and those with both should have more children. It is heady stuff.

Edgeworth seems to take the desirability of maximising happiness for granted. He simply states it as a first principle.

The end of conduct is argued to be Utilitarianism, as exactly defined in 'Methods of Ethics', by deduction from the general principle maxims of common sense; perhaps as the constitution of matter is proved by deducing from the theory experimental laws.[14]

Sidgwick is taken as the master in these matters, supported by another scientific analogy of dubious validity. In a review of Sidgwick's *Elements of Politics*, Edgeworth notes with approval the end of politics being defined as,

the greatest quantity, not of wealth, but of happiness. In applying the greatest happiness principle Dr Sidgwick follows Bentham rather than recent utilitarians. Like Bentham, Dr Sidgwick derives his precepts from the pure fount of utilitarian first principles, without admixture of turbid elements from alien sources.[15]

Bentham is, nevertheless, criticised at an earlier stage for adding the words 'of the greatest number' to 'the greatest happiness'. He might as well of talked of the greatest illumination with the greatest number of 'lamps'. Some lamps are more powerful than others, and if the greatest illumination is the object then the more powerful, not necessarily the greatest number, should be sought. Sidgwick and Mill are taken to task for confusing the greatest happiness with equality in the distribution of happiness. In Sidgwick's case, the mistake was due to a lack of the proper 'mathematical safeguards'. In Mill's case, the failure was more deep rooted. There is a suspicion that he is being held responsible for introducing many of the turbid and alien elements.[16]

As far as the proof of utilitarianism is concerned, Edgeworth is content to follow the lead of his predecessors. He constantly returns to the question of equality, but never bothers to make out a case for the greatest happiness as a first principle. Of all the classical utilitarians, he is the least impressive in philosophical argument, in spite of repeated use of philosophical terms and language. There are deeper discussions to be found in Jevons's own diaries, not to mention the relevant chapters of his *Theory of Political Economy* and his four articles, *John Stuart Mill's Philosophy Tested*. Edgeworth seems more interested in testing the implications of extreme utilitarianism to the point of destruction. For instance, he claims that it is 'indifferent to the means', looking only to 'the supreme end'. Again, it is he who rediscovers the concept of 'man as a pleasure machine', and employs it in mechanical and mathematical reasoning to produce exact and often unpalatable results.

Pleasure is defined as 'preferable feeling', and the absence of pain. The greatest happiness is a function of number of enjoyers multiplied by the duration and intensity of their enjoyment. Beacuse individuals differ in their capacities for pleasure, some can obtain both a greater amount of pleasure from any given means (consumption) than others, and a greater increment of pleasure from any given increment of that means. There are higher pleasures (affection and virtue), and the enjoyers of them might form a class which gains more happiness for any given level of means above the minimum; while the class which enjoys the sensual pleasures might gain more pleasure from any given increment of means above the minimum. Although Edgeworth is uncertain about these different categories (recognising that they could be difficult to measure, may be artificial in the sense of being a function of education, and more supposed than real), he will not abandon them. Heredity plays its part in explanation and improved hedonimetry gives more precise measurement. Those who are more apt to enjoy the higher pleasures tend to be more capable of happiness. It is part of the evolution of the human species. Similarly, there are those who can perform the same amount of work and suffer less fatigue, or perform the same increment of work and suffer a smaller increment of fatigue. He thinks that differences in the capacity to work are indisputable. However imperfect the relationship (there may be people for whom labour is sweet), it mirrors that between consumption and pleasure, simply reversing the signs from utility to disutility.

Having postulated both that the marginal utility of income eventually declines as income increases, and that the marginal disutility of labour increases as work increases, Edgeworth is ready to see maximum happiness as a balance between these two forces.

> Thus the distribution of means as between the equally capable of pleasure is equality; and generally is such that the more capable of pleasure shall have more means and more pleasure ... The distribution of labour as between the equally capable of work is equality, and generally is such that the more capable of work shall do more work.[17]

In a footnote, he offers an alternative version of the relationship between work and fatigue. Some can provide more work for the same amount of fatigue, or a greater increment of work for the same increment of fatigue. He wants to argue that this leads to the conclusion that they may have to suffer more fatigue than others. Of course, the more work they perform the greater will be the means of pleasure for other people (and themselves) to enjoy. The total surplus of pleasure over pain, therefore, could increase even though these particular workers had to bear more pain. Maybe that is what Edgeworth means.

The similarity between the problems of economics and utilitarianism, he says, is quite remarkable. Economics is concerned with the interaction between individual agents, each seeking to maximise their utilities; utilitarianism (or Politics) is concerned with the maximisation of total utility. The market has a role to play in both fields. Economists have long been prepared to accepted the results of its impersonal and impartial forces. Edgeworth refers to the 'reverence' they pay to competition, and how the 'majestic neutrality of Nature' commands their respect. On the other hand, his emphasis on the importance of imperfect competition, and on indeterminate market outcomes, has quite a different implication. Arbitration may be required. The advantage of utilitarianism is that it can provide a set of principles upon which the arbitration can be based. Ideal Edgeworthian solutions, it has to be remembered, demand rather more than acceptable contracts or compromises. Jobs have to be allocated to those most capable of bearing fatigue, and income distributed to those most capable of enjoying pleasure. Even a system of fully competitive factor and product markets, with utility-maximising agents, cannot guarantee such a perfect outcome. Edgeworth fails to reveal his correcting mechanisms. Driven back to the applied utilitarianism of the real world, he prefers instead to amend individual behaviour so that is selfishness is tempered with some consideration for the welfare of others, and to look for solutions in which 'the struggle for life is encouraged' but subjected to rough and ready, common-sense. These are approximations to the greatest happiness rule, and the status quo is often the best attainable state of affairs.

Consequentalism and Welfarism

Edgeworth nowhere seems to question that actions should be judged by their consequences or that their consequences should be ultimately assessed in terms of personal and collective utility. The principles of arbitration are sought in notions of justice and equity, but none of the authorities can tell him how they can be applied to the practical problems of economics.

> Justice requires to be informed by some more definite principle, as Mill and Mr Sidgwick reason well. The star of justice affords no certain guidance, for those

who have loosed from the moorings of custom, unless it reflect the rays of a superior luminary, utilitarianism.[18]

Mill, and perhaps Bentham, did not reason correctly when they tried to show that the interests of each are also the interests of all. Sidgwick was right to suggest that Egoistic and Universalistic Hedonism are not so easily reconciled. In economics, which deals with the 'lower elements of human nature', religion is unavailable to ease conflicts between the self and the other. There must be an appeal to mutual advantage in utilitarian contracts between opposing parties.

Although the 'rights of man' is a slogan for metaphysicians and demagogues, confusion about means and ends is not confined to the extremists and the misguided. Mill never succeeded in distinguishing between the proximate and final objectives of utilitarianism. His devotion to the ideals of liberty, freedom and equality blinded him to the requirement that they must all be deduced from the greatest happiness principle. Edgeworth has no such doubts. The very essence of the Utilitarian

is that he has put all practical principles in subjection, under the supreme principle. For, in that he has put all in subjection under it, he has left none that is not under it.[19]

When considering the virtues of equality, of opportunities as well as of income and wealth, his arguments are based entirely on how it affects aggregate utility; and when he comes to taxes, the aim is to devise a system that minimises aggregate sacrifice rather than one that satisfies equality of sacrifice.

Individualism and Equality

Edgeworth has little more to say about the ability of individuals to look after their own interests than he has about their entitlement to political rights and freedoms. He is not an advocate of extreme laisser faire. Sidgwick's long list of ways in which governments can justifiably intervene to improve the efficiency of production, is quoted with seeming approval. Pigou's *Wealth and Welfare* receives a less fulsome welcome, but no great exceptions are taken to its analysis of the possible divergence between private and public interests in market economies. As has aready been argued, Edgeworth's own reliance on examples of strife and indeterminacy in bargaining make him more receptive of the idea of market failure. It is just that these amendments to orthodox doctrine are framed in what might be called a paternalistic approach to economic problems. They are not allowed to weaken his strict interpretation of greatest happiness elsewhere.

Edgeworth's comments about the greatest number of lamps not necessarily providing the greatest illumination, for example, misses the point about the intrinsic value of the 'lamps'. Mill wanted each individual human being to be respected, and not just counted in terms of their contribution to the sum of happiness. Edgeworth is much more interested in the differences between individuals, and the effect these differences have on the utilitarian case for equality. Bentham's ideal that each should count for one, and Mill's ideal that all are equal and cultivated, are not necessarily desirable. Only if each is equal (as a pleasure and work machine) should they count for one. Edgeworth even manages to suggest approval for plural votes conferred upon capacity for happiness rather than sagacity. It may be unacceptable to democrats and aristocrats alike, but the utilitarian sees only quantity of pleasure as the ground for preference between human beings and the lower animals, and between human beings at every stage of evolution. As with capacity for pleasure, so with the capacity for work: it would be wrong to equalise objective circumstances without regard to subjective propensities. Why give the same income, or the same work, to individuals with very different physical and mental powers? Unexamined notions of equity, fairness and equal treatment can be opposed to the principle of utility.

As will been seen in the section on Aggregation below, Edgeworth worries about the quality of the population. If this is a matter of heredity, should those lowest in the order be discouraged from having children? Of course, Eugenics was more fashionable at the turn of the century and such comments would have been more acceptable than they are now. But even if it is true that some people are low achievers in utility terms (capable of only menial tasks and easily satisfied with subsistence levels of income), it does not mean they are less worthy of consideration; except, that is, to an extreme utilitarian. Nothing is certain in Edgeworth's treatment, and he gives no straight answers. At one point he speculates on past aristocratic privilege as reflecting superior talent to enjoy the higher pleasures of life.

> To lower classes was assigned the work of which they seemed most capable; the work of the higher classes being different in kind and not to be equated in severity. If we suppose that capacity for pleasure is an attribute of skill and talent ... ; if we consider that production is an unsymmetrical function of manual and scientific labour ... ; we may see a reason deeper than Economics may afford for the larger pay, though often more agreeable work of the aristocracy of skill and talent.[20]

Is he suggesting that the privileges of a new aristocracy can be similarly justified, or is it all a great tease?

He then toys with the link between natural superiority and gender. Men usually consider themselves better at both pleasure and work, but if women appreciate more things of beauty and refinement than men, and if they are physically weaker than men, then there is an argument on grounds of greater total happiness for giving them rather more of certain means and rather less of the hard work. No doubt Marshall's father[21] would have been among those who thought men were superior, but where exactly does Edgeworth stand? In a review of a book on problems after the war (of 1914/1918)[22], he records a number of very different statements about the unequal treatment of women in the labour market. Such discrimination cannot be excused on grounds of the inferiority of their work, their inability to acquire skills, or the allegation that they are only working for pocket money. Yet he refuses to take sides. Maybe women should get equal pay for equal results. Maybe if they did, they might be 'entirely excluded from a branch of industry'. Maybe the old story 'of men having dependants and women none' should be taken more seriously. It is the Edge coming out again.

He is much clearer on the subject of equality and taxation. In a long article written for the *Economic Journal* in 1897, the utilitarian theory of taxation is reformulated[23]. First, he rejects the benefit or quid pro quo principle which treats taxes as a kind of price for services rendered by the state. In the absence of competition, the relationship between the taxpayer and the government is not economic but political. Many services meet a common need. Not all benefits can be allocated to particular consumers. Thus when self-interested citizens enter into a political contract with the government to provide them with certain goods and services paid for out of general taxation, they are accepting that, in the long-run, they are unlikely to do better on their own. Decisions should be based on the maximisation of aggregate net benefits. On the tax side, this means devising a system of taxes that minimises the aggregate burden. It seems to be a matter of simple mathematics to conclude that the marginal disutility, or the marginal sacrifice of each taxpayer should be the same. Even if the rich are rich enough to pay for all government expenditure, the condition will still not be met. The rich have to be taxed, for the benefit of the poor, until there is complete equality in post-tax incomes.

Thus far Edgeworth is closely following Bentham, Mill and Sidgwick. He also repeats many of Mill's and Sidgwick's warnings about the dire consequences of too much equality. There may be a reduction in the total amount of output available. There may be a population increase. Individual liberty and cultural diversity may be threatened. (Edgeworth remarks on the fact that Mill gives this danger precedence over the other two; 'the weighty sentence in which he condenses the substance of his teaching on liberty deserves to be repeated'.) Savings and capital accumulation, particularly investment in education, may be discouraged. Finally, tax evasion may present an increasing problem. The parting of the ways comes when he points out that,

> the Benthamite argument that equality of means tends to maximum of happiness, presupposes a certain equality of natures; but if the capacity for happiness of different classes is different, the argument leads not to equal, but to unequal taxation.[24]

Quoting from the famous footnote of Sidgwick, he claims that the possibility of such differences would not have been denied by Bentham himself. Whatever the authority, Edgeworth realises that has completely undermined the utilitarian bias towards equality. There is now the possibility that greater inequalities in post-tax incomes will minimise total disutility. In working out the details of income taxation, however, this fundamental disagreement is almost completely ignored. He affirms that minimum sacrifice is the proper utilitarian principle of taxation. He agrees that it implies 'taking the whole tax from those few incomes which have the lowest final utility'. It should not be concluded, however, that lowest final utility is simply a matter of income size. Those with permanent incomes will have a lower final utility than those with impermanent incomes of the same size, for example. Similarly, single persons will have a lower final utility than married persons, as will parents with small families compared to parents with large families, the young compared to the old, and so on. Whereas most of these differences can be dealt with by granting tax allowances or exemptions (so much for each dependent, so much for age), there is still the problem of devising the best tax structure that relates income tax rates to income above subsistence level and the allowances.

Edgeworth's examination of the alternative principles of equal sacrifice is the foundation of much twentieth-century tax theory. The connection between principles of inter-personal equity (equal absolute, equal proportional, or equal marginal sacrifice) and the recommended system of income taxation (regressive, proportional or progressive) is shown to depend on the rate at which the marginal utility of income declines. It is much more complicated than assuming that 'utility diminishes in inverse ratio to means', where equal absolute sacrifice leads to proportional taxation and equal proportional sacrifice to progressive taxation. If anything, Edgeworth believes that utility probably declines at a faster rate than the law of Bernoulli, but concludes that all the speculation is pointless. The principle of minimum sacrifice is clear and simple, assuming no exact relationship between 'something psychical and something material', only that the law of diminishing utility is in operation. ('For all we know this might be the true law').[25] He even suggests that Mill could have muddled up equal sacrifice with the equal marginal sacrifice required for minimum disutility.

The pure utilitarian, he insists, has no difficulty with either equal or proportional sacrifice. They are both 'equally inexact but equally useful approximations to the true principle'. Substituting minimum for equal sacrifice will not greatly change practical advice. A long sentence explains this happy result.

> As of old, before the invention of the compass, the star-steered sailor would not sensibly have altered his course if he could have discovered, by the use of a telescope, that what he had regarded as a luminous point was really a star, composed of bodies separated from each other [by] many million miles; so in the present state of financial science, affairs being at such enormous difference from principle, the discovery that the sacrifice theory comprises several distinct ends is not calculated to result in a serious alteration of line of conduct indicated.[26]

What this apparently means is that income above the exemption limit should be taxed on a gently progressive scale. At least, that is what he concentrates on in several subsequent articles. Various formulae suggested by contemporary writers for progressive taxation are closely examined without any challenge to the general idea. His most explicit statement can be found in answers to questions about taxation, in particular, 'In considering the equity of any tax or system of taxation what tests should be applied?'

> the test which should be applied is the greatest happiness principle. From this principle it follows that ceteris paribus the sum of privation or sacrifice should be a minimum. Therefore, if a certain amount of taxation has to be raised (for the purposes of which the benefit cannot be allocated to particular persons) the prima facie best distribution is that the whole amount should be paid by the wealthiest citizens. The incomes above that level should all be reduced to that level; the incomes below that level should be untaxed, the level being determined by the amount which it is required to raise.[27]

Once again, Edgeworth immediately starts to pull back from extreme redistributive conclusion on grounds of prudence. Only now his language is more colourful. In addition to the usual warnings about increases in population and checks to accumulation, there is 'the danger of driving the rich, or at least their riches, from the country', and of 'awakening the predatory instincts of the poor, and precipitating revolution'. After repeating his argument that the equal sacrifice principle has no natural advantage over the principle of least sacrifice, he finishes on a comforting note. He tells his interrogators that his detailed investigations strengthen, somewhat, the case for progressive over proportional taxation, but that the rate of progression approximately satisfying the least sacrifice principle would, for high incomes, converge to a 'simple proportional rate of taxation'.

The Edgeworth of these 1890/1910 papers is some way from the author of *Mathematical Psychics*. If differences in the capacity for pleasure exist then differences in the final utility of personal income must extend beyond circumstances of family size and age. They will not be solved by instituting tax allowances. In other words, as Edgeworth acknowledges, least sacrifice only leads to complete equality of post-tax incomes given that marginal utility of income schedules are everywhere declining and identical. When this last condition (i.e. the schedules are not identical) is not met, translating least sacrifice into a tax structure is as difficult as for any variant of equal sacrifice. The outcome could be progressive, proportional or regressive taxation, as normally understood. Who are the most efficient pleasure machines? Are they roughly divided into classes? If the idle rich and the predatory poor are the most efficient, then the boring middle class will have to pay all the taxes. The Edgeworth of 1881 is inclined to think they include the rich, and doubted whether they always include the ignorant poor. But if differences in capacities for pleasure are more widely dispersed, then both speculation and calculation become practically impossible.

According to Sir John Hicks, Pareto accused Edgeworth of selling out to the Cambridge Left.[28] Hicks himself thought that Edgeworth had not so much changed his mind as adapted to the public debate on progression at the turn of the century. Provided the degree of progression was mild, governments could largely ignore the '(rather intangible) differences in capacity, of which he made so much in MP'. Edgeworth could also stop worrying about the destructive effects of progression. In fact, after he has made the reference in The Pure Theory of Taxation to the Benthamite assumption of 'a certain equality of natures', and the consequences of abandoning it for a policy on inequalities, he merely concludes that the

> possibility corroborated by so high evidence is calculated to temper the more drastic applications of utilitarianism.[29]

There has been a drastic change of emphasis, if nothing else. Differences in capacities are not ignored, but now their existence only justifies placing an 'intrinsic reservation' on the general drift of utilitarianism towards equality, not a move in opposite direction.

Measurement

Edgeworth often insists that it is enough to describe pleasure as increasing or decreasing, positive or negative, as well as more or less. There is no need for cardinal units of measurement. At other places, like all classical utilitarians (with the exception of John Mill), he wants to treat utility as just another 'quantity' in economics, having dimensions of number, intensity and time. He writes about pleasure increments, numbers of pleasure increments, and multiples of pleasure increments. He even dreams of summing up pleasures across different individuals and communities. But he is everywhere elusive and ambiguous, and there is no commitment to any particular scale of measurement. He vacillates between ordinal and cardinal utility.

Part of the difficulty is that he first tries to distinguish between the concept of utility used in the economical calculus and that used in the moral calculus. They serve different purposes. One is about marginal adjustments in exchange (final degrees of utility) and has dimensions of time and intensity. The other is about collective as well as individual pleasure.

> For moral calculus a further dimension is required; to compare the happiness of one person with the happiness of another, and generally the happiness of groups of different members and different average happiness.[30]

Later, in the Utilitarian Calculus, he introduces an axiom which would seem to leave nothing to doubt.

> Pleasure is measurable, and all pleasures are commensurable; so much of one sort of pleasure felt by one sentient being equatable to so much of other sorts of pleasure felt by other sentients.[31]

Moreover, he claims the basic units of pleasure, the just perceivable increments, the minimum sensible, of the economical calculus are the same as the units of pleasure of the moral.

Edgeworth carried on from Jevons the utilitarian habit of finding support in the associanist psychology of Alexander Bain.[32] Both quote Bain's *The Emotions and the Will* and his Law of Accommodation which they then use to explain diminishing marginal utility. Edgeworth also turns to experimental psychology which had begun to attempt the measurement of mental magnitudes, the sensations of touch and of feeling.[33] One of the ideas that attracted him was that if sensations could not be measured directly, they could be measured indirectly by the stimulus that produced them. Another was that there was a functional relationship between stimulus and sensation which possessed some stability. In particular, there was the just perceivable difference (a term which Jevons had used, and a subject upon which Galton gave a lecture to the Royal Institution in 1893) in sensations of weight or temperature which remained constant, whatever the absolute level of the stimulus. He saw the opportunity of translating this just perceivable difference into the basic unit of utility measurement. Utility or pleasure was to be the sensation, and the means to pleasure the stimulus.

Unlike Marshall and Pigou after them, Jevons and Edgeworth wanted to derive units of utility, of utility as such. They were not content to take units of money (prices offered in demand for commodities) as approximations to the utility consumers expected from the commodities. Edgeworth went further than Jevons in believing that measurable increments of stimulus (whether of a single commodity, or of commodities together as income or wealth) produce measurable increments of pleasure. Unfortunately, economics teaches (as Edgeworth believed) that the response need not be the same for all individuals, nor for the same individual when the means to pleasure increase. So there can be multiples of pleasure units for the same increment of means. At any rate, that seems to be the implication of the following passage from Edgeworth's On Hedonimetry:

> For if possible let one just perceivable increment be preferred to another. Then it must be preferred in virtue of some difference of pleasurability (non-hedonistic action not existing, or not being pertinent to the present inquiry). But, of one of the increments exceeds the other in pleasurability, then that one is not a just perceivable increment, but consists of at least two such increments.[34]

Diminishing marginal utility becomes explicable in terms of accommodation to 'increased repetition of the conditions of pleasure', and is marked by a falling number of just perceivable increments of pleasure for each increment in means. The possibility that individuals differ in the number of just perceivable increments of pleasure they get from the same increment of means, even at the same level of means, becomes attributable, 'to a large extent', to their varying susceptibilities to the compensations for (or counter-balancing forces to) diminishing marginal utility. Some people have stronger 'echoes of past pleasures', and others have 'active habits growing up in the decay of passive impressions'. The latter may be more likely to develop new pleasures to replace the old.

Edgeworth makes the now familiar utilitarian point about the underestimation of future pleasures. The cause is human imperfection. This presumably implies that the same increment of means in the future will generate a smaller number of just perceivable units of pleasure than it does to-day. No estimate is provided as to the exact relationship between depreciation and time. Indeed, his hedonimetry becomes very confused when he attempts to take into account intensity, as well as subjective time and objective time. (The 'state' referred to is state of mind, and the 'rate' that of intensity over objective time; at least that is what they seem to mean.)

> Suppose one state presents about three pleasure increments, another about two, above zero, that the rate of the former is double that of the latter, their objective duration being the same, is it better to give two marks to each state, say three and two to the former, two and one to the latter and then to multiply the marks of each; or by a sort of unconscious multiplication to mark at once six and two - about; for the comparison of pleasures as to quantity is here admitted to be vague; not vaguer perhaps than the comparisons made by an examiner as to excellence, where numerical marks are usually employed.[35]

He immediately attempts to corrects the vagueness by imagining a science of pleasure which would register the height of pleasure of each individual, from now to infinity, 'exactly according to the verdict of consciousness, or rather diverging therefrom according to the law of errors'. In a similar vein, tired and unpaid examiners often wish there was a machine to rank all their students at a touch of a button.

Examining provides an interesting illustration of the several problems, including that of cardinal measurement. Even with the most comprehensive of marking schemes and model answers, a subjective element remains. Examiners are forced to make judgements about the candidate's understanding of the subject, technical skills, ability to argue a case, and originality, as revealed in the objective evidence of the answer book. Perhaps it is easier than trying to determine someone's state of mind. Happiness may be more complex, and the objective evidence less tangible. Even so, examiners may feel more confident about ranking the candidates from best to worst, than in establishing an absolute standard of excellence or in supporting their ordering with precise differences on a complete scale in numerical marks. For example, they might only be prepared to mark in bands of ten. They have only a finite number of levels of discrimination. In much the same way, Edgeworth turns from the physical analogy to a more tentative and less precise concept of the just perceivable increment of pleasure, or the minimum sensible.

> Let us suppose for the same objective increase of temperature or weight ... I have at different times, or with different organs of my body, different subjective estimates. In one sense, certainly more usual, the quantities are the same. In another sense, the minima sensibilia being equated, *what is felt is*. And this latter sense, it is contended, not without hesitation, is appropriate to our subject.[36]

The increments in question are more like finite differences than genuine differentials. Where there are no discernible differences, or where 'we are equally undecided' between cases, indifferent between them, they should be put at the same level, or in the same band of pleasure. Then the distance between the bands will be finite.

In the Utilitarian Calculus chapter of *Mathematical Psychics* proper, on the other hand, he is still talking of continuous functions and making quite remarkable assumptions about the scope for equating and combining utility units.

> Equimultiples of equal pleasure are equatable; where the multiple of a pleasure signifies exactly similar pleasure (integral or differential) enjoyed by a multiple number of persons, or through a multiple time ... It suffices to postulate the practical proposition that when ... it requires n times more just-perceivable increments to get up to one pleasure from zero than to get up to another, then the former pleasure enjoyed by a given number of persons during a given time is to be sought as much as the latter pleasure enjoyed by n times the given number of persons during the given time, or by the given number during the multiple time.[37]

Here vagueness is replaced by another kind of certainty. An almost parallel development is to be found on the subject of inter-personal comparisons. In On Hedonimetry only at the limit of 'perfect evolution' can one person's pleasures be taken as equivalent to another's. Outside the bounds of this ideal world, the just perceivable increment is given in one's own consciousness, but has to be inferred in the other person's. Compensation for the inherent uncertainty is provided by increasing the number of observations, as suggested by the theory of probabilities. In the Utilitarian Calculus appendix, correctly estimating the pleasures of others becomes an exercise in 'accepting identical objective marks as showing identical subjective states'. In other words, Edgeworth deduces mental states from comparative behaviour. (Those who smile must be happy.) In spite of all the psychological baggage it carries, this argument that the just perceivable pleasure increments of different people are the same sounds like a leap of faith.

It is ironic that a another attempt to measure utility was about to be applied, with considerable success and greater clarity, accross the Atlantic by a non-utilitarian. In his thesis Mathematical Investigations in the Theory of Value and Prices, written ten years after the publication of *Mathematical Psychics*, Irving Fisher solves the problem, at least for those commodities whose marginal utilities are independent of each other. He had read Edgeworth but seemed to be influenced more by Auspitz and Lieben. For Fisher, the connection between psychology and economics is limited to desire, and desire reveals itself in preferences. There is no need to speculate about the nature of desire. Numbers can be generated for marginal and total utility, with the exactness of 'twice as hot', and with an arbitrarily chosen unit called the 'util'. The key to his solution is to be found in contrasting the desire (or the intensity of the preference) for the marginal units of one commodity, at different levels of consumption, with that of another commodity, which was kept constant in consumption. One person's utility did not have to be compared with another's, and total utility did not have to be integrable. Even if it was, the constants of integration did not have to be determined.[38]

Reviewing a number of recent contributions to Mathematical Economics, including W.E. Johnson's *The Pure Theory Utility Curves*, Edgeworth is still, in 1915, defending his concept of a measurable and comparable utility.

> The postulate here adopted that utility or welfare "can be brought under the category of the greater or less" rests primarily on the testimony of consciousness, the psychological observation that there are degrees of felt sensations. This personal experience is then extended by sympathy to the evaluation of other people's pleasures. Jevons's suggestion that the theory of utility is limited to the motions of a single mind, that "no common denominator of feeling seems to be possible" appears to us untenable.[39]

As Edgeworth points out, economists commonly weigh the welfare of one kind of person against that of another in the theory of taxation and arbitration, and by implication, in the theory of wages and distribution. The calculations may be rough but are based upon a comparison which,

> no doubt presupposes some homogeneity between the persons compared, such that presumably exists between "a thousand persons living in Sheffield and another thousand living in Leeds, each with about £100 a year".[40]

People from the same class or income bracket are more likely to have similar spending habits and changes in prices can then be used as an approximation to welfare changes. Marshall and Pigou might have agreed with Jevons about the lack of a common, psychological denominator of feeling, but they would have found the rest of Edgeworth's argument perfectly compatible with their notion of welfare economics.

Aggregation

Edgeworth's notion of the greatest happiness means the greatest possible value of the sum of the pleasures of consumption over the pains of production. When the number of people and their quality is constant, the grand utilitarian exercise might be seen as finding the distribution of means and of pain or fatigue of work that will maximise this value. The fact that people differ in their qualities, in their capacities for pleasure and work, causes him no qualms. On the contrary, he believes that (pure) utilitarianism only makes sense when it takes into account the consequences of changes in this dual dimension. The whole point of his criticism of Bentham, Mill, and to lesser extent Sidgwick, on the greatest happiness of the greatest number is that they tried to slip in an unwarranted egalitarian assumption. He does not hesitate before adding up the utilities of very different people, and he is quite prepared to consider, in theory at least, selection for the benefit of the next generation, emigration for the benefit of the present generation, and even sacrifices in the happiness of some of the lower classes for the benefit of the higher classes, all in the cause of the greatest happiness over time; or so it seems.

His most explicit reference to the problems of aggregation comes when he considers the effects of variations in the number of people. The third, fourth, fifth and sixth postulates of the Utilitarian Calculus concern population and utility in one way or another. The third expresses the hope that the quality of the population increases with time. Though even here, there may be inequalities.

For it is probable that the highest in order of evolution are most capable of
education and improvement. In general advance the most advanced should
advance most.[41]

The fourth postulate renews the utilitarian commitment to Malthus.
Means to pleasure increase at a slower rate than population. With all
other factors remaining constant, therefore, population growth should
be constrained. If not, future generations will enjoy less happiness. Of
course, there could be some amelioration in the form of increasing
returns. Then the outcome need not be unique. At low levels of
general activity the benefits of increasing returns may not be realised,
and a pessimistic estimate of the maximum population size would
seem sensible. At much higher levels, they might permit a much larger
optimal population to be maintained.

Aside from exceptions to the Malthusian rule, the sufferings of
future generations will depend on the average quality of the issue of
the previous generation. People with higher capacities will be
welcome, but if those sections of population with lower than average
capacities have most children, and their children inherit their parents'
attributes, the average might decline. So Edgeworth's fifth postulate is

that to substitute in one generation for any number of parents an equal number
each superior in capacity (evolution) is beneficial for the next generation ... the
average issue shall be as large as possible for all sections above a determinate
degree of capacity, but zero for all sections below that degree.[42]

It raises the question of why only the interests of the next generation
are being considered. One generation's issue will affect the next, and
that generation's the next after them, and so on. Edgeworth employs
the analogy of waves on the sea.

In the continuous series of generations, wave propagating wave onwards through
all time, it is required to determine what wavelet each section of each wave shall
contribute to the proximate propagated wave, so that the whole sum of light and
joy which glows in the long line of waves shall be the greatest possible.[43]

He worries about the possibility that population growth will be erratic.
The fifth postulate can cope with steady decline to an almost
stationary state. It will have to be amended for movements in
population 'not amenable to infinitesimal calculus'. So the sixth
postulate substitutes the words 'is beneficial for all time' for 'is
beneficial for the next generation', and it is hoped that the selection
need not be 'total'.

There is now a hint that Edgeworth can understand why some people might find these conclusions outlandish. He reminds the reader that practice is different from abstract theory. The rules of selection might be relaxed. People should only denied 'a share of domestic pleasures' if the policy is supported by scientific evidence and does not threaten political security. Those in the lower sections of the population could receive other compensations, including less arduous work. They might emigrate. (Getting rid of them in this way also raises the average capacity of those who remain. In a footnote, Francis Galton is quoted as suggesting that, 'the weak could find a welcome and a refuge in celibate monasteries'. Whether Edgeworth approves or disapproves, or thinks it a joke, is not clear.) Certainly, the sacrifices required by the utilitarian calculus seem very unjust. For a start, maximising total happiness could be satisfied by the transfer of the means of happiness from the poor and weak to the rich and strong. Then the same group could be stopped from having children in the future interests of the rich and strong. Their loss of the utility of having children is more than balanced by the increased capacities of the new generations.

Inter-generation sacrifices, however, do not stop there. Given the utilitarian lack of sympathy for discounting the present value of future pleasures, any amount of sacrifice might be demanded of present generations for the multitude of future generations. The maximisation of happiness to infinity is now the objective. In Edgeworth's seascape, for example, there is no suggestion that the very distant waves should glow with less light and joy than those closer to the observer on the shore. That some sacrifices can be justified, he is certain. Exactly how much, he admits, is 'as nice a question in political, as in personal prudence'. To be fair, several pages are taken to deal with the problem of the 'fortune of the least favoured class in the Utilitarian community'. He is anxious to put a floor beneath their deprivations. In situations where population growth is pushing up against total means, their lot might even be negative happiness. That is unsustainable because it will produce political instability. The greater happiness of abstract hedonics is saved from leading to extreme outcomes by practical and theoretical considerations, but there is little other positive guidance.

Nothing indeed appears to be certain from a quite abstract point of view, except that the required limit is above starving-point; both because in the neighbourhood of that point there would be no work done, and, before that consideration should come into force and above it, because the pleasures of the most favoured could not weigh much against the privations of the least favoured.[44]

He should perhaps have noted that at the neighbourhood of starvation levels, neither Bentham nor Mill took utilitarian comparisons to be possible.

The Edgeworth of *Mathematical Psychics* is in two minds. For much of the time he pushes utilitarianism in a community made up of individuals with different capacities to extreme and inegalitarian conclusions. How society is to move from its present imperfections to the purity of his lofty ideal is never explained. The end is all the theoretician seems to care about. Then, almost without warning, he suddenly comes down to earth and faces the practicalities. Instead of being overwhelmed by the problems of application, he turns to find comfort in common sense and evolutionary utilitarianism. Nature is a powerful force for the good, a 'first approximation to the best', and social reform should be pursued with great caution.

Notes

1. For biographical details see Keynes (1926) and (1972d), Webb (1982) pp.283-284, Creedy (1986), and Hicks (1984). Peter Newman's essay (1987) is invaluable for a proper understanding of Edgeworth's work. Newman was able to obtain copies of Edgeworth's early writing.
2. Edgeworth (1881), pp.64-66.
3. op. cit., p.4.
4. Pigou (1925)
5. *On the Present Crisis in Ireland*, Appendix VII in Edgeworth (1881), p. 138.
6. See Bowley (1934), and Hicks (1984).
7. An unpublished letter quoted in Jaffé (1983). See also Walras's Correspondence in Walras (1965) Vol. II.
8. From Marshall's otherwise favourable review of *Mathematical Psychics* in Marshall (1975).
9. Edgeworth (1925) Vol. III, p.189.
10. Edgeworth (1881) p.56.
11. Alfred Barrat (1844-1881), a philosophical writer and Balliol man, who believed in the harmony of all knowledge, and was an admirer of Spencer.
12. Edgeworth (1881), p.81.
13. For Galton's ideas see Forrest (1974). Edgeworth is at his most Spencerian around pp. 66-75 of *Mathematical Psychics*.
14. Edgeworth (1881), op. cit., p.76.
15. Edgeworth (1925), Vol. III, p.16.
16. Edgeworth (1881), Appendix VI.
17. op. cit., pp.64 and 66.
18. op. cit., p.52.
19. op. cit., p.129.

Notes continued

20. op. cit., p.78. See also *On the Present Crisis in Ireland* in the same volume, particlalrly pp.130-132.
21. William Marshall, according to Keynes, wrote a tract called *Man's Rights and Woman's Duties.*
22. Edgeworth (1925), Vol III, pp.230-233.
23. *The Pure Theory of Taxation*, in op. cit. Vol. II, pp.62-125
24. op. cit., p.105.
25. From a supplement to the main paper, Minimim Sacrifice Versus Equal Sacrifice, in op. cit., Vol. II, p. 234.
26. op. cit., p.117.
27. *Answers To Questions Put By The Local Taxation Commission*, (1899), op. cit., Vol. II, p. 130.
28. Hicks (1984).
29. Edgeworth (1925), Vol. II, p.105.
30. Edgeworth (1881), p.7.
31. op. cit., pp. 59-60.
32. (1818-1903), the biographer of James and John Mill,and Professor of Logic at Aberdeen.
33. E.H.Webber (1795-1878), anatomist and physiologist; Gustav Fechner (1801-1887), psychologist and physicist; Wilhelm Wundt (1822-1920), physiologist and psychologist; and J.L.R. Delboeuf (1831-1896), another psychophysicist.
34. Edgeworth (1881), p.98.
35. op. cit., pp.100-101.
36. op. cit., p.99.
37. op. cit., p.60.
38. Irving Fisher, (1925 and 1927). The thesis was written in 1891 and first published in 1892.
39. *On Some Theories Due To Pareto*, in Edgeworth (1925), Vol. II, p.475.
40. op. cit., same page.
41. Edgeworth (1881) p.68.
42. op. cit., p. 71.
43. op. cit., p.70.
44. op. cit., pp.74-75.

8. Conclusions

Schumpeter's giant and unfinished *History of Economic Analysis* may be often seem paradoxical and perverse, but his extraordinary mastery of the literature means that very little is missed. There is a price to be paid for this bounty. No one subject, whether branch of the discipline or contributor, is treated simply in one place. The reader has to hunt backwards and forwards, several times, to find everything that Schumpeter wanted to say about them. Wrong impressions can be gained from incomplete searches. For example, his much quoted under valuation of Adam Smith's *The Wealth of Nations* is neither so harsh nor so dismissive as has been suggested, and is balanced elsewhere by a strong endorsement of the *Theory of Moral Sentiments*. Such a judgement on the relative importance of moral philosophy to the founder of classical economics both reflects what the author himself thought and points forward to modern theories about the foundations of economic policy. In Bentham's case, though, Schumpeter's reaction is consistently one of intense dislike. Utilitarianism is ridiculed as a 'beefsteak philosophy'. In any struggle against established and ideas, Schumpeter rather condescendingly grants, simplicity and even triteness can be the best weapons. Unfortunately, the ideologues of reform are often persuaded to believe the nonsense they preach. Reducing everything worthwhile to individual happiness and conducting all public policy according to the greatest happiness of the greatest number, was (and is) a piece of nonsense.

Schumpeter is too much of a scholar to let his prejudices blind him to the strength of Bentham's influence. A comprehensive system of the social sciences which offers a philosophy of life, a political programme, and a an engine of analysis is bound to attract respect, however exaggerated Schumpeter believed the respect to be. (A doctrine which influenced leading figures in economics for so long, must have something going for it. When taking Edgeworth to task for keeping alive the 'unholy alliance between economics and Benthamite philosophy', Schumpeter would have been fully aware that one hundred years separated Bentham's and Edgeworth's early publications.) The only area in which he allows utilitarianism to have a role as an engine of economic analysis is welfare economics. Even here, showing that the transfer of a rich man's dollar to a poor man will increase the sum of happiness, is not allowed to stand for very much. For Schumpeter, the conclusions of utilitarian welfare economics are incomplete and convince no one who has not been convinced beforehand.[1]

While it may be possible to agree with him about the redundancy of the concept of subjective utility to the analysis of economic equilibrium, the relevance of the work of Bentham, the Mills, Jevons, Sidgwick and Edgeworth to issues of economic policy cannot be so lightly dismissed. Edgeworth, after all, tried to argue that the transfer of the rich man's dollar did not necessarily increase the sum of happiness, and all of them were concerned with the more sophisticated problem of how many of the rich man's dollars should be transferred before the sum of happiness started to decline. What they could claim was that their approach enabled them to weigh the merits of economic justice and the demands of economic efficiency in the same balance. Schumpeter may not have been persuaded that it took welfare economics very far forward, and others might think that the search for such a monothetic solution is misguided, but until the appearance John Rawls's *Theory of Justice* in 1972, there was no other 'workable and systematic moral conception'[2] on which economists could base their judgements.

This is not the place to argue whether economists find Rawls's justice principle, any more convincing than the utilitarian sum of happiness. The previous chapters have shown, however, that there was no complete and consistent set of answers bequeathed to twentieth century economists and philosophers by the classical utilitarians. It is the modern interpretations that seek to construct a utilitarian consensus. They are truly neo-classical. In other words, they represent a return to the ideas of the classical utilitarians, not in simple repetition but in selective reconstruction, smoothing out (what are seen as) some of the inconsistencies, filling in some of the gaps, and dropping some of the mistakes, much as neo-classical macroeconomic theory emerged after rather than before the publication of Keynes's *General Theory*. There is always a danger in these exercises that the past will be trawled for arguments to support one side or another in current controversies with little regard for textual accuracy or the context in which they were originally made. On the other hand, it is possible to gain great stimulus from the past by applying old ideas to new problems. Progress in the development of ideas is rarely linear. Classical utilitarianism certainly left much unfinished business behind.

First, it has to be remembered that the other classical utilitarians would have known far less, however hard they searched, about the work of Bentham than the neo-classical utilitarians know now. Its radicalism, its acceptance of the importance of differences in the quality of pleasures, and of the capacities of individual to enjoy them, its redefinition of the general happiness and the meaning of the greatest number, much even of its language (including its use of the term 'utilitarian'), was hidden from them. These discoveries can now be exploited in full. Second, many of the concepts introduced by the classical utilitarians have wide appeal. For example, it is possible to appreciate the value of Bentham's distinction between the security-providing and the disappointment-prevention principles, or the debate between Mill and Sidgwick about private spheres of action, or the analysis of 'bads' and 'goods' started by Jevons and Sidgwick, without being a committed utilitarian. Third, several of the main structures in neo-classical utilitarianism are derived from hints and suggestions in the writings of the classical utilitarians, rather than from completed ideas. There is no doubt that the distinction between act-utilitarianism (where the rights or wrongs of an individual act are judged by the consequences of the act itself) and rule-utilitarianism (where the rights or wrongs of an action is judged by the consequences of a rule that everyone should follow in like circumstances) appears in the writings of John Mill and Sidgwick, and perhaps even in Bentham. Yet there is little consistency in their treatment. They were content to advocate act-utilitarianism on some occasions and rule-utilitarianism on others. Again, though there are several references to the general happiness of all 'sentient beings', no attempt was made to draw out the detailed policy implications of including animals in the objective function. Similarly, references to the time at which these 'beings' live not being allowed to affect their contribution to general happiness, to the importance of future generations, were not developed into a theory of inter-generational equity. Sidgwick is often quoted on the utilitarian approach to population size, in particular on the issue of whether average or total happiness should be the proper test, but he did not spend much time worrying about it himself. Bentham and all the rest mention the significance of differences in human capacities for enjoyment; only (the early) Edgeworth drew the logical conclusion for the utilitarian doctrine on equality. Finally, they all took the measurement of utility to be a crucial problem for their science of society, and none of them (John Mill did not really try) produced a satisfactory solution.

Modern theorists have pursued these topics at great length. Perhaps it is possible to remain a utilitarian and not be committed to any particular method of measurement, to still count the happiness of animals but as lower than that of human beings, or to give more weight to the happiness of present compared to future generations, and so on. None of the seven characteristics of classical utilitarianism studied here appear preclude any of these positions. Neo-classicism, in contrast, has to strive for more uniformity and consistency. Part of the explanation is that it has to face a new set of critics. The pursuit of maximum aggregate utility, these have charged, leads to conclusions that are illiberal and unjust. It denies the importance of individual rights and differences in individual capabilities. It admits anti-social pleasures and ignores the way in which total happiness is distributed among the members of the community. In reply, modern theorists of utilitarianism argue that the notion of 'happiness' can be broadened to include all the 'good' things it is supposed to have excluded. Individual preferences can be 'purged' of their unpleasant consequences. A theory of distributive justice can be built on 'security' and 'expectation' rather than directly on maximum utility. Practical Benthamism, the search for policies that will probably increase general happiness, as Edgeworth found out, is much more difficult. It is the broadness of the target, its vagueness, which both attracts support and diminishes effectiveness. Almost everyone who is a welfare consequentalist will pay lip service to the utilitarian single objective and then propose their own (often very different) programme of implementation. On one side of the argument it can be claimed that classical utilitarianism had always 'left open the possibility' of these broader interpretations; and on the other, that these broader interpretations dilute the original philosophy to something indistinguishable from its alternatives.

Notes

1. Schumpeter (1954), pp 130-134. Schumpeter correctly attributes the term 'utilitarianism' to Bentham himself, and notes Smith's objections to happiness doctrines.
2. Rawls (1972), p.viii. He takes the work of Sidgwick as summarising the development of utilitarian moral theory.

Bibliography

Albee, Ernest (1957), *A History of English Utilitarianism*, Allen & Unwin, London.

Alexander, Edward (1965), *Mathew Arnold and John Stuart Mill*, Routledge, London.

Allen, Peter (1978), *The Cambridge Apostles*, Cambridge University, Cambridge.

Archibald, G.C. (1959), 'Welfare Economics, Ethics and Essentialism', *Economica*.

Arrow, K.J. (1963) *Social Choice and Individual Values*, 2nd ed.,Yale University, New Haven.

Arrow, K.J. (1984), *Social Choice and Justice*, Collected Papers,Vol. I, Blackwell, Oxford.

August, E. (1976), *J.S. Mill: a Mind at Large*, Vision Press, London.

Bain, Alexander (1882), *James Mill*, Longmans & Green, London.

Bain, Alexander (1969), *John Stuart Mill: A Criticism*, (reprint of 1882 ed.), Augustus Kelley, New York.

Barber, W.J. (1975), *British Economic Thought and India, 1600/1858*, Clarendon, Oxford.

Balfour, Arthur (1930), *Chapters of Autobiography*, ed. Dugdale, Mrs E., Cassell, London.

Beccaria, Cesare (1767), *Essays on Crimes and Punishment*, Almon, London.

Belback, Robert M., Rainbow, Paul and Sullivan, William M. eds, (1983), *Social Science as a Moral Inquiry*, Columbia University, New York.

Bell, David, Raiffa, Howard and Tversky, Amos (1988) 'Overview Paper' in their eds *Decision Making*, Cambridge University, Cambridge.

Bell, David (1984) 'The Insufficiency of Ethics' in Manser and Stock eds,(1984).

Bentham, Jeremy (1952), *Jeremy Bentham's Economic Writings*, ed. Stark, W., 3 Vols, Allen & Unwin.

Bentham, Jeremy (1962), *The Works of Jeremy Bentham*, ed. Bowring, John, Russell & Russell, New York.

Bentham, Jeremy (1968 continuing), *The Collected Works of Jeremy Bentham* eds Burns, J.H., Dinwiddy, J.R. and Rose, F., Universities of London (Athlone Press) and Oxford.

Bentham, Jeremy (1970a) *An Introduction to the Principles of Morals and Legislation*, eds Burns J.H. and Hart,H.L.A.

Bentham, Jeremy, (1970b) *Of Laws in General*, ed. Hart H.L.A.

Bentham, Jeremy (1977) *A Comment on the Commentaries: and a Fragment of Government*, ed. Burns J.H. and Hart H.L.A.

Bentham, Jeremy (1983a), *Constitutional Code*, Vol. 1, eds Rosen F. and Burns J.H.

Bentham, Jeremy(1983b) *Deontology together with A Table of the Springs of Action and the Articles on Utilitarianism*, ed. Goldworth, A.

Bentham, Jeremy (1988), *The Correspondence of Jeremy Bentham*, Vol. 7, ed. Dinwiddy, J.

Bentham, Jeremy (1993) *Official Aptitude Maximized, Expense Minimized*, ed. Schofield, P.

Black, R.D. Collison (1960), *Economic Thought and the Irish Question, 1817-1870*, Cambridge University, Cambridge.

Black, R.D. Collison (1972), 'Jevons, Bentham & De Morgan', *Economica*, Vol. 39.

Blaug, Mark (1957), 'The Classical Economists and the Factory Acts', *Quarterly Journal Of Economics*, Vol. 71.

Boskin, Michael J. (1979), *Economics and Human Welfare*, Academic Press, New York.

Bostaph, Samuel (1989), 'Jevons's Antipodean Interlude', *History of Political Economy*, Vol. 21.

Bowley, A.C. (1934), 'Edgeworth', *Econometrica*, Vol. 3.

Bowley, Marion (1937), *Nassau Senior and the Classical Economists*, Allen & Unwin, London.

Bradley, F.H. (1935), 'Mr Sidgwick's Hedonism' in *Collected Essays*, Clarendon, Oxford.

Bradley, F.H. (1962), *Ethical Studies*, 2nd ed., Clarendon, Oxford.

Broad, C.D., Elster, J. and Slote, M. eds (1984), *Common Sense Morality and Consequentalism*, Routledge, London.

Brink, David (1992), 'Mill's Deliberative Utilitarianism', *Philosphy and Public Affairs*, Vol. 41.

Burns, J.H. (1962), *Jeremy Bentham and University College*, (Pamphlet), Athlone Press, London.

Carlisle, Janice (1991), *John Stuart Mill and the Writing of Character*, Univerity of Georgia, Ithaca & London.

Chitnis, A. (1962), *A Scottish Enlightenment*, Croom Helm, London.

Chitnis, A. (1986), *The Scottish Enlightenment and Early Victorian English Society*, Croom Helm, London.

Clark, Ronald (1975), *Life of Bertrand Russell*, Cape and Weidenfeld, London.

Coats, A W.(1967), 'The Classical Economists and Labour' in Jones, E.L. and Mingay, G.E., eds *Land, Labour and Population in the Industrial Revolution*, Arnold, London.

Collard, David (1975), 'Edgeworth's Propositions in Altruism', *Economic Journal*, Vol. 85.

Collini, Stefan, Winch, Donald and Burrow, John (1983) *That Noble Science of Politics: a study in nineteenth-century intellectual history*, Cambridge University, Cambridge.

Colvin, Christina (1971), *Maria Edgeworth*, Clarendon, Oxford.

Conway, Stephen (1990), 'Bentham and the 19th century revolution in government' in Bellamy, Richard ed., *Victorian Liberalism*, Routledge, London.

Cowherd, Raymond (1977), *Political Economists and the English Poor Law*, Ohio University, Athens, Ohio.

Cowling, Maurice (1990), *Mill and Liberalism*, 2nd ed., Cambridge University, Cambridge.

Creedy, John (1986), *Edgeworth and the Development of Neoclassical Economics*, Blackwell, Oxford.

Creedy, John (1989) 'Edgeworth; utilitarianism and arbitration', *History of Political Economy*, Vol. 21.

Dasgupta, P.S. and Heal, G.M. (1979), *Economic Theory and Exhaustible Resources*, Nesbit, Cambridge University.

Dickens, Charles (1989), *Hard Times* ed. Schlicke, Paul, Oxford University, Oxford.

Donner, Wendy (1991), *The Liberal State*, Cornell University, Ithaca and London.

Dugdale, Blanche (1940), *Family Homespun*.

Eatwell, John, Milgate, Murray and Newman, Peter eds (1987), 4 Vols, *The New Palgrave: A Dictionary of Economics*, Macmillan, London.

Edgeworth, Francis Y. (1881), *Mathematical Psychics*, Kegan Paul, London.

Edgeworth, Francis Y. (1925), *Papers Relating to Political Economy*, 3 Vols, Macmillan, London.

Finer, Samuel (1952), *The Life and Times of Sir Edwin Chadwick*, Methuen, London.

Finer, Samuel (1972), 'The transmission of Benthamite ideas, 1820-50' in Sutherland, Gillian ed., *Studies in the Growth of Nineteenth Century Government*, Routledge, London.

Firneaux, Robin (1974), *William Wilberforce*, Hamish Hamilton, London.

Fisher, Irving (1925), *Mathematical Investigations in the Theory of Value and Prices*, Yale University, New Haven.

Fisher, Irving (1927), 'A Statistical Method of Measuring Marginal Utility and Testing the Justice of a Progressive Income Tax' in Hollander, Jacob H., ed., *Economic Essays in honour of John Bates Clark*, Macmillan, New York.

Foot, Philippa (1988), 'Utilitarianism and the Virtues' in Scheffler S. ed. (1988).

Forrest, D.W. (1974), *Francis Galton*, Taplinger Publishing, New York.

Gibbard, Alan (1982), 'Inchoately Utilitarian Common Sense: The Bearing of a Thesis of Sidgwick on Moral Theory' in Miller and Williams eds (1982).

Godwin, William (1985), *Enquiry Concerning Political Justice*, Penguin Classics, London.

Gossen, Hermann Heinrich (1983), *The Laws of Human Relations*, MIT Press, Cambridge, Mass.

Green, T.H. (1986), *Lectures on the Principles of Political Obligation: and Other Writings*, Harris, Paul and Morrow, John eds, Cambridge University, Cambridge.

Griffin, James (1982), 'Modern Utilitarianism' *Internation Journal of Social Science.*

Griffin, James (1986), *Well-Being*, Clarendon, Oxford.

Haakonssen, K. (1981), *The Science of a Legislator: The Natural Jurisprudence of David Hume and Adam Smith*, Cambridge University, Cambridge.

Haakonssen, K. (1985), 'James Mill and Scottish Moral Philosphy', *Political Studies*, Vol. 85.

Haakonssen, K. ed. (1988), *Traditions of Liberalism*, Center for Independent Studies, London.

Hahn, Frank (1982), 'On some difficulties of the utilitarian economist' in Sen and Williams eds (1982).

Hahnel, Robin and Albert, Michael (1990), *The Quiet Revolution in Welfare Economics*, Princton University, Princeton N.J.

Halévy, E. (1928), *The Growth of Philosphical Radicalism*, Faber, London.

Hammond, Peter (1982), 'Utilitarianism, uncertainty and information', in Sen and Williams eds (1982).

Hammond, Peter (1986), 'Consequentalist Social Norms for Public Decisions' in Heller, Walter, Starr, Ross M. and Starret, David A. eds *Social Choice and Public Decision Making*, Cambridge University, Cambridge.

Hare, R.M. (1961), *The Language of Morals*, 2nd ed., Clarendon, Oxford.

Hare, R.M. (1982), 'Ethical theory and utilitarianism' in Sen and Williams eds (1982).

Harrison, Ross (1983), *Bentham*, Routledege, London.

Harrod, R.F. (1936), 'Utilitarianism Revisited' *Mind*, Vol. 45.

Harsanji, John C. (1976), *Essays in Ethics, Social Behaviour and Scientific Explanation*, Reidel, Dordrecht.

Harsanji, John C. (1982), 'Morality and the theory of rational behaviour'in Sen and Williams eds (1982).

Harsanji, John C. (1985), 'Rule Utilitarianism, Equality and Justice' in Paul, Paul and Miller eds (1988).

Harsanji, John C,. (1986), 'Utilitarian morality in a world of very half-hearted altruists',in Heller, Ross and Starret eds (as for Hammond 1986).

Hart, H.L.A. (1982), *Essays on Bentham*, Clarendon, Oxford.

Harvard, W.C. (1959), *Henry Sidgwick*, Florida University, Gainsville.

Hausman, Daniel M. (1981), 'John Stuart Mill's Philosophy of Economics', *Philosophy of Science*.

Hausman, Daniel M. ed.(1984), *The Philosophy of Economics*, Cambridge University, Cambridge.

Hazlitt, William (1969), *The Spirit of the Age*, ed. Mackerness, Collins, London & Glasgow.

Held, Virginia (1970), *The Public interst and Individual Interests*, Basic books, New York.

Helvetius, C-A. (1758) *De L'Esprit*.

Hey, John D. and Winch, Donald (1990), *A Century of Economics*, Blackwell, Oxford.

Hicks, John R. (1981) 'A Manifesto' in *Wealth and Welfare: Collected Essays on Economic Theory*, Vol. 1, Blackwell, Oxford.

Hicks, John R. (1984), 'Francis Ysidro Edgeworth' in Murphy A.E. ed. *Economics and the Irish Economy; from the 18th Century to the Present Day*, Irish Academic Press, Dublin.

Hirschman, Albert O. (1981), *Essays in Trepassing*, Cambridge University, Cambridge.

Hirschman, Albert O.(1983), 'Morality and the Social Sciences: A Durable Tension' in Belback, Rainbow and Sullivan eds (1983).

Hoag, Robert W. (1992), 'J.S. Mill's Language of Pleasure', *Utilitas*.

Hodgson, D.A. (1967), *Consequences of Utilitarianism*, Clarendon, Oxford.

Hollander, Samuel (1985), *The Economics of John Stuart Mill*, Vol. II, *Political Economy*, Blackwell, Oxford.

Hollander, Samuel (1987), *Classical Economics*, Blackwell,Oxford.

Hope, V. (1984), *Philosophy of the Scottish Enlightenment*, Edinburgh University, Edinburgh.

Hurley, Susan (1989), *Natural Reasons*, Oxford University, New York.

Hutchison, T. W. (1953) *A Review of Economic Doctrines:1870-1929*, Oxford University, Oxford.

Hutchison, T.W. (1956), 'Bentham as an Economist' *Economic Journal*, Vol. 66.

Hutchison, T.W. (1978), *On Revolution and Progression in Economic Knowledge*, Cambridge University, Cambridge.

Hutchison, T.W. (1982), 'The Politics and Philosophy of Jevons's Political Economy' *Manchester School*, Vol. 50.

Jaffé, W. (1983), *William Jaffé's Essay on Walras*, ed. Walker, Donald A., Cambridge University, Cambridge.

James, D.W. (1970), *Henry Sidgwick*, Oxford University, London.

Jevons, William S. (1879), 'John Stuart Mill's Philosophy Tested; IV, Utilitarianism', *Contemporary Review*.

Jevons, William S. (1882), *The State in Relation to Labour: The English Citizen; His Rights and Responsibilities*, Macmillan, London.

Jevons, William S.(1905), *The Principles of Economics*, Macmillan, London.

Jevons, William S. (1906), *The Coal Question*, Macmillan, London.

Jevons, William S.(1970), *The Theory of Political Economy*, ed. Black, Collison R.D., Penguin Books, London.

Jevons, William S.(1972-1981), *Papers and Correspondence of William Stanley Jevons*, ed. Black, R.D. Collison, 7 Vols., Macmillan, London.

Jevons, William S. (1972), Vol. I, Biographical Notes and Journal, with Könekamp, Rosamond.

Jevons, William S. (1973), Vol. II. Correspondence (1850-1862).

Jevons, William S. (1977), Vol. III Correspondence (1863-1872).

Jevons, William S. (1977), Vol. IV Correspondence (1873-1878).

Jevons, William S. (1977), Vol. V Correspondence (1879-1882).

Jevons, William S. (1981), Vol. VII Papers on Political Economy.

Kant, I. (1948), *The Moral Law*, trans. and analysed by Paton, H.J., Hutchison, London.

Kelly, P.J. (1991), *Utilitarianism and Distributive Justice*, Clarendon, Oxford.

Keynes, John M. (1926), 'Obituary for Edgeworth' *Economic Journal*

Keynes, John M. (1972a), 'The End of Laisser Faire' in *Essays in Persuasion*, Vol. IX. of *Collected Writings*, Macmillan, London.

Keynes, John M. (1972b), 'My Early Beliefs' in *Essays in Biography*, Vol. X of *Collected Works*.

Keynes, John M. (1972c), 'William Stanley Jevons' in *Essays in Biography*.

Keynes, John M. (1972d), 'F.Y.Edgeworth' in *Essays in Biography*.

Keynes, John M. (1972e), 'Marshall' in *Essays in Biography*.

Kinzer Bruce L., Robson Ann N. and Robson John M. (1992), *A Moralist in and Out of Parliament,: John Stuart Mill and Westminster*, Toronto University, Toronto.

Kivey, Peter (1973), *Frances Hutcheson*, M. Nijhoff, the Hague.

Klappholz, Kurt (1964), 'Value Judgements and Economics', *British Journal of the Philosophy of Science*, reprinted in Hausman ed.(1984).

Kurer, Oskar (1991), *John Stuart Mill: The Politics of Progress*, Grand Publicity Press, New York.

Le Mahier, D.L. (1976), *The Mind of William Paley*, University of Nebraska, Lincoln.

Lewis, R.A. (1952), *Edwin Chadwick and the Public Health Movement 1832-1854*, Longmans, London.

Lively, Jack and Rees, John (1978), *Utilitarian Logic and Politics*, Clarendon, Oxford.

Long, Richard T. (1992), 'Mill's Higher Pleasures and Choice of Character', *Utilitas*, Vol. 3.

Lyons, David (1965), *Forms and Limits of Utilitarianism*, Clarendon, Oxford.

Mack, Ruth M. (1962), *Jeremy Bentham*, Heineman, London.

Mack, Ruth M. (1968), 'Bentham' in Sils, David L. ed., *Encyclopaedia of the Social Sciences*, Macmillan & Free Press, London.

MacKay, Alfred F. (1986), 'Extended Sympathy and Interpersonal Utility Comparisons', *Journal of Philosphy*, Vol. 83.

Majumdar, Tapas (1958), *The Measurement of Utility*, Macmillan, London.

Maloney, John (1982), *Marshall, Orthodoxy and the Professionalisation of Economics*, Cambridge University, Cambridge.

Manser, Anthony and Stock, Guy eds (1984), *The Philosphy of F. H. Bradley*, Clarendon, Oxford.

Marshall, Alfred (1959), *The Principles of Economics*, 8th ed., Macmillan, London.

Marshall, Alfred (1975), 'On Utilitarianism: A Summum Bonum' in Whitaker, J.K. ed., *The Early Writings of Alfred Marshall 1867/1890*, Macmillan, London.

Marx, Karl (1938), *Capital Vol. I*, ed. Torr, Dona, Allen & Unwin, London.

Maurice, F.D. (1970), *Sketches of Contemporary Authors*, ed. Hartley A.J., Anchor Books, London.

Maurice, Frederick (1884), *Life of F.D. Maurice*.

McCulloch, J.R. (1825), *The Principles of Political Economy*, Wm Tait, Edinburgh.

Meek, R.L. (1976), *Social Science and the Ignoble Savage*, Cambridge University, Cambridge.

Mill, James (1824), *Elements of Political Economy*, Baldwin, Cradock & Joy, London.

Mill, James (1826), *History of British India*, 6 Vols, Baldwin, Cradock & Joy, London.

Mill, James (1966), *James Mill: Selected Economic Writings*, ed. Winch, Donald, Oliver & Boyd, Edinburgh.

Mill, James (1967), *An Analysis of the Phenomenon of the Human Mind*, 2 Vols, 2nd ed. (reprint of 1869), Augustus Kelley, New York.

Mill, James (1992), *James Mill: Political Writings*, ed. Ball, Terence, Cambridge University, Cambridge.

Mill, John S. (1963/1986), *Collected Works of John Stuart Mill*, 33 Vols, General Editor Robson, John M., Toronto University, Toronto.

Mill, John S. (1963), *The Earlier Letters of John Stuart Mill*, Vols XII and XIII, ed. Mineka, Francis E.

Mill, John S. (1965), *Principles of Political Economy*, Vols II and III, eds Robson, John M., with Bladon, V.W.

Mill, John S. (1967), *Essays on Economics and Society*, Vols IV and V, ed. Robson, John M. with an Introduction by Robbins, Lionel.

Mill, John S. (1969) *Essays on Ethics, Religion and Society*, Vol. X, eds Robson, John M., Priestley, F.E.L. and Dryer, D.P.

Mill, John S. (1972), *Later Letters of John Stuart Mill*, Vols XV and XVI, eds Mineka, Francis E. and Lindley, D.N.

Mill, John S. (1974), *A System of Logic*, Vols VII and VIII, eds Robson John M. and McRae, R.F.

Mill, John S. (1977), *Essays on Politics and Society*, Vol. XIX, ed. Robson John M., with an Introduction by Brady, Alexander.

Mill, John S. (1981), *Autobiography and Literary Essays*, Vol. I, eds Robson, John M.and Stillinger, Jack.

Mill, John S. (1982), *Essays on England, Ireland and the Empire*, Vol.VI, eds Robson, John M.and Hamburger, Joseph.

Mill, John S. (1984), *Essays on Equality, Law and Education*, Vol. XXI, ed. Robson John M. with an Introduction by Collini, Stefan.

Mill, John S. (1986), *Newspaper Writings*, Vols XXII to XXV, eds Robson, John and Ann.

Miller, Harlan P. and Williams, William H. eds (1982), *The Limits of Utilitarianism*, Minnesota University, Minneapolis.

Narveson, J. (1967), *Morality and Utility*, Johns Hopkins University, Baltimore.

Newman, Peter (1987), 'Edgeworth' in Eatwell, Milgate and Newman eds.

Ogden, C.K.(1932) *Jeremy Bentham: 1832-2032*, Kegan Paul, London.

Owen, Robert (1972), *A New View of Society*, ed. Saville, John, Macmillan, London.

Packe, Michel St J. (1954), *The Life of John Stuart Mill*, Secker and Warburg, London.

Paley, William (1825), *Principles of Morals and Political Philosphy*, in Works of William Paley, 7 Vols, London.

Palgrave, R.H. Inglis ed. *Dictionary of Political Economy*, Macmillan, London,(1900).

Parekh, B. ed. (1974), *Jeremy Bentham : Ten Critical Essays*, Frank Cass, London.

Park, Roy (1971), *Hazlitt and the Spirit of the Age*, Clarendon, Oxford.

Paul, Ellen F., Paul, Jeffrey and Miller, F. D. eds (1985) *Ethics and Economics*, Blackwell, Oxford.

Peacock, Thomas Love (1968), *Halliford Edition of Peacock's Work*, ed. Brett-Smith, H.F.B. and Jones, C.E. (reprint of 1924/34 ed.).

Philips, C.H. (1940), *The East India Company*, Manchester Universtity, Manchester.

Pigou, A.C. (1925) Review of Edgeworth's 'Papers Relating to Political   Economy', *Economic Journal*, Vol. 35.

Pigou, A.C. (1960), *The Economics of Welfare*, 4th ed. Macmillan, London.

Pigou, A.C. (1962) *A Study in Public Finance*, 3rd revised ed.,Macmillan, London.

Pitt, Joseph C. ed.(1979), *Philosophy and Economics*, Reidel, Dordrecht.

Plamenatz, John (1949), *The English Utilitarians*, Blackwell, Oxford.

Posner, Richard A. (1981), *The Economics of Justice*, Harvard University, Cambridge Mass.

Quinton, Anthony (1974), 'Utilitarian Ethics' in *New Studies in Ethics*, eds Findlay, J.N. and others.

Rawls, John (1971), *A Theory of Justice*, Harvard University, Cambridge, Mass.

Rawls, John (1988), 'Classical Utilitarianism' in Scheffler ed. (1988).

Rawls, John (1993), *Political Liberalism*, Columbia University, New York.

Redman, Deborah (1991), *Economics and the Philosophy of Science*, Oxford University, New York.

Rees, John C. (1986), *John Stuart Mill's Liberty*, ed. Williams, G.L., Clarendon, Oxford.

Ricardo, David (1951/1952), *Works and Correspondence of David Ricardo*, eds Sraffa, P. and Dobb, M., 8 Vols, Cambridge University, Cambridge.

Riley, Jonathan (1988), *Liberal Utilitarianism*, Cambridge University, Cambridge.

Riley, Jonathan (1993), 'On Quantities and Qualities of Pleasure', *Utilitas*, Vol. 4.

Robbins, Lionel (1936), 'The Place of Jevons in the History of Economic Thought', *Manchester School*, Vol. 7. Reprinted in Robbins (1970) and *Manchester School*, 1982.

Robbins, Lionel (1938), 'Interpersonal Comparisons of Utility', *Economic Journal*, Vol. 48.

Robbins, Lionel (1952), *The Theory of Economic Policy*, Macmillan, London.

Robbins, Lionel (1962), *An Essay on the Nature and Significance of Economic Science*, Macmillan, London.

Robbins, Lionel (1970), *The Evolution of Modern Economic Theory*, Macmillan, London.

Roberts, David (1974), 'Bentham and the Victorian Administrative State', in Parekh ed. (1974).

Rosen, F. (1992), *Bentham, Byron and Greece*, Clarendon, Oxford.

Rosenblum, Nancy L. (1978), *Bentham's Theory of the Modern State*, Harvard University, Cambridge Mass.

Roy, Subrato (1989), *Philosophy of Economics*, Routledge, London.

Ryan, Alan (1987a), *The Philosophy of John Stuart Mill*, 2nd ed., Macmillan, London.

Ryan, Alan (1987b) 'J.S. Mill' in Eatwell, Milgate and Newman eds.

Scanlon, Thomas (1973) 'Contractarianism and Utilitarianism' in Smart and Williams eds.

Schabas, Margaret (1990), *A World Ruled by Number: W.S. Jevons and the Rise of Mathematical Economics*, Princeton University, Princeton.

Scheffler, Samuel (1982), *The Rejection of Consequentalism*, Clarendon, Oxford.

Scheffler, Samuel ed. (1988), *Consequentalism and its Critics*, Oxford University, Oxford.

Schelling, Thomas (1984), *Choice and Consequence*, Harvard University, Cambridge Mass.

Schneider, H.W. (1948), *Adam Smith's Moral and Political Philosophy*, Harper, New York.

Schneewind, J.B. (1977), *Sidgwick's Ethics and Victorian Moral Philosophy*, Clarendon, Oxford.

Schumpeter, Joseph (1954), *History of Economic Analysis*, ed. Schumpeter, Elizabeth Boody, Allen and Unwin, London.

Sen, Amartya K. (1966), 'Hume's Law and Hare's Rule', *Philosophy*.

Sen, Amartya (1970), *Collective Choice and Social Welfare*, Oliver and Boyd, Edinburgh.

Sen, Amartya (1973), *On Economic Inequality*, Clarendon, Oxford.

Sen, Amartya (1976), 'Liberty, Unanimity and Rights', *Economica*.

Sen, Amartya (1979a), 'Interpersonal Comparisons of Utility', in *Economics of Human Welfare*, ed. Boskin, M., Academic Press, New York.

Sen, Amartya (1979b), 'Personal Utilities and Public Judgements: What's Wrong with Welfare Economics', *Economic Journal*.

Sen, Amartya (1979c), 'Utilitarianism and Welfare', *Journal of Philosophy*, Vol. 76.

Sen, Amartya and Williams, Bernard eds (1982), (with an Introduction), *Utilitarianism and beyond*, Cambridge University, Cambridge.

Sen, Amartya (1985), 'The Moral Standing of the Market' in Paul, Paul and Miller eds.

Sen, Amartys (1987), *On Ethics and Economics*, Blackwell, Oxford.

Sen, Amartya (1990), 'Justice: Means versus Resources', *Philosophy and Public Affairs*.

Sen, Amartya (1993), 'Markets and Freedom', *Oxford Economic Papers*, Vol. 45.

Senior, Nassau (1836), *An Outline of the Science of Political Economy*, Clowes, London.

Sidgwick, Arthur and Eleanor M. (1906), *Henry Sidgwick: A Memoir*, Macmillan, London.

Sidgwick, Henry (1919), *The Elements of Politics*, Macmillan, London.

Sidgwick, Henry (1967), *The Methods of Ethics*, 7th ed., Macmillan, London.

Sidgwick, Henry (1969), *The Principles of Political Economy*, 3rd ed. (Kraus reprint), Macmillan, London.

Skinner, Andrew and Campbell, R.H. eds (1982) *The Origins and Nature of the Scottish Enlightenment*, John Donald, Edinburgh.

Skorupski, John (1989), *John Stuart Mill*, Routledge, London.

Smart, J.C. and Williams, Bernard (1973), *Utilitarianism: for and against*, Cambridge University, Cambridge.

Smith, Adam (1976), *Theory of Moral Sentiments*, eds (with an Introduction) Raphael, D.D. and Macfie, A.C., Clarendon, Oxford.

Smith, Adam (1976), *Wealth of Nations*, eds (with an Introduction) Campbell, R.H. and Skinner, A.S., Clarendon, Oxford.

Smith, Adam (1977), *The Correspondence of Adam Smith*, eds Mossner, E.C. and Ross, I.S., Clarendon, Oxford.

Stephen, Leslie (1950), *The English Utilitarians*, (LSE reprint), Duckworth, London.

Stigler, George (1941), *Production and Distribution Theories*, (Essays on Edgeworth and Jevons), Macmillan, New York.

Stigler, George (1950), 'The Development of Utility Theory', *Journal of Political Economy*, reprinted in 1962 *Landmarks of Political Economy*, eds Hamilton, Earl J., Rees, Albert and Johnson, Harry G., University of Chicago, Chicago.

Stillinger, Jack (1961), *The Early Draft of John Stuart Mill's Autobiography*, University of Illinois, Urbana.

Stokes, Eric, (1959), *The English Utilitarians and India*, Clarendon, Oxford.

Strasnick, Steven (1979), 'Neo-Utilitarian Ethics and the Ordinal Representation Assumption' in Pitt ed.

Sumner, L.W. (1992), 'Welfare, Happiness and Pleasure', *Utilitas*.

Taylor, Charles (1979), *Hegel and Modern Society*, Cambridge University, Cambridge.

Taylor, W.L. (1965), *Frances Hutcheson and David Hume as Predecessors of Adam Smith*, Duke University, Durham N.C.

Thomas, Geoffrey (1987), *The Moral Philosophy of T.H. Green*, Clarendon, Oxford.

Thomas, William (1979), *The Philosophical Radicals*, Clarendon, Oxford.

Viner, Jacob (1949), 'Bentham and J.S. Mill: the Utilitarian Background', *American Economic Review*, Vol. 39. Reprinted in Viner (1958), *The Long View and the Short*, Free Press, Glencoe Ill.

Walsh V (1987) 'Philosophy and Economics' in Eatwell, Milgate andNewman eds.

Walras, Leon (1965), *Correspondence of Leon Walras and Related Papers*, ed. Jaffé, W., Vol. II, North Holland, Amsterdam.

Webb., Beatrice (1982), *Diary of Beatrice Webb*, ed. McKenzie, Norman and Jeanne, Virago, London.

Welch, Colin (1987), 'Utilitarianism' in Eatwell, Milgate and Newman eds.(1987).

Whewell, William (1862), *Lectures on the History of Moral Philosophy*, Bell & Dalby, London.

Williams, Bernard (1973), 'A Critique of Utilitarianism' in Smart and Williams eds.

Williams, Bernard (1976), 'Persons, Character and Morality' in *The Identitiy of Persons*, ed. Rorty A., California University, Berkeley.

Williams, Bernard (1985), *Ethics and the Limits of Philosophy*, Fontana, London.

Williams, Bernard (1988), 'Consequentalism and Integrity' in Scheffler ed. (1988).

Winch, Donald (1965), *Classical Political Economy and Colonies*, Bell, London.

Winch, Donald (1969), *Economics and Policy: a Historical Study*, Hodder, London.

Index